Understanding AJAX

DATE DUE

Prentice Hall
Open Source Software Development Series
Arnold Robbins, Series Editor

"Real world code from real world applications"

Open Source technology has revolutionized the computing world. Many large-scale projects are in production use worldwide, such as Apache, MySQL, and Postgres, with programmers writing applications in a variety of languages including Perl, Python, and PHP. These technologies are in use on many different systems, ranging from proprietary systems, to Linux systems, to traditional UNIX systems, to mainframes.

The **Prentice Hall Open Source Software Development Series** is designed to bring you the best of these Open Source technologies. Not only will you learn how to use them for your projects, but you will learn *from* them. By seeing real code from real applications, you will learn the best practices of Open Source developers the world over.

Titles currently in the series include:

Linux® Debugging and Performance Tuning: Tips and Techniques
Steve Best
0131492470, Paper, ©2006

Understanding AJAX: Using JavaScript to Create Rich Internet Applications
Joshua Eichorn
0132216353, Paper, ©2007

Embedded Linux Primer
Christopher Hallinan
0131679848, Paper, ©2007

SELinux by Example
Frank Mayer, David Caplan, Karl MacMillan
0131963694, Paper, ©2007

UNIX to Linux® Porting
Alfredo Mendoza, Chakarat Skawratananond, Artis Walker
0131871099, Paper, ©2006

Linux Programming by Example: The Fundamentals
Arnold Robbins
0131429647, Paper, ©2004

The Linux® Kernel Primer: A Top-Down Approach for x86 and PowerPC Architectures
Claudia Salzberg, Gordon Fischer, Steven Smolski
0131181637, Paper, ©2006

Understanding AJAX

Using JavaScript to Create Rich Internet Applications

Joshua Eichorn

PRENTICE
HALL

Upper Saddle River, NJ · Boston · Indianapolis · San Francisco
New York · Toronto · Montreal · London · Munich · Paris · Madrid
Cape Town · Sydney · Tokyo · Singapore · Mexico City

 This Book Is Safari Enabled

The Safari® Enabled icon on the cover of your favorite technology book means the book is available through Safari Bookshelf. When you buy this book, you get free access to the online edition for 45 days. Safari Bookshelf is an electronic reference library that lets you easily search thousands of technical books, find code samples, download chapters, and access technical information whenever and wherever you need it.

To gain 45-day Safari Enabled access to this book:

* Go to http://www.awprofessional.com/safarienabled
* Complete the brief registration form
* Enter the coupon code 2XCS-DTJE-TIFN-54EP-MLHC

If you have difficulty registering on Safari Bookshelf or accessing the online edition, please e-mail customer-service@safaribooksonline.com.

Visit us on the Web: www.prenhallprofessional.com

Copyright © 2007 Pearson Education, Inc.

Java and all Java-based trademarks are trademarks of Sun Microsystems, Inc. in the United States, other countries, or both. Other company, product, or service names mentioned herein may be trademarks or service marks of their respective owners.

Information is provided "as is" without warranty of any kind.

All rights reserved. Printed in the United States of America. This publication is protected by copyright, and permission must be obtained from the publisher prior to any prohibited reproduction, storage in a retrieval system, or transmission in any form or by any means, electronic, mechanical, photocopying, recording, or likewise. For information regarding permissions, write to:

> Pearson Education, Inc.
> Rights and Contracts Department
> One Lake Street
> Upper Saddle River, NJ 07458
> Fax: (201) 236-3290

ISBN 0-13-221635-3
Text printed in the United States on recycled paper at R.R. Donnelley & Sons in Crawfordsville, IN.
First printing, August 2006.

Library of Congress Cataloging-in-Publication Data

Eichorn, Joshua.
 Understanding AJAX: using JavaScript to create rich Internet applications / Joshua Eichorn.
  p. cm.
 ISBN 0-13-221635-3 (pbk.) 1. JavaScript (Computer program language). 2. Asynchronous transfer mode. 3. World Wide Web. I. Title.
 QA76.73.J39E43 2006
 005.13'3—dc22
                    2006019443

Contents

PART II

Acknowledgments

Writing this book has been a lot of work, and I couldn't have done it without the help of many people. This project was initiated by Pearson, and it never would have started without the research done by Andrew Wait, who found my blog and brought me to the attention of his father at Pearson. The readers of my blog have also been a great help, as their questions and feedback have helped me hone my thinking about AJAX. The HTML_AJAX project was also important in my growth as an AJAX developer; Laurent Yaish and Arpad Ray have helped me with it, and our talks led to a number of improvements in this book.

I would especially like to thank Mark L. Taub of Pearson Education for initiating this project and walking this first-time author through the many steps that it takes to complete a book. Mark has a wealth of knowledge, and I wouldn't have made it through the process without him. The production teams at Pearson did an excellent job and were a pleasure to work with. Terra Dalton was the production editor, Alan Clements designed the book's cover, Daniel Knott helped with the figures, and Curt Johnson managed the marketing.

I had a lot of help during the writing process; Sheri Cain was my development editor and helped me improve my writing abilities. Arnold Robbins, the series editor, provided a lot of great feedback at the end of the writing process, helping me improve the rough spots and greatly increasing the focus and quality of the book. Myles Grant and David Coallier were my technical reviewers and gave a lot of useful feedback.

I would also like to thank Travis Swicegood and Gordon Forsythe, my coworkers at Uversa, who have shown me many new ways to use AJAX while building Clearhealth. Finally I would like to thank my wife, Megan, for putting up with my complaints when I was tired of working on the book and for always encouraging me to put more effort into it.

Joshua Eichorn
Phoenix, Arizona

About the Author

Joshua Eichorn is a web developer living in Arizona. He holds a Computer Information Systems Degree from Arizona State University. Josh has contributed to several open source projects over the years and is the creator of phpDocumentor, the most popular documentation solution for PHP. Josh is currently the project lead for the HTML_AJAX library in PEAR.

Preface

Audience

This book is intended for Web developers who understand how to build Web applications and have a basic understanding of JavaScript. JavaScript knowledge should include the ability to do Document Object Model (DOM) manipulation and the ability to use object-oriented libraries. Basic understanding of PHP is also helpful for understanding many of the examples in the book, but it isn't required because this book focuses on client-side JavaScript programming. Understanding the stateless nature of HTTP and how tools (such as cookies) can be used to work around this stateless nature is also useful.

As I wrote this book, I assumed that you had knowledge of Hypertext Markup Language (HTML) and Cascading Style Sheets (CSS). If you are a Web developer who has used JavaScript before, you should be able to use what you've learned from this book to add Asynchronous JavaScript and XML (AJAX) to your sites. If this is the first time you've looked at JavaScript, you will want to find an introductory reference source before delving into AJAX. I recommend the Mozilla developer Web site at http:// developer.mozilla.org/en/docs/JavaScript. It contains a comprehensive JavaScript reference and an introduction to the language.

What You Will Learn

This book focuses on using AJAX to create a new style of Web applications. It covers the following topics:

- Ways to perform AJAX communications

- AJAX communications models, both Remote Procedure Call (RPC) and document-centric

- Usability guidelines and tips

- How to choose an AJAX library

- Ways to measure improvements in task completion speeds

- How to add AJAX to an existing application

- How to build rich applications

- How to debug AJAX applications

- The Sarissa Extensible Markup Language (XML) AJAX library

- Scriptaculous effects and widgets

- HTML_AJAX, which is an AJAX library with PHP support

The goal of this book is to add AJAX as a tool in your arsenal, not to cover every aspect of JavaScript and Web programming. To do this, we cover AJAX in a number of different ways, starting with basic implementation. We then move on to more theoretical topics, such as usability, and then finish by building actual applications.

Organization of the Book

This book is divided into two main parts and three appendixes. The first part, which encompasses Chapters 1–7, covers the basics of AJAX and how it fits into the rest of the Web development world. It includes introductions to the basic technology (such as `XMLHttpRequest`), facts about how to get the most out of AJAX, and tips regarding usability. Chapter 7 covers debugging, because bugs are bound to happen in any development environment, and AJAX affects how you implement many current Web-development debugging techniques.

The second part, which encompasses Chapters 8–12, contains three use cases. These use cases show how you can use AJAX to solve usability problems and improve performance on your current Web sites. The final use case also shows what is involved in building a JavaScript-powered application.

Finally, the appendixes summarize a large number of open source libraries. These include AJAX libraries and various JavaScript support libraries. I know that everyone requires different features from an AJAX library; these features range from specific server-side language support to DHTML features such as visual effects and drag-and-drop support. However, it's impossible for me to give detailed coverage of all the libraries, so I've chosen to focus only on those that I use on a regular basis. These libraries may not meet your needs, especially if you're using a server-side language other than PHP and you want complete server-side integration. To help with the process of picking a different library, the appendixes give you a starting point for picking a library to use if the ones covered in detail in this book don't meet your needs.

Web Browsers

Any book that includes JavaScript code needs to make some assumptions about the Web browsers that will be used. All examples shown in this book have been tested on Internet Explorer 6 and Firefox 1.5. The code should work in newer versions without much trouble, but it may have small problems with other browsers. This is especially true for older browsers such as Internet Explorer 4 or Netscape 4.7; in fact, none of the examples in this book would run on these browsers without a lot of changes. Browsers have advanced over time, and the vast majority of users have upgraded. If you need to support old browsers, do it with non-JavaScript versions of your application; supporting AJAX on ancient technology will make support a nightmare.

Why PHP?

The main focus of this book is on the client-side JavaScript code, but in many of the examples, server code is also shown to present the complete processes. PHP was chosen as the language for these examples because of its widespread use and my familiarity with it. The concepts shown on the server-side code should be easily transferable to any other language, although each language will have its own implementation details.

Summary of Chapters

The first part of the book builds a basic understanding of AJAX and shows how the technology works. It builds a foundation that will allow you to build complete applications. Specifically, it covers the following:

• Chapter 1, "What Is AJAX?" page 3, provides an overview of AJAX, what it actually means, and where it came from.

- Chapter 2, "Getting Started," page 15, is a guide to basic AJAX implementation covering AJAX communications powered by `XMLHttpRequest`, `IFrames`, and cookies.

- Chapter 3, "Consuming the Sent Data," page 41, shows the various ways to use the data that you learned how to transmit between the client and server in Chapter 2. It includes both document-centric approaches (such as processing XML and displaying HTML) and RPC approaches.

- Chapter 4, "Adding AJAX to Your Web Development Process," page 77, covers some of the ways that AJAX will change the development process and the ways in which you can deal with these changes. It also covers how to pick an AJAX library.

- Chapter 5, "Getting the Most from AJAX," page 99, provides a mental framework for thinking about AJAX and deciding when to use it. The chapter also provides some basic tools for measuring the time it takes for a task to be completed.

- Chapter 6, "Usability Guidelines," page 119, provides a set of usability guidelines for building AJAX applications.

- Chapter 7, "AJAX Debugging Guide," page 137, covers the various debugging options, from logging techniques to handling JavaScript exceptions, and a number of useful tools. These include the Firebug Firefox extension and Fiddler, which is a debugging HTTP proxy.

The second part of this book introduces you to three AJAX libraries and then looks at use cases in which they are used. Specifically, it covers the following:

- Chapter 8, "Libraries Used in Part II: Sarissa, Scriptaculous," page 167, provides an overview of the Sarissa and scriptaculous JavaScript libraries.

- Chapter 9, "Libraries Used in Part II: HTML_AJAX," page 195, provides an overview of HTML_AJAX, which is a JavaScript and PHP AJAX library.

- Chapter 10, "Speeding Up Data Display," page 217, builds a small application for browsing large amounts of data and dealing with a graph that is very slow to generate.

- Chapter 11, "Adding an AJAX Login to a Blog" page 249, adds an AJAX login to a sample blog application, showing how an AJAX login could work and how it could be used to load additional information at the time it is needed.

- Chapter 12, "Building a Trouble-Ticket System," page 271, builds a complete JavaScript-powered application. All the control and view logic is managed on the client side, and a set of services for interacting with the database is provided by the server.

Several appendixes cover various AJAX and JavaScript libraries that you might find useful while implementing your own AJAX application. Specifically, they cover the following:

- Appendix A, "JavaScript AJAX Libraries," page 333, covers AJAX libraries that have only a JavaScript component.

- Appendix B, "AJAX Libraries with Server Ties," page 339, details AJAX libraries that have a server-side component and a JavaScript component; the list is organized by server language.

- Appendix C, "JavaScript DHTML Libraries," page 347, gives information about JavaScript libraries that is useful for adding rich, JavaScript elements to your Web applications.

Typographical Conventions

Typographic conventions are used throughout this book to convey information. Italic font is used for emphasis and for citations of others' work. Code-based items are shown `like this` and include variable names, function and class names, and filenames.

Where to Get Examples Used in This book

The example programs used in this book can be found at http://understandingajax.net.

PART I

Chapter 1

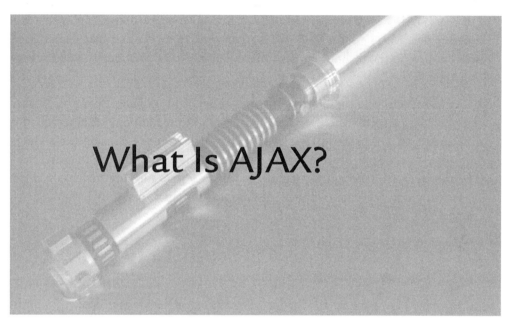

What Is AJAX?

In this chapter

Web 2.0, **Rich Internet Application (RIA)**, Asynchronous JavaScript and XML (AJAX) are terms that explain some of the new technologies that are changing the World Wide Web. These changes focus on the user experience instead of just on the technology, and this collective focus will create the next version of the Web.

This chapter examines these terms, defines them, and looks at their basic composition. The main focus is AJAX because it is the technology that makes the others possible. A short history is provided to give you the context into which AJAX fits. In addition, the chapter discusses some reasons why AJAX didn't take off before 2005 even though the technical obstacles were solved years before. This chapter concludes with an overview of Google's Gmail, gives an overview of the various AJAX features it uses, and shows how Gmail brought AJAX to the mainstream.

1.1 Rich Internet Applications

The Internet has changed a lot since its initial creation. It started with simple text-based communication and has built on its past to create ever more powerful means of communicating. In today's World Wide Web, you can create interactive multimedia presentations and powerful applications. Although these applications are powerful, they aren't without their drawbacks. Most are incredibly clumsy when compared to their native application counterparts (Hotmail versus Outlook Express, for instance), and many more have massive usability problems. However, problems or not, the Web—and especially Web applications—is one of the fastest growing and most important fields of software development.

Internet applications bring huge benefits to the table when compared to a normal application. They are highly accessible, require no installation, can be upgraded at any time, and offer access to large amounts of data without complex networks. These advantages allow for a shorter time to market, as well as lower development and support costs, when compared to a native application. Even though Internet applications usually have poorer usability due to their simpler, less interactive interfaces and slow update times, they are replacing native applications everywhere you look.

A Rich Internet Application (RIA) is an Internet application that attempts to bridge the usability gap between native applications and normal Internet ones. It contains more code on the browser, which offers higher levels of interactivity and an experience similar to native applications. With RIAs, it's possible to use many technologies, such as Flash, Java, and ActiveX, but the most important one is JavaScript. Because JavaScript is provided directly by the browser instead of being an add-on like the other technologies, you can get the most benefit from the least amount of work.

One of the driving technologies behind RIA in the JavaScript language is a technology called AJAX. AJAX offers the ability to communicate with your Web server outside of the normal load flow.

1.2 AJAX Defined

AJAX, originally defined by an article written by Jesse James Garrett in February 2005, meant "Asynchronous JavaScript+XML." Although that acronym is amusing, it doesn't tell the full story. AJAX is a secondary path of communication from the JavaScript environment on the user's Web browser to your server. The use of AJAX causes changes in the typical page flow that you see in a normal Web application. With AJAX, requests now happen more often and may result in smaller responses of non-HTML data.

To get a true sense of what this really means, let's look at the communication flow of a normal Web application (see Figure 1-1). It's composed of two types of network activity: user-initiated HyperText Transfer Protocol (HTTP) requests (typing in a URL or clicking on a link) and responses from the server. In Web applications, most of the user requests contain data from a form, and the server responses are generated on the fly by a programming language such as PHP or Java. In the normal Web application model, the user always generates requests, so it's possible for a high rate of page requests to happen by someone clicking quickly, but in general, the request rate is low, with random amounts of time between each request.

An AJAX Web application takes the normal communication flow of a Web application and adds a new type of request. To your server, this looks just like a normal page request (although in most cases, its data will be in a different format), but to the Web browser, it is different. It's a request that won't require a page reload on completion, and it doesn't have to be directly initiated by a user. In many cases, these AJAX requests will be small and might, for instance, take the form of a request to validate a field or to preload some data. However, the requests can also be large. For instance, they might submit a form through JavaScript or return Hypertext

Markup Language (HTML) that will be used to replace the content on part of the page. A sample AJAX communication flow is shown in Figure 1-2. If you look at an AJAX application's requests over time and compare them to a normal Web application, you can pick out which is which just by seeing their request frequency. A comparison between the two is shown in Figure 1-3.

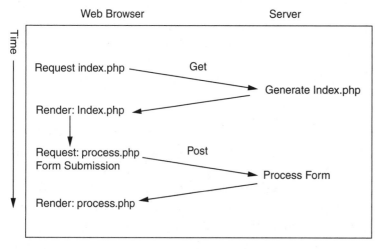

FIGURE 1-1
Web application request flow

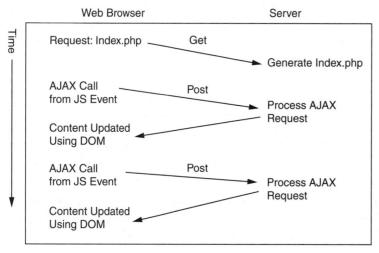

FIGURE 1-2
AJAX application request flow

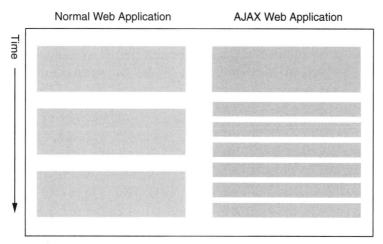

FIGURE 1-3
Normal Web application requests versus AJAX requests

This change in frequency can greatly affect your ability to host an AJAX Web application. Your servers now have to be able to handle much higher request rates from the same number of users. This can be especially hard if each AJAX request takes just as much processing as a normal page load.

1.3 Technologies of AJAX

If you search the Internet for AJAX, you are likely to notice a large number of items popping up under the AJAX name that don't seem to fit my definition. In most cases, these libraries provide the related functionality needed to finish your AJAX application, but other times, these libraries are just someone trying to jump on the AJAX bandwagon. When looking at these libraries and techniques, I divide them into three groups:

- Those directly used in AJAX

- Those closely related to AJAX

- Those that are just part of the rest of the RIA world

Most of the technologies directly related to AJAX are those that make up the "asynchronous" and the "XML" parts of the AJAX acronym. These are the libraries and techniques that provide the communication layer and the ways to encode the data that moves over it. In many cases, this is the XMLHttpRequest object, but

`IFrames` are also popular, and cookies or embedded ActiveX/Java are yet another possibility. The "X" in AJAX is the technique used in the data encoding, and it's an area with a huge number of possibilities. Data can be transferred as plain text, HTML, XML, or any other type of format that might be convenient for the situation.

XML is extremely popular as a data format because it's supported by so many languages and because it is easy to describe arbitrary data types with it. Many times, XML is used to facilitate Remote Procedure Call (RPC) mechanisms, but it can also be used to directly describe the data being transferred. RPC allows for the direct mapping of JavaScript types to the server's data types (PHP, Java, and so on) and vice versa. XML has been used for this purpose before, so it includes many standardized formats such as those used in SOAP, XML-RPC, and WDDX. It can also include a custom XML format created for a specific AJAX implementation.

Another popular approach is to generate JavaScript directly on the server and send it to the client where it can be used directly. This approach is possible because JavaScript can run code from a string using its `eval` statement. This approach is often used in conjunction with others because the server-side language can't evaluate JavaScript directly, but a specific JavaScript Notation (JSON) can allow JavaScript to be used in both directions. This notation, called JavaScript Object Notation, is often used in RPC approaches because it can describe any data type JavaScript can support while still being easily parseable by other languages.

As we move beyond what is needed to allow for AJAX communication, we get the large set of related technologies. These provide the extra glue and user-interface elements that are needed for a complete AJAX application. These are generally JavaScript libraries; some are stand-alone and just provide a few features; others provide an entire framework for creating dynamic Web pages. In most cases, you'll need some sort of effects library. This library provides fades, swipes, and many other visual effects that can be used to draw attention to the HTML element that you've updated using AJAX.

In addition, there are a number of libraries that provide drag-and-drop functionality, which is less closely related to AJAX but is most useful when used in conjunction with AJAX. Some of these libraries allow AJAX communication in some setups, while they are just a related add-on in other setups. This mix-and-match of libraries is great because you use only what you need to get the job done. Keep in mind, however, that the Web browser will need to download all this JavaScript to actually run.

In the wider world of technologies related to AJAX, you get the JavaScript libraries and other technologies, such as Scalable Vector Graphics (SVG), that might be in an AJAX Web application, but they really don't have a direct relation to AJAX. These technologies make up the wider world of RIA, but they are also more expansive and harder to integrate into existing applications.

1.4 Remote Scripting

At the heart of improving the usability of a Web application is removing the communications bottleneck between the user and the Web application. Using most Web applications means spending tons of time in search screens looking up an item's ID or waiting for a page to reload. The simplest way to solve these problems is to talk to your server from JavaScript and skip the page reload.

Experimentation down this new path began in 2001; at the time, it was called *remote scripting*. A couple of different approaches were used, but most ended up being an RPC-style approach using JavaScript's XMLHttpRequest object for sending the data. This same approach is used in many AJAX implementations today, so why did it take four years for its use to become widespread? It may have been that most developers weren't comfortable using JavaScript. It also might be that questions about why a specific Web technology is used or not seemed impossible to answer. However, I think it was just a case where it took a long time for a critical mass of acceptance to be reached.

1.5 Gmail Brings XMLHttpRequest into the Mainstream

In March 2004, the use of XMLHttpRequest to create highly interactive Web applications came to the forefront of the public's attention. Google released a beta form of Gmail, a highly interactive, JavaScript-based Web mail application. Gmail (see Figure 1-4) made waves not only for its user interface, but also for its large storage capacity. It also had an innovative invitation-based method of joining the preview, which made it even more exciting because Gmail was not open to all. Gmail was one of the first mainstream applications to make widespread use of AJAX, although the term hadn't yet been invented in 2004.

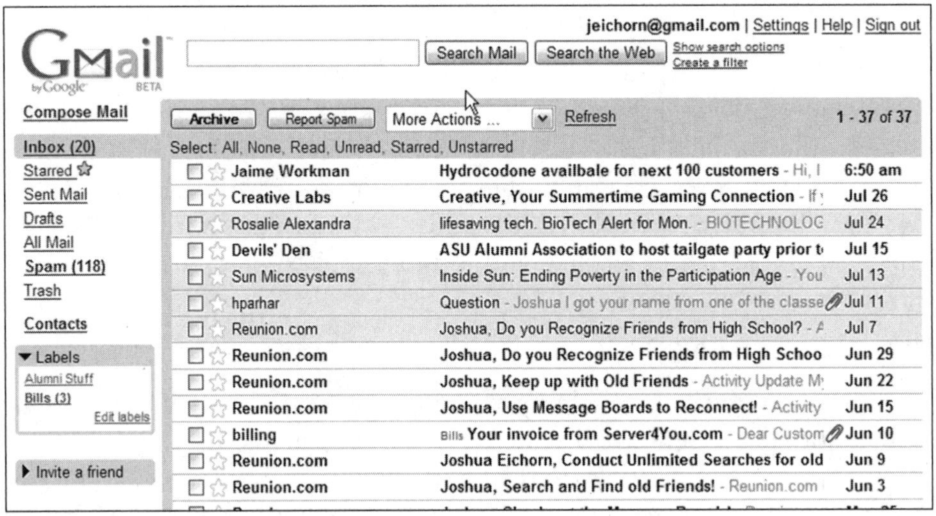

FIGURE 1-4
Gmail Web mail interface

Google applications spend a lot of time in beta before their final release, and Gmail is no exception. While I was writing this book (in May 2006), Gmail was still in beta. This extended beta period is useful for a large-scale application like this because it allows time for polishing the user interface and to work out any scalability issues. When you look at Gmail, this polish shows in a number of ways. AJAX and other JavaScript techniques are used throughout, minimizing full-page reloads and providing all the features you would expect in a high-quality mail reader. Gmail features available through the use of AJAX include the ability to do the following:

- Read messages without a page reload

- Tag messages (labels) without a page reload

- Change folders

- Check the spelling of messages

- Compose messages

- Check for new mail on a regular basis

- View news headlines without a page reload

- Search messages without a page reload

- Add messages to a quick group and view just that group without a page reload

- Save drafts automatically

The features in the preceding list provide the bulk of the rich experience, but it's the extras that complete it. For instance, users can receive feedback while they are waiting on data. This feedback comes in the form of an icon (see Figure 1-5) in the upper-right corner. Dynamic HTML (DHTML) features, such as a JavaScript rich text editor, are also available. With its large resources, Google has also made a non-JavaScript version of Gmail. It looks the same but has none of the advanced features and the continuous reloads that you see in most Web applications. This two-application approach might be difficult to replicate for some, simply due to the large amount of work involved, but it's a great way to make sure your application is accessible to everyone.

FIGURE 1-5
Gmail's loading indicator

There are still some minor issues with the Gmail application, and many AJAX applications will run into these issues. For instance, the browser's bookmark feature becomes useless because the URL doesn't change when content is updated, and the URL is the only identifier that the browser stores. In addition, the user interface looks similar to a native application, but it behaves differently, which can be a problem for some users because the application will fail to meet their expectations. Still, the application does attempt to alleviate this problem by giving feedback messages that tell users that an action is complete. The messages include notices that labels have been added to emails (see Figure 1-6).

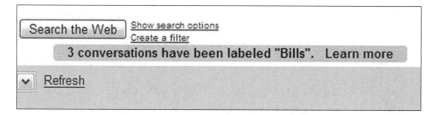

FIGURE 1-6
Gmail provides feedback for completed actions

Because Gmail was one of the first mainstream AJAX-powered applications, it set a baseline for what users could expect. For instance, its replacement of standard browser functions, such as refresh, with links inside the application is a technique that has been copied by many other applications. This has helped increase the quality of many AJAX applications because Gmail does a good job of providing a consistent and highly usable experience.

1.6 New Name: AJAX

In February 2005, Jesse James Garrett published an article that created the term AJAX and moved it from something neat that Google and a couple of other cutting-edge companies were using to a technique that could be used by anyone. While many people have complained about the acronym he coined, it did get people's attention. This article began a period of widespread experimentation and implementation in the Open Source Software (OSS) and blogging communities that has made AJAX a possibility for anyone.

By 2006, developers were using AJAX in a number of exciting new applications, from online mapping sites to to-do lists and calendars. However, the driver of innovation was not the large consumer-targeted applications, but the tools that allowed AJAX to be used by developers everywhere.

1.7 Summary

RIAs are modern Web applications that provide high levels of interactivity and perform similarly to native applications. RIA is made possible by a number of enabling technologies and techniques. These include JavaScript, DHTML, SVG, and AJAX.

AJAX is a JavaScript technology that provides an extra communication channel with the Web server. AJAX is one of the enabling technologies that allow the creation of RIAs, together with DHTML and other JavaScript techniques; with them, you can make powerful applications that can rival native applications.

AJAX isn't a new technology, but it's one that has taken awhile to become ready for mainstream consumption. It has been driven by the Web's constant need for innovation and by companies such as Google pushing it into the mainstream. Open source has made it possible for developers to add advanced AJAX techniques without having to develop everything themselves.

Chapter 2

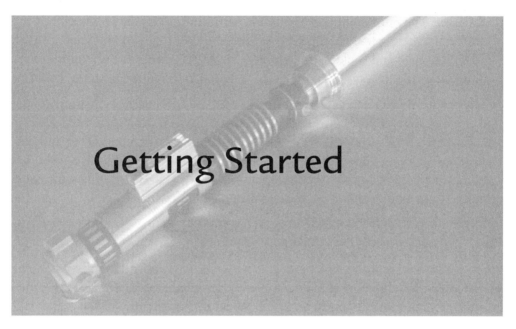

Getting Started

In this chapter

The foundation that makes AJAX possible is the communication layer with the server. The most complete option for performing this communication is the JavaScript `XMLHttpRequest` object. If `XMLHttpRequest` is not suitable to you, hidden `IFrames` and cookies can also be used. We will examine both options later in this chapter.

This chapter introduces you to the `XMLHttpRequest` object, showing you how to work around its implementation differences between browsers. After that, we make some actual page requests, both in a synchronous fashion and in an asynchronous fashion. This chapter finishes with some various fallback approaches that can be used if a browser doesn't support `XMLHttpRequest`, including how to use `IFrames` and cookies as your communication channel.

2.1 `XMLHttpRequest` **Overview**

Originally, Microsoft designed `XMLHttpRequest` to allow Internet Explorer (IE) to load XML documents from JavaScript. Even though it has XML in its name, `XMLHttpRequest` really is a generic HTTP client for JavaScript. With it, JavaScript can make `GET` and `POST` `HTTP` requests. (For `POST` requests, data can be sent to the server in a format of your choosing.) The main limitations to `XMLHttpRequest` are due to the browser security sandbox. It can make only HTTP(S) requests (file URLs, for example, won't work), and it can make requests only to the same domain as the currently loaded page.

The security limitations of `XMLHttpRequest` do limit the ways in which you can use it, but the trade-off in added security is well worth it. Most attacks against JavaScript applications center around injecting malicious code into the Web page. If `XMLHttpRequest` allowed requests to any Web site, it would become a major player in these attacks. The security sandbox reduces these potential problems. In addition, it simplifies the programming model because the JavaScript code can implicitly trust any data it loads from `XMLHttpRequest`. It can trust the data because the new data is just as secure as the page that loaded the initial page.

Despite the fact that `XMLHttpRequest` provides only a small API and just a handful of methods and properties, it has its differences between browsers. These differences are mainly in event handling and object instantiation (in IE, `XMLHttpRequest` is actually an ActiveX object), so they aren't hard to work around. In the following overview of the XMLHttpRequest API, the Mozilla syntax for XMLHttpRequest instantiation is used. If you want to run the examples in IE, you need to replace new XMLHttpRequest(); with either new ActiveXObject("MSXML2.XMLHTTP. 3.0"); or the full cross-browser instantiation method shown in the "Cross-Browser XMLHttpRequest" section of this chapter.

XMLHttpRequest is the most-used method for AJAX communications because it provides two unique features. The first feature provides the ability to load new content without that content being changed in any way, which makes it extremely easy to fit AJAX into your normal development patterns. The second feature allows JavaScript to make synchronous calls. A synchronous call stops all other operations until it's complete, and while this isn't an option that is usually used, it can be useful in cases in which the current request must be completed before further actions are taken.

2.1.1 XMLHttpRequest::Open()

The open method is used to set the request type (GET, POST, PUT, or PROPFIND), the URL of the page being requested, and whether the call will be asynchronous. A username and password for HTTP authentication can also be optionally passed. The URL can be either a relative path (such as page.html) or a complete one that includes the server's address (such as http://blog.joshuaeichorn. com/page.html). The basic method signature is:

```
open(type,url,isAsync,username,password)
```

In the JavaScript environment, security restrictions are in place. These security restrictions cause the open method to throw an exception if the URL is from a different domain than the current page. The following example uses open to set up a synchronous GET request to index.html:

```
1 var req = new XMLHttpRequest();
2 req.open('GET', 'index.html', false);
3 req.send(null);
4 if(req.status == 200)
5 alert(req.responseText);
```

2.1.2 XMLHttpRequest::Send()

The send method makes the connection to the URL specified in open. If the request is asynchronous, the call will return it immediately; otherwise, the call will block further execution until the page has been downloaded. If the request type is POST, the payload will be sent as the body of the request that is sent to the server. The method signature is:

```
send(payload)
```

When you make a POST request, you will need to set the Content-type header. This way, the server knows what to do with the uploaded content. To mimic sending a form using HTTP POST, you set the content type to application/x-www-form-urlencoded. URLencoded data is the same format that you see in a URL after the "?". You can see an example of this encoded data by making a form and setting its method to GET. The following example shows a synchronous POST request to index.php that is sending a URLencoded payload. If index.php contains `<?php var_dump($_POST); ?>`, you can see the submitted data translated as if it's a normal form in the alert:

```
1 var req = new XMLHttpRequest();
2 req.open('POST', 'index.php', false);
3 req.setRequestHeader('Content-type',
4          'application/x-www-form-urlencoded;charset=UTF-8;');
5 req.send('hello=world&XMLHttpRequest=test');
6 if(req.status == 200)
7   alert(req.responseText);
```

2.1.3 XMLHttpRequest::setRequestHeader()

There are many different cases in which setting a header on a request might be useful. The most common use of setRequestHeader() is to set the Content-type, because most Web applications already know how to deal with certain types, such as URLencoded. The setRequestHeader method signature takes two parameters: the header to set and its value:

```
setRequestHeader(header,value)
```

Because requests sent using XMLHttpRequest send the same standard headers, including cookie headers and HTTP authentication headers, as a normal browser request, the header name will usually be the name of the HTTP header that you want to override. In addition to overriding default headers, setRequestHeader is useful for setting custom, application-specific headers. Custom headers are generally prefixed with x- to distinguish them from standard ones. The following example makes a synchronous GET request adding a header called X-foo to test.php. If test.php contains `<?php var_dump($_SERVER); ?>`, you will see the submitted header in the alert:

```
1 var req = new XMLHttpRequest();
2 req.open('GET', 'test.php', false);
3 req.setRequestHeader('X-foo','bar');
4 req.send(null);
5
6 if(req.status == 200)
7     alert(req.responseText);
```

2.1.4 XMLHttpRequest::getResponseHeader() and getAllResponseHeaders()

The getResponseHeader method allows you to get a single header from the response; this is especially useful when all you need is a header like Content-type; note that the specified header is case-insensitive. The method signature is as follows:

getResponseHeader(header)

getAllResponseHeaders returns all the headers from the response in a single string; this is useful for debugging or searching for a value. The following example makes a synchronous GET request to test.html. When the client receives a response, the Content-type is alerted and all the headers are alerted:

```
1 var req = new XMLHttpRequest();
2 req.open('GET', 'test.html', false);
3 req.send(null);
4
5 if(req.status == 200) {
6     alert(req.getResponseHeader('Content-type'));
7      alert(req.getAllResponseHeaders());
8 }
```

2.1.5 Other XMLHttpRequest Methods

All browsers implement an abort() method, which is used to cancel an in-progress asynchronous request. (An example of this is shown in the "Sending Asynchronous Requests" section in this chapter.) Mozilla-based browsers also offer some extra methods on top of the basic API; for instance, addEventListener() and removeEventListener() provide a way to catch status events without using the on* properties. There is also an overrideMimeType() method that makes it possible to force the Content-type to text/xml so that it will be parsed into a DOM document even if the server doesn't report it as such. The Mozilla-specific methods can be useful in certain circumstances, but in most cases, you should stay away from them because not all browsers support them.

2.1.6 `XMLHttpRequest` **Properties**

`XMLHttpRequest` provides a number of properties that provide information or results about the request. Most of the properties are self-explanatory; you simply read the value and act on it. The on* properties are event handlers that are used by assigning a function to them. A list of all the properties follows:

- **`status`**. The HTTP status code of the request response.

- **`statusText`**. The HTTP status code that goes with the code.

- **`readyState`**. The state of the request. (See Table 2-1 in the next section of this chapter for values.)

- **`responseText`**. Unparsed text of the response.

- **`responseXML`**. Response parsed into a DOM Document object; happens only if Content-type is `text/xml`.

- **`onreadystatechange`**. Event handler that is called when `readyState` changes.

- **`onerror`**. Mozilla-only event handler that is called when an error happens during a request.

- **`onprogress`**. Mozilla-only event handler that is called at an interval as content is loaded.

- **`onload`**. Mozilla-only event handler that is called when the document is finished loading.

> **NOTE** Mozilla resets event handlers, such as `onreadystatechange`, after a request is completed, so you need to reset them if you are making multiple calls with the same object.

2.1.7 `readyState` **Reference**

Table 2-1 shows the possible values for the `readyState` variable. It will return a number representing the current state of the object. Each request will progress through the list of `readyStates`.

TABLE 2-1
readyState **Levels**

readyState **Status Code**	Status of the XMLHttpRequest **Object**
(0) UNINITIALIZED	The object has been created but not initialized. (The open method has not been called.)
(1) LOADING	The object has been created, but the send method has not been called.
(2) LOADED	The send method has been called, but the status and headers are not yet available.
(3) INTERACTIVE	Some data has been received. Calling the responseBody and responseText properties at this state to obtain partial results will return an error, because status and response headers are not fully available.
(4) COMPLETED	All the data has been received, and the complete data is available in the responseBody and responseText properties.

The readyState variable and the onreadystatechange event handler are linked in such a way that each time the readyState variable is changed, the onreadystatechange event handler is called.

2.2 Cross-Browser XMLHttpRequest

One of the attributes that have made XMLHttpRequest such a popular transport for AJAX requests is that it is easy to use in a way that is compatible across multiple browsers. The big two browsers, IE and Firefox, provide the same basic API. This consistency makes for a similar development experience. Opera and Safari also support the same basic API, but only in their more recent versions.

When you are writing cross-browser, the first problem you need to overcome is that XMLHttpRequest is an ActiveX object in IE, and it's a normal JavaScript object in Mozilla and the other browsers. There are a number of approaches to overcoming this problem, including optional JScript code for IE, but I find that the simplest solution is just to use exceptions. Listing 2-1 shows an example that tries every version of the XMLHTTP ActiveX object, if needed. This helps make our implementation as robust as possible. The function also throws an exception if it's not possible to create an XMLHttpRequest object. This gives us a way to give error messages or to fall back to IFrame requests, if needed.

Listing 2-1
Cross-Browser XMLHttpRequest *Creation*

```
1   // function to create an XMLHttpClient in a cross-browser manner
2   function initXMLHttpClient() {
3       var xmlhttp;
4       try {
5           // Mozilla / Safari / IE7
6           xmlhttp = new XMLHttpRequest();
7       } catch (e) {
8           // IE
9           var XMLHTTP_IDS = new Array('MSXML2.XMLHTTP.5.0',
10                                      'MSXML2.XMLHTTP.4.0',
11                                      'MSXML2.XMLHTTP.3.0',
12                                      'MSXML2.XMLHTTP',
13                                      'Microsoft.XMLHTTP' );
14          var success = false;
15          for (var i=0;i < XMLHTTP_IDS.length && !success; i++) {
16              try {
17                  xmlhttp = new ActiveXObject(XMLHTTP_IDS[i]);
18                      success = true;
19                  } catch (e) {}
20          }
21          if (!success) {
22              throw new Error('Unable to create XMLHttpRequest.');
23          }
24      }
25      return xmlhttp;
26  }
```

The overall pattern of this code is simple: Create an XMLHttpRequest instance in the most optimal way possible, as shown in line 6. This creation should always succeed on Mozilla-based browsers, such as Firefox, on Opera, and on the upcoming IE 7.

If XMLHttpRequest doesn't exist, catch the exception that is thrown, as shown in line 7. Getting an exception means you're on IE or an old browser. To test for IE, attempt to create an ActiveX version of XMLHttpRequest, which is accomplished by the following:

1. Looping over all possible ActiveX identifiers. This action will create an ActiveX instance for each identifier until the creation succeeds, setting the success flag to `true`, as shown in lines 9–20.

2. If creation is successful, returning an `XMLHttpRequest` instance, as shown in line 25. Otherwise, throwing a JavaScript exception, as shown in line 22.

This approach allows for minimal overhead if the browser supports a native `XMLHttpRequest` object while fully supporting IE. It also gives us an error if `XMLHttpRequest` isn't supported at all. This error could be displayed to the user at this point, or you could insert another communication approach, such as hidden `IFrames`.

2.3 Sending Asynchronous Requests

Synchronous requests are easier to use than asynchronous requests because they return data directly and remove the hassle of creating callback functions. However, they aren't the standard use case for `XMLHttpRequest` because the entire browser is locked while the request is happening. There are some circumstances in which blocking is useful (mainly when a decision needs to be made before the current function ends), but in most cases, you'll want these requests to happen in the background. An asynchronous request allows the browser to continue running JavaScript code and users to continue interacting with the page while the new data is loaded. With the proper user interface, asynchronous communication allows an AJAX application to be useful even when the user's connection to the site is slow.

To make an asynchronous call, we need to accomplish two tasks: set the asynchronous flag on open to `true`, and add a `readyStateChanged` event handler. This event handler will wait for a ready state of 4, which means the response is loaded. It will then check the status property. If the status is 200, we can use `responseText`; if it's another value, we have an error, so we'll need to create an alert dialog to show it. An asynchronous call to `test.php` is shown in Listing 2-2. The `initXMLHttpClient` function from an earlier chapter section, "Cross-Browser `XMLHttpRequest`," is used to create our `XMLHttpRequest` object.

Listing 2-2

Making an Asynchronous Request

```
1   var req = initXMLHttpClient();
2   req.onreadystatechange = function() {
3       if (req.readyState == 4) {
4           if (req.status == 200) {
5               alert(req.responseText);
6           } else {
7               alert('Loading Error: ['+req.status+'] '
8                       +req.statusText);
9           }
10      }
11  }
12  req.open('GET','test.php',true);
13  req.send(null);
```

Although this code gets the job done, it's not a great long-term solution because we will have to write a new onreadystatechange method for each call. The solution to this is to create our own HttpClient class that wraps XMLHttpRequest. Such a class gives us an easy-to-use API and a property to use for the callback that has to deal only with successful requests. Just adding some helper methods would be a simpler solution, but that's not a possibility because IE doesn't allow you to add methods to an ActiveX object.

A sample XMLHttpRequest wrapper class is shown in Listing 2-3. The main features of the HttpClient class are a callback property that is called when a successful asynchronous request is complete and a makeRequest method that combines the open and send functions. It also provides event properties that are called when a request is made (onSend), when it ends (onload), and when an errors occurs (onError). A default onSend and onLoad implementation is provided, which creates a basic loading message while requests are being made.

Listing 2-3

HttpClient XMLHttpRequest *Wrapper*

```
1   function HttpClient() { }
2   HttpClient.prototype = {
3       // type GET,POST passed to open
4       requestType:'GET',
5       // when set to true, async calls are made
6       isAsync:false,
7
8       // where an XMLHttpRequest instance is stored
```

```
9      xmlhttp:false,
10
11       // what is called when a successful async call is made
12       callback:false,
13
14       // what is called when send is called on XMLHttpRequest
15       // set your own function to onSend to have a custom loading
16       // effect
        onSend:function() {
17          document.getElementById('HttpClientStatus').style.display =
18                              'block';
19       },
20
21       // what is called when readyState 4 is reached, this is
22       // called before your callback
23        onload:function() {
24           document.getElementById('HttpClientStatus').style.display =
25                              'none';
26        },
27
28       // what is called when an http error happens
29       onError:function(error) {
30          alert(error);
31       },
32
33       // method to initialize an xmlhttpclient
34       init:function() {
35         try {
36            // Mozilla / Safari
37              this.xmlhttp = new XMLHttpRequest();
38         } catch (e) {
39            // IE
40            var XMLHTTP_IDS = new Array('MSXML2.
                                          XMLHTTP.5.0',
41                                        'MSXML2.XMLHTTP.4.0',
42                                        'MSXML2.XMLHTTP.3.0',
43                                        'MSXML2.XMLHTTP',
44                                        'Microsoft.XMLHTTP');
45            var success = false;
46            for (var i=0;i < XMLHTTP_IDS.length &&
              !success; i++) {
47                try {
48                    this.xmlhttp = new ActiveXObject
                      (XMLHTTP_IDS[i]);
49                    success = true;
50                } catch (e) {}
51            }
52            if (!success) {
53                this.onError('Unable to create XMLHttpRequest.');
```

```
54                  }
55              }
56          },
57
58      // method to make a page request
59      // @param string url   The page to make the request to
60      // @param string payload   What you're sending if this is a POST
61      //                           request
62      makeRequest: function(url,payload) {
63              if (!this.xmlhttp) {
64                  this.init();
65              }
66          this.xmlhttp.open(this.requestType,url,this.isAsync);
67
68              // set onreadystatechange here since it will be reset after a
69          //completed call in Mozilla
70          var self = this;
71          this.xmlhttp.onreadystatechange = function() {
72          self._readyStateChangeCallback(); }
73
74          this.xmlhttp.send(payload);
75
76          if (!this.isAsync) {
77              return this.xmlhttp.responseText;
78          }
79      },
80
81      // internal method used to handle ready state changes
82      _readyStateChangeCallback:function() {
83          switch(this.xmlhttp.readyState) {
84              case 2:
85                  this.onSend();
86                  break;
87            case 4:
88                  this.onload();
89                  if (this.xmlhttp.status == 200) {
90                      this.callback(this.xmlhttp.responseText);
91                  } else {
92                      this.onError('HTTP Error Making Request: '+
93                                    '['+this.xmlhttp.
                                      status+']'+
94                                    '+this.xmlhttp.
                                      statusText));
95                  }
96                  break;
97          }
98      }
99  }
```

The `HttpClient` class contains comments explaining its basic functionality, but you will want to look at a couple of areas in detail. The first areas are the properties you'll want to set while interacting with the class; these include the following:

- **`requestType`** (**line 4**). Used to set the HTTP request type, GET is used to request content that doesn't perform an action whereas POST is used for requests that do.

- **`isAsync`** (**line 6**). A Boolean value used to set the request method. The default is false, which makes an synchronous request. If you're making an asynchronous request, `isAsync` is set to `true`. When making an asynchronous request, you also need to set the `callback` property.

- **`callback`** (**line 12**). This property takes a function that takes a single parameter result and is called when a request is successfully completed.

Lines 16–31 contain simple functions for handling some basic user feedback. When a request is sent to the server, a DOM element with the ID of `HttpClientStatus` is shown (lines 16–19). When it completes, it is hidden again (lines 23–26). The class also defines a function to call when an error happens (lines 29–31); it creates an alert box with the error message. Common errors include receiving a `404 page not found` HTTP error message or not being able to create an `XMLHttpRequest` object. The implementation of these three functions is simple, and you'll likely want to override them with more sophisticated application-specific versions.

Lines 33–56 contain the `init` method, which is identical to the `initXMLHttpClient` function we created in Listing 2-1, except for what it does with its error message. Now it sends it to the `onError` method. You won't be dealing with this function directly because the `makeRequest` method will take care of it for you. The `makeRequest` method (lines 62–79) is your main interaction with the class. It takes two parameters: a URL to which to make the request and a payload that is sent to the server if you're making a POST request. The actual implementation is a more generic version of the code shown in Listing 2-2. The `_readyStateChangeCallback` (lines 82–99) method is set as the `readyState` handler by `makeRequest`. It handles calling `onSend` when the initial request is sent and then calling `onload` when the request completes. It also checks for a `200 HTTP` status code and calls `onError` if some other status is returned.

Listing 2-4 uses the `HttpClient` class and shows its basic usage. A wrapper class like this helps cut down the amount of code you need to write per request while giving a single place to make future changes.

Listing 2-4

Using the `HttpClient` `XMLHttpRequest` ***Wrapper***

```
1   <html>
2   <head>
3   <title>Simple XMLHttpRequest Wrapper Test Page</title>
4
5   <script type="text/javascript" src="HttpClient.js"></script>
6   <body>
7   <script type="text/javascript">
8
9   var client = new HttpClient();
10  client.isAsync = true;
11
12  function test() {
13      client.callback = function(result) {
14          document.getElementById('target').innerHTML = result;
15      }
16        client.makeRequest('.',null);
17  }
18  </script>
19
20  <div id="HttpClientStatus" style="display:none">Loading ...</div>
21  <a href='javascript:test()'>Make an Async Test call</a>
22  <div id="target"></div>
23  </body>
24  </html>
```

Using the `HttpClient` `XMLHttpRequest` wrapper is a simple task. You start by including it in the header of your HTML page (line 5), and then you can proceed to use it. You do this by creating an instance of the class (line 9), configuring its basic properties (in this case, setting `isAsync` to true (line 10)), and then setting up some code to call `makeRequest`. In most cases, this code will be contained in a function so that it can be tied to a user-driven event, such as clicking a link. The call is made by the `test` function (lines 12–17); the `test` function first sets up a callback to run when the request is complete (lines 13–15), and then it calls `makeRequest` (line 16), which starts the AJAX call.

2.4 AJAX Without XMLHttpRequest

There are a number of cases in which you might not have XMLHttpRequest support. The most common would be in the case of an older browser. This is the hardest to work around, not because there is no AJAX fallback, but because all the other DOM manipulation that you do within the application won't work. Another problem case is when your browser supports everything that is needed except for XMLHttpRequest. This problem could occur when IE is in a mode where it can't use ActiveXObjects or when you are using a pre-7.6 version of Opera. In some cases, especially intranet applications, it's easy to just require an upgrade, but if you want to use AJAX on a public site, you'll want to think about using some sort of fallback mechanism. The best candidate for a fallback is to use hidden IFrames. Another option is to use cookies, but they can send only a limited amount of data per request, so it is hard to drop in cookie-based approaches as a replacement for code that has been written with XMLHttpRequest in mind. Only XMLHttpRequest supports synchronous calls, so if they are necessary for your application, then using it as a fallback will not be possible.

If you're using a fully wrapped XMLHttpRequest and you don't use synchronous calls, providing transparent fallback to your program should be possible. You need only to replace the final throwing of an exception in the example init method with the instantiation of your IFrame HTTP client. The main item to remember about using another approach instead of XMLHttpRequest is that it's not going to gain you huge leaps in compatibility. The major browsers already support XMLHttpRequest. This support makes browsers with JavaScript turned off, not those running an unsupported browser, the biggest group that can't use your AJAX application. The advantages and disadvantages of the AJAX communication techniques are shown in Table 2-2.

TABLE 2-2
Advantages and Disadvantages of AJAX Techniques

Technique	Advantages	Disadvantages
XMLHttpRequest	Can make requests to pages not set up for AJAX Can set/get all HTTP headers Can make HTTP requests using any type (GET, POST, PROPFIND, and so on) Supports full control over POST requests, allowing for any type of data encoding	Requests ActiveX to be enabled in IE 5 and 6 Is only available in newer versions of Opera and Safari Has small implementation differences between browsers
IFrame	Can make POST and GET HTTP requests Supportes all modern browsers Supports asynchronous file uploads	Prohibits synchronous requests Server pages must be designed to work with IFrame requests Has implementation differences between browsers Can leave extra entries in browser history (depends on browser and implementation) All request data is URL-encoded, increasing request size
Cookies	Supports the largest number of browsers Few implementation differences between browsers	Prohibits no synchronous requests Doesn't work with large requests/results Requires server pages to be designed to work with cookie requests Requires polling on the client Can make only GET HTTP requests

2.5 Fallback Option 1: Sending a Request Using an `IFrame`

`IFrames` make a suitable transport for asynchronous calls because they can load content without causing the entire page to reload, and new `IFrame` elements can be created using JavaScript. The nicest attribute about an `IFrame` is that a form can use one as its target, reloading that `IFrame` instead of the entire page; this approach allows large amounts of data to be sent to the server using `POST`.

One difficulty in using an `IFrame` as a transport is that the page we're loading needs to be HTML, and it needs to have a JavaScript `onload` event handler to tell the parent document when it's done loading. This need forces all requests being made with `IFrames` to be made to pages designed to deal with `IFrame` requests. (Code can't just grab an XML file in the way that `XMLHttpRequest` allows.)

Note that the use of `IFrames` does have a number of further limitations:

- Support of only asynchronous requests
- Server pages needing changed
- Phantom entries in browser's history
- Odd back/forward button behavior in some browsers
- Large differences in browser implementations, especially in older browsers

One advantage that an `IFrame` has over `XMLHttpRequest` is that it can be used to make file uploads. Due to browser security limitations, only user actions, such as clicking a form, can interact with files on the user's machine. This makes targeting a form to an `IFrame` the only option for file uploads that do not involve a normal form `POST` and page reload cycle. However, there is no reason you can't fall back to using an `IFrame` for file uploads and `XMLHttpRequest` for the rest of your AJAX requests. Unless you are making remote scripting-style AJAX requests (which is covered in Chapter 3, "Consuming the Sent Data"), working around `IFrame` limitations will add a significant amount of work to any AJAX development project.

2.5.1 Creating a Hidden `IFrame`

To get maximum compatibility with older browsers, you could just add the `IFrame` to your HTML and give it a size of 0x0. (You can't just hide it, or some browsers won't load it.) However, this approach isn't flexible, so you will want to create the frame dynamically. Not all older browsers support `document.createElement`, but browsers without that support will generally lack the other dynamic capabilities needed to use the data you're loading, so it's best to provide support to them with a static HTML version of the page. In the following example, the `IFrame` is created using `innerHTML` because it's simpler than creating it using DOM methods. Note, however, that it could also be created with `document.createElement`, just like the `div` to which it's being added:

```
1 var rDiv = document.createElement('div');
2 rDiv.id = 'remotingDiv';
3 var style = 'border:0;width:0;height:0;';
4 rDiv.innerHTML = "<iframe name='"+id+"' id='"+id+"'
5 style='"+style+"'></iframe>";
6
7 document.body.appendChild(rDiv);
```

2.5.2 Creating a Form

If you want to make only a GET request, you can change the value of the `IFrame`'s `src` property, but to do POST, you need to use a targeted form. GET isn't a good solution for AJAX requests for two reasons: it can send only a limited amount of data (an amount that changes depending on the browser), and GET can be cached and/or preloaded by proxy servers, so you never want to use it to perform an action such as updating your database.

Using a form with an `IFrame` is easy. Just set the form's `target` attribute, and when you submit the form, the result loads in the `IFrame`. The following example creates our form and sets its targets to the `IFrame` we created earlier in the "Creating a Hidden `IFrame`" section of the chapter:

```
1 rDiv.form = document.createElement('form');
2 rDiv.form.setAttribute('id', id+'RemotingForm');
3 rDiv.form.setAttribute('action', url);
4 rDiv.form.setAttribute('target', id);
5 rDiv.form.target = id;
6 rDiv.form.setAttribute('method', 'post');
7 rDiv.form.innerHTML = '<input type="hidden" name="data"
8                        id="'+id+'Data">';
```

2.5.3 Send Data from the Loaded Content to the Original Document

The only way to know that the content of the `IFrame` has loaded is to have the content page run some JavaScript that notifies the parent page in which the `IFrame` is embedded. The simplest way to do this is to set the `onload` event handler on the document you are loading. This limitation means you can't use an IFrame for loading arbitrary content like you can with XMLHttpRequest. However, it's still useful for cases in which a single server page is already being used as an AJAX gateway. Here is an example of `onload`:

```
<body onload="parent.document.callback(result)">
```

2.5.4 Complete IFrame AJAX Example

A full example of an IFrame that AJAX requests includes two pieces. The first piece is the client-side code to create the IFrame and form. The second piece is the server-side code, which prepares some data and sends it back to the parent document in its `onload` event handler.

The first part of the example (Listing 2-5) is the JavaScript code in a simple HTML file. This page is used for testing; the callback function just alerts the contents of the results. The second part of the example (Listing 2-6) is a simple PHP script, which takes the data from POST and sends it back to the parent document. To make a useful system, you might also want to include some extra variables in the form, which would tell the PHP code what to do with the uploaded data, or you could put the logic directly into the script and use a different target page for each task you wanted to accomplish.

Listing 2-5

Making an AJAX Request Using an IFrame

```
1  <html>
2  <head>
3  <script type="text/javascript">
4  var remotingDiv;
5  function createRemotingDiv(id,url) {
6      var rDiv = document.createElement('div');
7      rDiv.id = 'remotingDiv';
8      var style = 'border:0;width:0;height:0;';
9      rDiv.innerHTML = "<iframe name='"+id+"' id='"+id+"'
10                      style='"+style+"'></iframe>";
11
12     document.body.appendChild(rDiv);
13     rDiv.iframe = document.getElementById(id);
14
15     rDiv.form = document.createElement('form');
16     rDiv.form.setAttribute('id', id+'RemotingForm');
17     rDiv.form.setAttribute('action', url);
```

```
18      rDiv.form.setAttribute('target', id);
19      rDiv.form.target = id;
20      rDiv.form.setAttribute('method', 'post');
21      rDiv.form.innerHTML = '<input type="hidden" name="data"
22                            id="'+id+'Data">';
23
24      rDiv.appendChild(rDiv.form);
25      rDiv.data = document.getElementById(id+'Data');
26
27      return rDiv;
28 }
29
30 function sendRequest(url,payload,callback) {
31      if (!remotingDiv) {
32          remotingDiv = createRemotingDiv('remotingFrame',
33                                          'blank.html');
34      }
35      remotingDiv.form.action = url;
36       remotingDiv.data.value = payload;
37       remotingDiv.callback = callback;
38       remotingDiv.form.submit();
39
40 }
41
42 function test() {
43      sendRequest('test.php','This is some test data',
44                  function(result){ alert(result) });
45 }
46
47
48
49 </script>
50 </head>
51
52 <body id="body">
53
54
55 <a href="javascript:test()">Test</a>
56
57 </body>
58 </html>
```

Listing 2-5 is made up of three functions:

- createRemotingDiv for setting up the IFrame.

- sendRequest for making an AJAX request.

- test for making an AJAX request. The test function is tied to a link (line 55) in the pages' HTML. Clicking on this link allows the user to start an AJAX request.

The createRemotingDiv function (lines 5–28) combines the previously described code for creating a hidden IFrame with the code for creating a form to submit to it. When the form is created, it's targeted against the newly created IFrame, making the form submission use it instead of reloading the current page. Showing the IFrame during development is often useful in the debugging process so that you can see any output generated by the page you're calling. You can do this by editing the style on line 8 and changing it to width:200;height:200;.

The sendRequest function (lines 30–40) makes an AJAX request. It takes the URL to which to make the request, a payload to send to the server, and a callback function to run when the request is complete. The function uses createRemotingDiv to set up the process (lines 31–34). Then sendRequest updates the action on the IFrame form (line 35), adds the payload value on the form, and submits the form using the IFrame. When the new page is loaded into the IFrame, the new document uses a JavaScript onload handler to call the callback function that was passed into the sendRequest method. The PHP page that processes the form POST and creates the onload JavaScript is shown in Listing 2-6.

Listing 2-6

PHP Server Page That Handles an IFrame ***AJAX Request***

```
1   <html>
2   <head>
3   <script type="text/javascript">
4   var result = "<?php
5                   echo $_POST['data'];
6                   ?>";
7   </script>
8   </head>
9   <body
10  onload =
11  "parent.document.getElementById('remotingDiv').callback(result)">
12  </body>
13  </html>
```

On the server side, the form is processed and output is created in the form of an HTML page. The simplest way to add new data is to generate JavaScript containing the new data. In this case, we are just echoing the data back to the client by putting it in the result variable (lines 4–6). Normally, you'll be running server-side code here and either outputting a string (as in this case) or adding new JavaScript code to run against the parent document. The `callback` function on the parent is called by the `onload` handler on the body tag (line 11).

2.6 Fallback Option 2: Sending a Request Using a Cookie

You can transfer data to your server using cookies, but any implementation using them will be severely limited. Cookies have a maximum size of 4k, and each domain can set only 20 of them, which means that each request is going to be size-limited. Cookie-based AJAX is most useful when your site is designed for it, because its limitations make it hard to use it as a fallback. The basic functionality is provided by setting a cookie, loading an image, and then polling on an interval while waiting for the response to appear. The implementation is simple; to do something besides alerting the contents of the result, you just set your own custom `onComplete` event handler. An example where the server returns the input and the number of times it has been called is shown in Listings 2-7 and 2-8. The example's JavaScript is shown in Listing 2-7, and the PHP code, which reads the cookie and then sets a response, is shown in Listing 2-8.

Listing 2-7
Cookie-Powered AJAX

```
1   <html>
2   <head>
3     <title>Cookie Test</title>
4
5   <script type="text/javascript">
6   function CookieRequest() { }
7   CookieRequest.prototype = {
8       interval: 500,
9       attempts: 5,
10      attemptCounter: 0,
11      call: function(url,payload) {
12          var d = new Date();
13          var i = new Image();
14          this.setCookie('CR',payload);
15          i.src = url + '?u=' + d.getTime();
16          var self = this;
17          this.timerId = setTimeout(function()
18                              { self.read(); }, this.interval);
19      },
```

```
20      read: function() {
21          this.attemptCounter++;
22          // check for data
23          var data = this.getCookie('CR');
24          if (data != false) {
25              this.attemptCounter = 0;
26              this.onComplete(data);
27              return true;
28          }
29
30          // check for error
31          if (this.attemptCounter > this.attempts) {
32              this.onError();
33          } else {
34              var self = this;
35              this.timerId = setTimeout(function() { self.read(); },
36                              this.interval);
37          }
38      },
39      onComplete: function(result) {
40          alert(result)
41      },
42      onError: function() {
43          alert('Request timed out');
44      },
45      setCookie: function(name, value, expires) {
46          document.cookie = name + "=" + escape(value) +
47                          ((expires) ? "; expires=" +
48                          expires.toGMTString() : "");
49      },
50      getCookie: function(name) {
51          var docCookie = document.cookie.split("; ");
52          for (var i=0; i < docCookie.length; i++){
53              var piece = docCookie[i].split("=");
54              if (piece[0] == name) {
55                  return unescape(String(piece[1]).
                    replace(/\+/g, " "));
56              }
57          }
58          return false;
59      }
60  }
61  function test() {
62      var cr = new CookieRequest();
63      cr.call('cookie.php','Some Example Data');
64  }
65  </script>
66  </head>
67  <body>
68      <a href='javascript:test()'>Test</a>
69  </body>
```

In Listing 2-7, the cookie-powered AJAX functionality is wrapped inside the JavaScript class `CookieRequest`. Requests to the server are made with the `call` method (lines 11–19). The `call` method takes a URL to which to send the request. It also takes a payload (the content we want to send to the server), which is sent in the request cookie. The method then uses the `setCookie` method to set a cookie named CR (line 14); it then creates a new `Image` object and sets its `src` to the requested URL (line 15). The method finishes by starting a timer, which runs the `read` method every 500 milliseconds.

The `read` method (lines 20–38) checks for the presence of the CR cookie (lines 23–24). If it exists, the data in it is passed to the `onComplete` method (line 26). If the data isn't present, we check for errors; this is done by comparing the number of checks we've completed against the max checks set in the `attempts` property (line 31). If there is an error, the `onError` method is called (line 32). If no error is present, we start another timer to do the next check (lines 34–35).

Lines 39–44 contain methods that you'll override when using the class. The `onComplete` method is called when data is successfully loaded. This is the equivalent of the `callback` property in the `HttpClient` class. The `onError` method is called if the request doesn't complete successfully; of course, you could leave this as an alert, but, in most cases, you'll want to provide a more understandable error message to your users or even retry the request.

The `CookieRequest` class also contains helper methods for dealing with getting and setting cookies. `setCookie` (lines 45–49) works by setting the value of `document.cookie` to a `urlencoded` string in the format of `cookie name=value`. `getCookie` (lines 50–59) works by splitting `document.cookie` into one part for each cookie (the cookies are separated by ";") and then looping over these parts looking for a cookie with the specified name. If a matching name is found, the value is returned; otherwise, false is returned.

The PHP page that is used with Listing 2-7 is shown in Listing 2-8. It is used as the URL in the `call` method and processes the payload that is set; it then sets a response for read to grab.

Listing 2-8

PHP Server Page for Handling a Cookie AJAX Request

```
1   <?php
2   session_start();
3   if (!isset($_SESSION['i'])) {
4       $_SESSION['i'] = 0;
5   }
6   if (isset($_COOKIE['CR'])) {
7       $_SESSION['i']++;
8       setcookie('CR','Server Responds: '.$_SESSION['i'].',
9                   '.$_COOKIE['CR']);
10  }
11  ?>
```

This PHP code provides the basic functionality needed to interact with cookie-based AJAX requests. It uses PHP sessions to store a counter and increments it as each request is made. As you extend this code, you could use different PHP pages to decide which action to perform, or you could include that information in the cookie that is sent from the client. Lines 2–5 handle basic session setup, setting the counter to 0 if this is the first call. Lines 6–10 handle the checking of the client cookie and the sending of the response. This is done by setting a cookie that then will be sent with the response (line 8–9). If you want to handle large server responses, you would need to include code to split the data among multiple cookies.

2.7 Summary

At the heart of AJAX is the communication channel with your server. The best way to accomplish AJAX communication is by using XMLHttpRequest. XMLHttpRequest provides the ability to make synchronous and asynchronous requests while providing an easy-to-use programming model. XMLHttpRequest's biggest disadvantage is that it doesn't work on IE6 when ActiveX is disabled, which can cause problems for security-conscious users. For cases in which XMLHttpRequest can't be used, you do have a number of different options. The best of these options is the use of hidden IFrames. IFrames require server pages to be specially tailored to respond to their requests. This shortcoming makes for a much less flexible implementation but one that is still capable of getting the job done for many AJAX applications.

When you need to support old browsers, you can use either IFrames or cookie-based solutions. Cookie-based solutions can even be used on version 3 browsers, if needed. Note, however, that the limited dynamic ability of a browser from that period makes building any large-scale AJAX applications a very difficult task. When targeting modern browsers, compatibility isn't a huge concern, and you can choose the AJAX communication layer with the best features: XMLHttpRequest.

Chapter 3

Consuming the Sent Data

In this chapter

There are two main ways you can use the data you receive from XMLHttpRequest or one of the fallback methods: the document-centric approach, and the other is remote scripting. In this chapter, we look at different ways to implement these techniques and use the data we learned to send in the previous chapter.

3.1 Document-Centric Approaches

A document-centric approach to AJAX simply means that your main interaction with the server is pulling down pages of content. This doesn't mean that the pages aren't dynamically generated, but it does mean you're pulling down the content in a ready-to-use or parse format. The simplest use case is to download a chunk of HTML from your server and insert it into the page using innerHTML.

The biggest differentiator between document-centric approaches and remote scripting is how the design relates with the server. Remote scripting-style AJAX is tightly coupled to the server and gives you a direct interface to the server-side code, using a standardized system to transfer the call and request between the client and the server. Document-centric approaches are loosely tied to the server; the only requirement is that the data be in the usable format, allowing you to generate plain text, HTML, or XML in whatever manner you want. One advantage that document-centric approaches have is that they are highly scalable because more of the work happens on the client. Document-centric approaches are not a magic bullet for scalability or performance, because dynamically generated content can have many bottlenecks; however, they do closely resemble current Web models, which allow the same optimization strategies to be used.

3.1.1 Adding New HTML Content to a Page with AJAX

One of the basic actions performed on every Web page is the displaying of new content when a user clicks a link. In many circumstances, this works fine, but when you want to keep the original content, you have a problem. HTML offers two solutions to the problem: frames and IFrames. Both allow multiple pages to be embedded into a single page. The problem with frame-based solutions is that you're still stuck loading entire pages; that being said, you can easily use frame-based solutions to add a new row to a table or provide a status message. AJAX offers an easy way

out: load the HTML directly using XMLHttpRequest and add it to your page by
replacing the content of a DIV using innerHTML. An example of using the
HttpClient.js XMLHttpRequest wrapper we built earlier (Listing 2-3) is shown
in Listing 3-1. The pages that are being loaded, content1.html and content2.
html, are also shown; they can be any fragment of HTML or other text you want
to load into the DIV.

Listing 3-1

Adding HTML Content.html

```
1   <html>
2   <head>
3   <title>Adding HTML Content</title>
4   <script type="text/javascript" src="HttpClient.js"></script>
5   <script type="text/javascript">
6
7   var client = new HttpClient();
8   client.isAsync = true;
9
10  client.callback = function(result) {
11      document.getElementById('target').innerHTML = result;
12  }
13
14  function replaceContent(page) {
15      client.makeRequest(page,null);
16  }
17  </script>
18  </head>
19  <body>
20
21  <ul>
22      <li><a href="javascript:replaceContent('content1.html')">
23          Load Document 1</a></li>
24      <li><a href="javascript:replaceContent('content2.html')">
25          Load Document 2</a></li>
26  </ul>
27
28  <div style="position: absolute; width:100px; height:20px;
29      top: 5px; right: 5px; display:none"
30      id="HttpClientStatus">Loading ...</div>
31
32  <div id="target" style="width:300px; height:300px;
33      border: solid 1px black"> </div>
34  </body>
35  </html>
```

Line 4 includes the `XMLHttpRequest` wrapper, `HttpClient`, which is instantiated on line 7. Because we want to make an asynchronous request, we turn that mode on at line 8 and then create our callback function (lines 10–12). This callback will take the result from the load and set the `innerHTML` of the target element to it. Lines 14–16 create a JavaScript function that we can call from HTML links. This function, `replaceContent`, takes a single parameter, `page`, which is the URL we want to load. Line 15 makes the remote request. The second parameter is `null` because we have no `POST` data that we want to send as a payload.

The rest of the example is a list of test calls to `replaceContent` and the user interface (UI) elements used by the JavaScript code. Lines 22–23 load `Content1.html`, and lines 24–25 load `Content2.html`. Lines 28–30 create a DIV element with an ID of `HttpClientStatus`. Whenever you are using `HttpClient.js`, you need to provide an element with this ID. The element should be hidden by default; this is accomplished by setting `display:none` in the style attribute. When the `XMLHttpRequest` object downloads content from the server, the `HttpClientStatus` element will be shown by setting the `style.display` attribute to `block`. Lines 32–33 provide a DIV with an ID of `target`; this is where the downloaded content is displayed. The results of Listing 3-1 loading `content1.html` are shown in Figure 3-1.

```
content1.html
```

```
<p>I'm an HTML fragment.  Any <b>html</b> can be used.</p>
```

```
content2.html
```

```
I'm some other content. In this case I don't contain anything but text.
```

In Listing 3-1, we took a normal HTML document and used AJAX to load in new content at will. This basic technique can be accomplished through the use of frames, but AJAX gives you a lot more flexibility. We can divide the page in any way we choose, dynamically updating something as small as a single word or as large as the majority of the page. Dynamically updating a page with content is powerful, and it fits well into any server-side development model, because you're simply increasing the number of pages you generate while decreasing their size and scope.

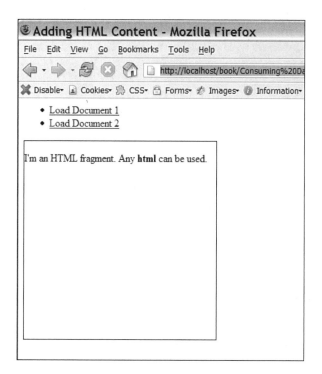

FIGURE 3-1
Using AJAX to perform basic content replacement

3.1.2 Consuming XML Using DOM

Another popular way to load new data is to use XML. XML is useful when you want abstraction between the code on the server that produces the data and the JavaScript client code that uses it. This allows you to change out the back end without affecting the front end. It also allows you to expose data for other clients through the same generic API. The XML Document Object Model (DOM) is similar to the HTML one that we've used in other examples.

An easy way to visualize the DOM is to picture a tree of objects, one for each XML element on the page. For example, the following sample XML document will make DOM with four nodes: the root Document node, an Element node for the rootTag, and an Element node for the childTag. The childTag has a Text node containing Some Text.

```
<rootTag>
  <childTag>Some Text</childTag>
</rootTag>
```

A visual representation of this tree is shown here:

```
Document
        Element (rootTag)
                Element (childTag)
                        Text
```

To turn this DOM model into HTML, we will need to use a couple basic methods and properties:

- **getElementsByTagName(tagName).** Gets an array of tags of the specified name as a result

- **getAttribute(attributeName).** Gives you the value of one of the tag's attributes

- **firstChild().** Returns the first child node of any node

The other step we need to take is to get the XML document result from XMLHttpRequest instead of the plain text. To do this, set the Content-type of the downloaded page to text/xml. This causes the responseXML property of XMLHttpRequest to create a DOM document from the contents.

In the following examples, we take an XML list of resource links about a subject and turn them into a simple HTML list. The two test lists contain PHP resource links and a list of book sellers. Listing 3-2 contains the list of PHP resources, whereas Listing 3-3 contains the list of sellers. These files are used by Listing 3-4, which uses the DOM to update the current page and build the list.

Listing 3-2

PhpResources.xml

```
<sites type="PHP Resources">
    <site url="http://php.net">PHP Website</site>
    <site url="http://php.net/manual">PHP Manual</site>
    <site url="http://phpdoc.org">phpDocumentor Code Documentation Tool</site>
</sites>
```

Listing 3-3

BookSellers.xml

```
<sites type="A List of Book Sellers">
     <site url="http://amazon.com">Amazon</site>
     <site url="http://bn.com">Barnes and Noble</site>
</sites>
```

Listing 3-4

DOMExample.html

```
1   <html>
2   <head>
3   <title>DOM Example - Displaying URL Lists from XML</title>
4   <script type="text/javascript" src="HttpClient.js"></script>
5   <script type="text/javascript">
6
7   var client = new HttpClient();
8   client.isAsync = true;
9
10  client.callback = function() {
11     var newDom = client.xmlhttp.responseXML;
12
13     var content = "<h2>"+
14         newDom.firstChild.getAttribute('type')
15         +"</h2><ul>";
16
17     var sites = newDom.getElementsByTagName('site');
18     for(var i = 0; i < sites.length; i++) {
19       content += "<li><a href='"+
20             sites[i].getAttribute('url')+"'>"+
21             sites[i].firstChild.nodeValue+
22             "</a></li>";
23     }
24     content += "</li>";
25
26     document.getElementById('target').innerHTML =
27         content;
28  }
29
30   function displayResources(url) {
31      client.makeRequest(url,null);
32  }
33  </script>
34  </head>
35  <body>
36
37  <ul>
```

```
38      <li><a href="javascript:displayResources('PhpResources.xml')">
39          Display PHP Links</a></li>
40      <li><a href="javascript:displayResources('BookSellers.xml')">
41          Display Book Seller Links</a></li>
42  </ul>
43
44  <div style="position: absolute; width:100px; height:20px;
45      top: 5px; right: 5px; display:none"
46      id="HttpClientStatus">Loading ...</div>
47
48  <div id="target" style="width:300px; height:300px;
49      border: solid 1px black"> </div>
50  </body>
51  </html>
```

The JavaScript `HttpClient` class (from Chapter 2, "Getting Started") gives us cross-browser `XMLHttpRequest` support. On line 4, we include the library, and on line 7, we create an instance of the client. Then, on line 8, we set `isAsync` to `true` because we want to make an asynchronous request for the XML data file. Next, on lines 10–28, we add our callback function; this function takes the downloaded XML document, creates an HTML list, and then shows the list using `innerHTML`.

On line 11, we grab the XML DOM document from response XML. We have to use the `XMLHttpRequest` object directly because `HttpClient` doesn't wrap this. Depending on the complexity of the HTML page, updating a node with `innerHTML` can be an expensive operation. To keep this to a minimum, we use a variable to hold our HTML content and then update it all at once at the end of the function. On lines 13–15, we read the type attribute from the site's tag and use it to make a title for our list. Then on line 17, we get an array of all the site nodes in our XML document, which is looped through on lines 18–23. In each iteration of the site's array, we build one list element. This is a pretty straightforward process; the only item of note is the use of `firstChild()` and `nodeValue()` to get to the text content of the site tag. These calls are needed because text content exists in its own node in the DOM, and there is no `innerHTML` attribute to read from the text content and its markup, as is the case with the HTML DOM.

The rest of the page gives you a basic UI for testing. Lines 30–32 provide a helper function that requests the download of new XML files. When the download is done, the callback function that builds the output will be called. Lines 37–42 contain a list with links to process the sample XML files, and lines 44–46 contain a basic loading DIV that is shown while waiting for the XML documents to be downloaded. Finally, we have a target DIV that is used by the callback function as a place to display the generated list. The output of Listing 3-4, showing the PHP resources list, is shown in Figure 3-2.

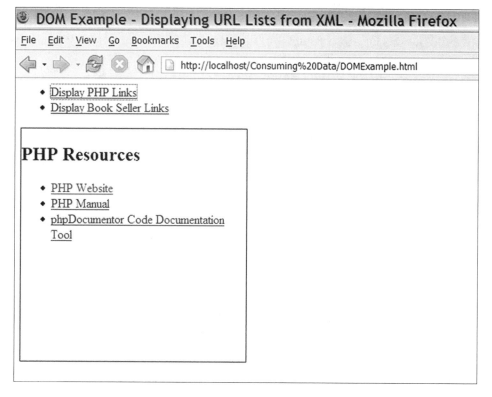

FIGURE 3-2
Updating an HTML page by consuming XML documents using the DOM

When tied with dynamically updates, DOM-based consumption of XML can be an efficient way to dynamically display data on the browser. Using the DOM manipulation function can make for tedious programming, so it isn't usually the best approach for generating a large amount of content from nonstructured data.

3.1.3 Consuming XML Using XSLT

eXtensible Stylesheet Language Transformations (XSLT) is another popular way to take a DOM document and generate new output. The advantage it has over DOM is that the transformation and the data are in an XML file. XSLT has been used by many successful AJAX applications, such as Google Maps, but it does have a number of drawbacks. XSLT browser support is uneven, and even when two browsers, such as Internet Explorer 6 and Firefox 1.0, support the same main features, the application programming interfaces (APIs) for controlling the transformations from JavaScript are completely different. This difference is large enough that you can't just write a simple wrapper like you can for XMLHttpRequest. If you need cross-browser support, you'll need to rely on a library like Sarissa instead. (The Sarissa library is explained in detail in Chapter 8, "Libraries Used in Part II: Sarissa, Scriptaculous.")

XSLT can also be problematic simply due to its complexity. Not only will you need to learn how to write the XSLT style sheets that drive the actual transformation, but you'll also need to learn XPath, which is used to refer to XML nodes inside the style sheet. Because XSLT is a World Wide Web Consortium standard, there are tools and documentation out there to help, but in many cases, the added effort required over a DOM approach isn't worth the effort.

Although the purpose of this book isn't to teach you how to write an XSLT style, I will explain the basics of the one used. Listing 3-5 replaces the JavaScript DOM code in Listing 3-4 with an XSLT transformation. The same XML data files (`PhpResources.xml` and `Booksellers.xml`) that are used in the DOM example are used here. The Mozilla XSLT API is used in these examples because it's easier to understand, and all you have to do to make it work in IE is include the Sarissa library.

Listing 3-5

XSLTExample.html

```
1   <html>
2   <head>
3   <title>XSLT Example - Displaying URL Lists from XML</title>
4   <script type="text/javascript" src="HttpClient.js"></script>
5   <script type="text/javascript" src="sarissa/sarissa.js">
</script>
6   <script type="text/javascript">
7   var client = new HttpClient();
```

```
8   client.isAsync = true;
9   var xsltProcessor = new XSLTProcessor();
10
11  function setup() {
12      // set up an xsltprocessor and import the stylesheet
13      client.callback = function() {
14          var xslRef = client.xmlhttp.responseXML;
15          xsltProcessor.importStylesheet(xslRef);
16      }
17      client.makeRequest('Resources.xsl');
18  }
19
20  function displayResources(url) {
21      client.callback = function() {
22          var newDom = client.xmlhttp.responseXML;
23          var output = xsltProcessor.transformToDocument(newDom);
24          document.getElementById('target').innerHTML = "";
25          document.getElementById('target').appendChild(
26              document.importNode(output.firstChild,true));
27      }
28
29      client.makeRequest(url,null);
30  }
31  </script>
32  </head>
33  <body onload="setup()">
34
35  <ul>
36      <li><a href="javascript:displayResources('PhpResources.xml')">
37          Display PHP Links</a></li>
38      <li><a href="javascript:displayResources('BookSellers.xml')">
39          Display Book Seller Links</a></li>
40  </ul>
41
42  <div style="position: absolute; width:100px; height:20px;
43      top: 5px; right: 5px; display:none"
44      id="HttpClientStatus">Loading ...</div>
45
46  <div id="target" style="width:300px; height:300px;
47      border: solid 1px black"> </div>
48  </body>
49  </html>
```

The first 18 lines cover the basic setup; we include our HttpClient
XMLHttpRequest wrapper and the Sarissa XML compatibility library. On line 7,
we create an HttpClient instance; this will be used to load both the style sheet and
the XML files we're going to transform; on line 8, we set isAsync to true because

we will be making only asynchronous requests. On line 9, we create a new `xsltProcessor` instance; this will be loaded with a style sheet in the `setup` function (lines 11–18) and then used to transform XML files loaded by the `displayResources` function (lines 20–30). On lines 13–16, we create a callback to run when the style sheet is loaded. It grabs the new XML DOM from the client (line 14) and then adds it to the `xsltProcessor` using its `importStylesheet` method (line 15); this style sheet is shown in Listing 3-6. The setup function completes by making the actual request (line 17) and is run by an `onload` handler (line 33).

The `displayResources` function is called by links in the HTML page; it loads new XML files and then transforms them. Lines 21–27 add a callback method that processes the downloaded XML document. Line 23 uses the processor we created to generate a new DOM document formatted by the style sheet we imported on line 15. Line 24 clears the target element on the HTML page, and then on lines 25–26, we append the content of the transformed DOM document. `document.importNode` has to be used for this process to work in a cross-browser manner. The rest of the HTML page (lines 34–49) has no changes from the DOM example. It's just a basic list of actions to be performed and a target to display the results.

Listing 3-6 finishes up the process; it is run on each XML file to produce HTML that is similar to the DOM example. Line 8 creates the list title using `value-of` to output the `type` attribute. Lines 10–19 loop over each site tag in the file, outputting a list item with the link inside it. You can see the output of this script showing the PHP resource list in Figure 3-3.

Listing 3-6

```
Resources.xsl
```

```
1    <?xml version="1.0"?>
2    <xsl:stylesheet version="1.0"
3        xmlns:xsl="http://www.w3.org/1999/XSL/Transform">
4
5    <xsl:output method="html" />
6    <xsl:template match="/sites">
7    <div>
8        <h2><xsl:value-of select="@type" /></h2>
9        <ul>
10       <xsl:for-each select="//site">
11           <li>
12           <xsl:element name="a">
13               <xsl:attribute name="href">
```

```
14                            <xsl:value-of select="@url" />
15                    </xsl:attribute>
16                    <xsl:value-of select="." />
17            </xsl:element>
18            </li>
19      </xsl:for-each>
20      </ul>
21 </div>
22 </xsl:template>
23 </xsl:stylesheet>
```

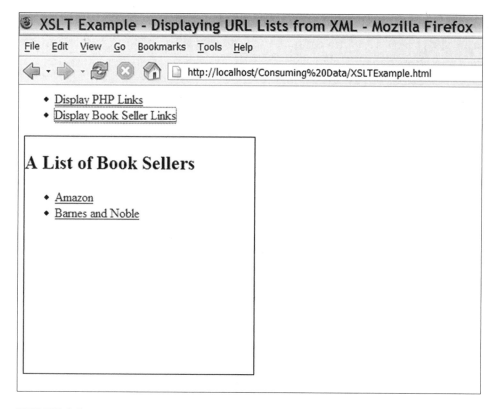

FIGURE 3-3
Using XSLT to transform XML documents loaded using AJAX

XSLT is an extremely powerful technique for managing AJAX transformation, and because it's supported by most browsers, it's easy to see how it could be paired with AJAX. XSLT's strength lies in its ability to create rules that will work against nonstructured or structured schemas. This trait allows it to easily transform any type of XML document and generate new content to add to the current HTML page. If you are already dealing with XML on the server side, XSLT makes a great choice because there is a good chance you're already familiar with its basics.

3.2 Remote Scripting

Remote scripting is a technique in which you make a request to the server that directly maps to a function on the server. In most environments, this is usually referred to as a *Remote Procedure Call* (RPC). Remote scripting approaches differ from document-centric ones mainly in how tightly coupled the server side is to the JavaScript client side. The data formats used are of a more generic nature and are designed to move standard data types, such as arrays or strings, and are not application-specific, such as the schema used by our data XML files in the DOM or XSLT examples.

The general RPC pattern is shown in Figure 3-4 and is as follows:

1. The JavaScript client code serializes the request data into a standard format.

2. The serialized data is sent to the server.

3. The data is userialized to a native data type.

4. The data in native format is used to perform an action, usually calling a preregistered function or method.

5. The results of the server action are serialized back to the standard format.

6. The serialized data is returned to the JavaScript client.

7. The JavaScript client unserializes the data to a native JavaScript type.

8. An action is performed on the result.

Any approach that follows this basic pattern can be considered an RPC approach. This can be anything from a simple technique that passes plain strings back and forth to something as complex as an entire Simple Object Access Protocol (SOAP) stack.

RPC approaches fit into four main subgroups:

- Approaches that use plain text or basic serialization such as URL encoding

- Approaches that use standardized XML schemas, such as SOAP or XML-RPC

- Approaches that use custom XML schemas

- Approaches that send JavaScript or its subset, JavaScript Object Notation (JSON)

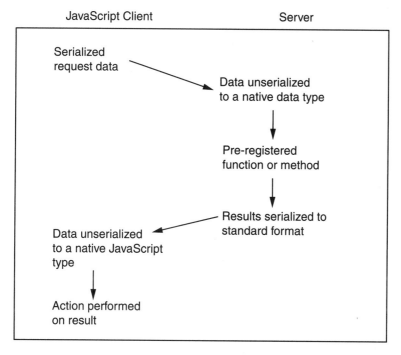

FIGURE 3-4
The RPC pattern

All these approaches are used in various AJAX implementations and, in many cases, are even combined; this is especially prevalent with approaches that generate JavaScript because few server-side languages have the ability to natively parse it.

3.2.1 Basic RPC

The simplest RPC approaches send plain text between the client and the server. What distinguishes them from document-centric approaches is that they usually call only a single page on the server, and the results come directly from what a function on the server returns. Like any remote scripting approach, there is a server component and a client component. The server component has a list of functions that can be called by the client (for security reasons, any RPC server should allow calls only to preregistered functions), and it manages dispatching client requests to a function and returning its results. The application flow is this: The JavaScript client makes a call using XMLHttpRequest to the server, sending the function to call and a payload. The server calls the requested functions and outputs the results, and the JavaScript client does something useful with the result. The process is shown in Listings 3-7 and 3-8; Listing 3-7 shows the server side written in PHP, and Listing 3-8 shows the client-side HTML and JavaScript.

Listing 3-7

rpc-basic-plain.php

```php
1   <?php
2   // functions that can be called remotely
3   function rot13($string) {
4       return str_rot13($string);
5   }
6
7   function reverse($string) {
8       return strrev($string);
9   }
10
11  // list of functions that can be called
12  $functionList = array(
13          'rot13',
14          'reverse'
15      );
16
17
18  // function to call
19  $funcToCall = $_REQUEST['function'];
20
21
22  // set the content type
23  header('Content-Type: text/plain');
24
```

```
25 // check whether the function is registered
26 if (!in_array($funcToCall,$functionList)) {
27     die('Unable to call'.$funcToCall);
28 }
29
30 // Get the content from the client
31 $payload = "";
32 if (isset($HTTP_RAW_POST_DATA)) {
33     $payload = $HTTP_RAW_POST_DATA;
34 }
35
36 // call a function and output its results
37 echo $funcToCall($payload);
38 ?>
```

The server-side component of this basic RPC arrangement is as simple as it could be; this works for small pages, but to build a full site, you would want to move to a more feature-rich solution, like one of the toolkits listed in Appendix A, "JavaScript AJAX Libraries." In Listing 3-7, lines 2–8 define two small string-processing functions; these could just as easily contain calls to a database or code that builds HTML. Lines 11–15 provide an array of functions that can be called remotely; this provides security, locking remote access to a small set of functions that expect input from JavaScript. On line 23, we set the Content-type header. text/plain is used because we're merely sending back string data. Lines 25–28 show the security check; it uses the $functionList array we built on lines 12–15; it also uses $funcToCall, which we read on line 19. The function we're trying to call isn't in this array; we end the script execution using the die command. The script ends by reading in the POST data that was sent from the form and then calling the requested function with that data as its only parameter.

The HTML page contains an input box and some links to perform some remote actions on the contents of the box. The actions run the two functions registered on the PHP page, reverse and rot13, against the content in the input box. The reverse function returns a string in reverse order, whereas rot13 replaces each character with the one that is 13 characters ahead of it in the alphabet. Now that we have a server to call, we need to build our client HTML and JavaScript page. We will reuse the same HttpClient class, adding in a helper function to allow us to make remote function calls. An HTML page that makes RPCs to the PHP script we built in Listing 3-7 is shown in Listing 3-8.

Listing 3-8

rpc-basic-plan.html

```
1   <html>
2   <head>
3   <title>Basic RPC Example, No data serialization</title>
4   <script type="text/javascript" src="HttpClient.js"></script>
5   <script type="text/javascript">
6   var serverUrl = 'rpc-basic-plain.php';
7   function remoteCall(func,payload,callback) {
8      var client = new HttpClient();
9      client.isAsync = true;
10     client.requestType = 'POST';
11     client.callback = callback;
12     client.makeRequest(serverUrl+'?function='+escape(func),
13               payload,'text/plain');
14  }
15
16  function reverseString() {
17     remoteCall('reverse',document.getElementById('string').value,
18           function(result) {
19                 document.getElementById('string').value = result;
20           }
21     );
22  }
23
24  function rot13String() {
25     remoteCall('rot13',document.getElementById('string').value,
26           function(result) {
27                 document.getElementById('string').value = result;
28           }
29     );
30  }
31  </script>
32  </head>
33  <body>
34     <label for="string">Source String:</label> <input id="string">
35  <ul>
36     <li><a href="javascript:reverseString()">Reverse String</a></li>
37     <li><a href="javascript:rot13String()">ROT 13 String</a></li>
38  </ul>
39
40  <div style="position: absolute; width:100px; height:20px;
41     top: 5px; right: 5px; display:none"
42     id="HttpClientStatus">Loading ...</div>
43
44  </body>
45  </html>
```

Like the earlier example pages, this one is broken into two main sections. The JavaScript code is at the top, followed by the HTML interface that calls it. Lines 7–14 contain the `remoteCall` function, which creates a new `HttpClient`. It sets up this new client to make an asynchronous POST request, and it uses the callback parameter as the callback function for the request. The function finishes by sending the request to the server. Each request is made to the same PHP page; we just change the query string, setting function to the PHP function we want to call. A new `HttpClient` instance is created for each request. If you didn't do this, you would need to add in extra logic to keep a new request from being made before an earlier one had finished, because each `HttpClient` instance can have only a single outstanding request.

Lines 16–30 provide the two helper functions that initiate the remote function calls. The first is for `reverse`, and the second is for `rot13`. The two functions are nearly identical; they both call `remoteCall`, passing in the remote function to run, the value of the input box as the payload, and a callback to handle the results. The callback functions get the result from the PHP server and set the value of the input box to it.

The rest of the page is the basic UI. Line 34 contains the input box we're reading from to make remote calls; the input box also gets updated with the results of the calls. Lines 36–37 contain links to run the JavaScript functions that make the remote calls. The script ends with a DIV (lines 40–42), which is shown while we wait for the server to respond. Figure 3-5 illustrates example output showing a reversed string.

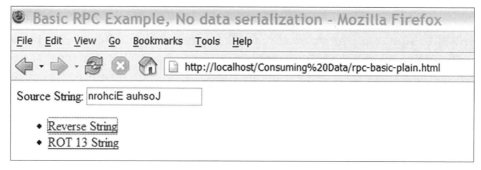

FIGURE 3-5
Using a basic RPC example to reverse a string

A simple RPC system is quick to build and has little overhead, but it lacks enough functionality that it's not usually used in larger projects. Normally, you want the ability to pass multiple arguments to the functions on the server side and an easy way to get back something besides a string on the client.

3.2.1.1 Mimicking a Form POST

Another option for performing AJAX-based RPC is to mimic a form POST. This entails URL encoding the data. URL encoding is the format used in the query string of a GET request; key value pairs are separated by an ampersand, and a basic example is shown here:

```
ajax=asynchronous+javascript+and+xml&hello=world
```

As you can see in this example, spaces are encoded as + characters. In addition, =, &, and other non-ASCII characters are escaped as hexadecimal entities. Knowing the actual details of the encoding isn't that important because JavaScript contains the encodeURIComponent() to handle the encoding of each key and value, and PHP will automatically handle the decoding for you. URL encoding can be used to perform basic RPC, allowing multiple variables to be passed, or to submit a form over AJAX. The form submission method is especially useful because you can easily fall back to normal form submission for users who don't have JavaScript enabled.

The example of this takes an HTML form and uses a drop-down element to decide how it's submitted. One mode does a submission to a slightly modified version of Listing 3-8; another submits the form using AJAX, and one mode does a normal form submission. The AJAX and normal form submission submit to the same page, showing you how you can detect an AJAX form submission. Because the AJAX code mimics a normal form submission, the server side can treat the data sent from either input method identically. You'll generally create different output from an AJAX form submission because you need to return only that content that needs to be updated (instead of generating an entire page). The fake form submission example is shown in Listing 3-9, starting with the HTML page and finishing with the two back ends.

Listing 3-9

Ajax-form.html

```
1   <html>
2   <head>
3   <title>Basic RPC Example, No data serialization</title>
```

```
4  <script type="text/javascript" src="HttpClient.js"></script>
5  <script type="text/javascript">
6  function handleForm(form) {
7     var serverUrl = '';
8     switch(document.getElementById('formAction').value) {
9          case 'normal':
10                return true;
11                break;
12         case 'ajax':
13                serverUrl = 'Ajax-form.php';
14                break;
15         case 'rpc':
16                serverUrl = 'Rpc-basic-urlencoded.php';
17                break;
18     }
19
20     var client = new HttpClient();
21     client.isAsync = true;
22     client.requestType = 'POST';
23
24     // urlencode the payload
25     payload = "ajax=true";
26     for(var i =0; i < form.elements.length; i++) {
27       if (form.elements[i].name) {
28             if (payload != "")  {
29                   payload += "&";
30             }
31             payload +=  encodeURIComponent(form.elements[i].name)
32             + '=' + encodeURIComponent(form.elements[i].value);
33       }
34     }
35
36     client.callback = function(result) {
37           document.getElementById('target').innerHTML = result;
38     };
39
40     client.makeRequest(serverUrl,payload,
41                 'application/x-www-form-urlencoded');
42     return false;
43  }
44
45  </script>
46  </head>
47  <body>
48  <form action="Ajax-form.php" method="POST"
49          onsubmit="return handleForm(this)">
50    <p><label>Source String:</label>
51    <input name="payload" id="string"></p>
52
53    <p>
```

```
54    <label>Submit As:</label>
55    <select id="formAction">
56         <option value='normal'>Normal Form</option>
57         <option value='ajax'>AJAX Form</option>
58         <option value='rpc'>RPC Form</option>
59    </select>
60    </p>
61
62    <p>
63    <select name='function'>
64         <option value="reverse">Reverse String</option>
64         <option value="rot13">ROT 13 String</option>
65    </select>
66    </p>
67
68    <p><input type="submit" value="Submit Form"></p>
69 </form>
70
71 <div id="target"></div>
72
73 <div style="position: absolute; width:100px; height:20px;
74    top: 5px; right: 5px; display:none"
75    id="HttpClientStatus">Loading ...</div>
76
77 </body>
78 </html>
```

Listing 3-9 makes a form submission perform different actions; this basic setup leads us to a different layout in our JavaScript code than most of the RPC examples. Instead of having a number of smaller helper functions, we end up with a large form handler function that performs many of the same actions, no matter how we submitted the form. In its definition, this function handle Form, which starts on line 6 and continues to line 43, expects the form to be submitted as a parameter. Lines 7–18 decide how we're going to submit the form. To do this, we create a switch statement around the value of a select element. If we do a normal form submission, we return true, which allows normal form submission to take place. For AJAX or RPC form submission, we set the URL to submit content, too. The rest of the logic is the same because the data is formatted the same—whether we're treating it as a normal form POST or a URL-encoded RPC submission.

Lines 20–23 set up an HttpClient instance to make an asynchronous POST submission; HttpClient is the XMLHttpRequest we built earlier and included on line 4. After that, we prepare a payload to send as the POST body. This is done on lines

26–34. We loop over each element in the form, and if `name` is set on it, we add it to the form as the string `name=value`. Both `name` and `value` are escaped using `encodeURIComponent`, with each form element's value being separated from the next by an ampersand (&). Then a callback handler (lines 36–38) is created to perform an action on the results of our remote calls; in this case, it just updates the contents of a DIV using `innerHTML`. The form handler finishes by making a remote request and returning `false`. When making a request (lines 40–41), it's important to include the correct `Content-type`, because `$_POST` will be automatically populated in PHP only when the content-type is `application/x-www-form-urlencoded`. The final action of returning `false` is also important. Without it, the form would submit over our `HttpClient` and then as a normal form.

The rest of the file creates a basic user interface: an HTML form, an output target, and an element to show while we're waiting for the server to respond. Lines 48–49 define the form, and the `action` attribute sets the page that will handle normal form submission requests. `onsubmit` ties our form-handling function to this form, and the value from this function is returned, allowing it to cancel the normal form submission. Line 51 creates the source string; this will be the payload sent to our RPC functions when doing an RPC submission. Lines 55–59 define the `select` element that lets us select how the form will be submitted; the value of each option matches up with the `switch` statement in the handler function. Lines 63–65 define a `select` element that lets us pick an RPC function to call on the string payload, and the values of these options match functions registered on the PHP RPC page. The page finishes with a submit button (line 68), a DIV with an ID of `target` that is used to show the output of our calls (line 71), and a status DIV (lines 73–75).

The output from `ajax-form.html` can be sent to one of two pages: `rpc-basic-urlencoded.php` or `ajax-form.php`. Each page interacts with the data in the same way because our encoding works in the form submission handler, which makes each `POST` request look like a normal form submission. `ajax-form.php` is shown in Listing 3-10; it's a simple page that checks if this is an AJAX submission or a normal submission and then shows the value of `$_POST` using `var_dump`. The check for an AJAX submission is done by looking for the `ajax` element in the `$_POST` being set. Unless you set a marker like this, there is no way to tell that `XMLHttpRequest` was used instead of a normal form submission.

Listing 3-10

`ajax-form.php`

```
<pre>
<?php

if (isset($_POST['ajax'])) {
    echo "AJAX Form submission\n";
}
else {
    echo "Standard Form submission\n";
}
var_dump($_POST);
?>
</pre>
```

3.2.1.2 URL-Encoded AJAX RPC

The RPC handler, `rpc-basic-urlencoded.php`, is the same code as `rpc-basic-plain.php`, except for a change to how the payload is read. Lines 31–34 of `rpc-basic-plain.php` are replaced with the code shown next. This code sets `$payload` with the value of the `payload` index in `$_POST`:

```
31  $payload = "";
32  if (isset($_POST)) {
33      $payload = $_POST['payload'];
34  }
```

You can experiment with the example by loading Listing 3-9. Figure 3-6 shows what the listing's output should look like. Notice how easy it is to move between a normal form submission and an AJAX form submission. AJAX form submissions can be used with document-based approaches as well as with remote scripting approaches.

Adding some basic data encoding to our AJAX requests adds a lot of power and flexibility to AJAX-based RPC. It's a great way to send multiple parameters to the server, and it is a great fit for form type data. The same encoding technique can also be used with non-RPC-based approaches when you want to emulate a normal form submission.

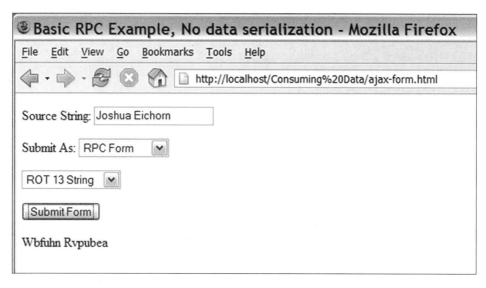

FIGURE 3-6
URL-encoded AJAX RPC

3.2.2 SOAP and XML-RPC

SOAP and XML-RPC are standardized XML protocols for doing remote requests. Many people who have used them before will wonder why they are not used more often. There are a variety of reasons for this, but the mains ones are as follows:

- The standards are complex and require large client libraries.

- Their encodings are verbose, making for slower interaction.

- The biggest benefits of talking to any Web service are negated by the fact that XMLHttpRequest's security model limits you to talking to the same server that sent the HTML page.

At present, there are no successful cross-browser implementations in JavaScript for either SOAP or XML-RPC. There don't seem to be technical issues stopping SOAP or XML-RPC from being implemented, except that any implementation will be much larger than the RPC options. SOAP or XML-RPC may become more popular in the future if browsers add native clients, but, so far, any implementations such as the SOAP client in Mozilla have been restricted to signed code or custom browsers built from the Mozilla base.

3.2.3 Custom XML

Some AJAX implementations use various custom XML schemas for transferring data. Although these formats suffer from some of the same data-bloat problems as SOAP or XML-RPC, they are generally much simpler and make a better fit because of this. One advantage of custom XML formats is that a format can be constructed to drive actions on the client side instead of just transferring data. Custom XML schemas based off the current schemas in your application's workflow might also be useful, but these generally fit a document-centric approach better because most of the schemas will be data-specific and don't fit into a generic RPC approach.

The XML example server pages, `Rpc-xml.html` and `Rpc-xml.php`, build off the RPC plain-encoded example. One advantage of using this approach over the basic RPC code is that it makes your client code more dynamic, because you can use a set of generic content-replacement functions that are put into action as needed from the server. You can use these generic functions instead of coding lots of custom callbacks. Depending on your needs, you may want to use a different XML schema in each direction, but for this example, we use the same one. It's a basic schema that tells which function to call and the parameters to pass to the function. An example of the schema is shown in Listing 3-11.

Listing 3-11

Example Call XML

```
<call function="reverse">
    <param>Test</param>
</call>
```

On the JavaScript side, we can use the DOM to read the XML, turning it into a string that can be run through the `eval` function to make the actual call. This works well from a security standpoint because the browser security sandbox keeps any remote requests on the same server, so you can trust any new content just as much as you trusted the original page load. On the PHP side, you don't have that same level of trust, because a request can come from anywhere on the Internet. Instead, you'll want to compare the function to call against a white list and use a method like `call_user_func` instead of `eval`. XML processing is also slightly harder than in

JavaScript, because versions older than 5.0 don't have DOM support by default. An easy way to support PHP 4 and 5 is to use a library from PEAR called XML_Serializer. XML_Serializer has the capability to take an XML file and turn it into a native PHP array. Most recent PHP installs come with the PEAR package manager, allowing you to install the library by running pear install XML_Serializer. (Detailed installation instructions are available at http://pear.php. net.) An example using XML to build an AJAX RPC system is shown in Listing 3-12.

Listing 3-12

Rpc-xml.html

```
1   <html>
2   <head>
3   <title>XML RPC Example</title>
4   <script type="text/javascript" src="HttpClient.js"></script>
5   <script type="text/javascript">
6   var serverUrl = 'Rpc-xml.php';
7   function remoteCall(func,payload) {
8      var client = new HttpClient();
9      client.isAsync = true;
10     client.requestType = 'POST';
11     client.callback = function(result) {
12         var call = '';
13         var callNode = client.xmlhttp.responseXML.firstChild;
14         call += callNode.getAttribute('function')+'(';
15         var params = callNode.getElementsByTagName('param');
16
17         for(var i = 0; i < params.length; i++) {
18         call += "'"+escape(params[i].firstChild.nodeValue)+"',";
19     }
20
21         call = call.substring(0,call.length-1)+')';
22
23         eval(call);
24     }
25
26     payload = '<call function="'+escape(func)+'"><param>'+
27              escape(payload)+'</param></call>';
28
29     client.makeRequest(serverUrl,payload,'text/xml');
30 }
31
32 function replace(id,value) {
33     document.getElementById(id).innerHTML = value;
34 }
35
```

```
36 function append(id,value) {
37     document.getElementById(id).innerHTML += value;
38 }
39
40 function remote(func) {
41     remoteCall(func,document.getElementById('string').value);
42 }
43
44 </script>
45 </head>
46 body>
47   <label for="string">Source String:</label> <input id="string">
48 <ul>
49   <li><a href="javascript:remote('reverse')">Reverse String</a></li>
50   <li><a href="javascript:remote('rot13')">ROT 13 String</a></li>
50 </ul>
51
52 Output:<div id="target"></div>
53 <div style="position: absolute; width:100px; height:20px;
54    top: 5px; right: 5px; display:none"
55    id="HttpClientStatus">Loading ...</div>
56
57 </body>
58 </html>
```

Listing 3-12 follows the normal pattern of a JavaScript section at the top and then a small UI to interact with it below. The JavaScript starts on line 4 by including the standard XMLHttpRequest wrapper. After that, we define the remoteCall method. This method is based on remoteCall in rpc-basic-plain.html; the biggest different is that instead of a callback being passed in, it is built from the XML. Lines 8–10 create an HttpClient instance and set it up for an asynchronous POST request. Lines 11–24 build the callback handler that handles this result; this code uses the DOM representation of the resulting XML file to perform an action.

The basic process is to build a string and evaluate it. This process starts on line 13 by grabbing the root node of the XML document (the call tag) and putting it into callNode. Next, we append the function name and an "(" to the call string. After that, we use getElementsByTagName() (line 15) to get an array of all the param tags. We loop through these tags, appending each one inside single quotes to the string (lines 17–19). Each value is also run through the escape function in case it contains a single quote or another character that would cause our eval() to fail. At the end of this process, we will get a string like "functionName('param1', 'param2', ". To finish up the process of building our call string, we remove the extra

"," from the end and append the closing ")" on line 21. Finally, the string is run through `eval()` on line 23, calling the function.

Lines 26–27 prepare the XML payload to be sent to the server. Because this is just a simple example with one parameter, it is just a matter of escaping the input and putting it together with the XML tags using string concatenation. Line 26 finishes `remoteCall()` by making the actual server request.

Next, the file contains a couple of generic callback functions and a helper function for making the remote calls. Lines 32–34 contain a generic function that replaces the content of an HTML element using `innerHTML`. This method takes two parameters: the ID of the element and the content to use for `innerHTML`. Lines 36–38 contain an `append()` function that follows the same pattern as the `replace()` function on lines 32–34; the only difference is that `append()` appends to `innerHTML`. The `remote()` function on lines 40–42 grabs the input value from the string input box and calls `remoteCall()` with it, passing it the function in the `func` variable.

The rest of the file (lines 46–57) contains the basic HTML UI. Line 47 contains our source input box, and lines 48–50 contain a list of action links that call the JavaScript `remote()` function. Line 52 contains our target DIV, which can be used by the `append` and `replace` functions. The file is finished by a `status` DIV on lines 53–55. The back end for this page is shown in Listing 3-13.

Listing 3-13

Rpc-xml.php

```
1   <?php
2   require_once 'XML/Unserializer.php';
3
4   // functions that can be called remotely
5   function rot13($string) {
6       $xml = '
7       <call function="replace">
8             <param>target</param>
9             <param>'.str_rot13($string).'</param>
10      </call>
11      ';
12      return $xml;
13  }
14
15  function reverse($string) {
16      $xml = '
17      <call function="append">
```

```
18      <param>target</param>
19      <param>'.strrev($string).'</param>
20    </call>
21    ';
22    return $xml;
23 }
24
25
26 // list of functions that can be called
27 $functionList = array(
28      'rot13',
29      'reverse'
30      );
31
32
33 // set the content type
34 header('Content-Type: text/xml');
35
36
37 // Get the content from the client
38 if (isset($HTTP_RAW_POST_DATA)) {
39    $xml = $HTTP_RAW_POST_DATA;
40
41    $unserializer = new XML_Unserializer(
42    array('returnResult'=>true,'parseAttributes'=>true));
43    $data = $unserializer->unserialize($xml);
44
45    // function to call
46    $funcToCall = $data['function'];
47
48    // params to function
49    $params = array();
50    if (isset($data['param'])) {
51          if (is_array($data['param'])) {
52                $params = $data['param'];
53          }
54          else {
55                $params = array($data['param']);
56          }
57    }
58 }
59
60 // check whether the function is registered
61 if (!in_array($funcToCall,$functionList)) {
62    die('Unable to call'.$funcToCall);
63 }
64
65 // call a function and output its results
66 echo call_user_func_array($funcToCall,$params);
67 ?>
```

The first section of the file contains the same small function wrappers around basic PHP string handling functions as the plain example. The difference is that returned small chunks of XML define what to do with the results instead of just sending the results back. The `rot13` function on lines 5–13 returns XML to replace the content of the element with an ID of `target` with a `rot13` of the input string. The `reverse()` function on lines 15–23 returns XML to append to the contents of the `target` element with the reverse output of the input string. These two functions are then added to our function white list on lines 27–30.

The latter half of the file (lines 33–66) takes an incoming request and prepares the results. Line 34 sets the content-type; if it's not set to `text/xml`, then `responseXML` will never be populated on the client without this header being set. Lines 37–58 parse the XML, getting the function to call and building an array of parameters to call it with. Lines 41–42 create a new `XML_Unserializer` instance. Options are set to parse XML attributes (line 42) and to return the parsed data form unserialized instead of using an extra method call to get it. Line 43 parses the actual XML and sets its output array to the `$data` variable. Line 46 uses this array to get the function we're calling, and then lines 49–57 grab the array of parameters. We first check whether the `param` index is set (line 50), allowing us to call functions without input. If it is set, we check whether it's an array (line 51). If it is, we just set that to `$params`; if it's not, we wrap it in an array as we set it to `$params`. This is done because `XML_Serializer` makes `$data['param']` an array when multiple `param` tags exist, but if just one exists, `XML_Serializer` makes `$data['param']` index string. Lines 60–63 do a basic security check, canceling script execution if the function isn't in our white list of AJAX-callable functions. Finally on line 66, we use `call_user_func_array` to call the function and echo its results to the client. This example is shown in Figure 3-7.

Using XML to move the data in our AJAX RPC system, we can build a system that can transfer any type of data. Using the concepts of standard XML-based RPC systems, we can encode any type of data and get the flexibility needed to build complex applications. If we optimize the schema for the server-side language that is being used, we can also limit the overhead created by the XML tags needed to describe the data. XML is used in many AJAX RPC libraries and provides everything you need to make a complete RPC solution.

FIGURE 3-7
XML-based AJAX RPC

3.2.4 JavaScript and JSON

Generating JavaScript and sending it to the client where it is run through `eval()` is a popular way to move data in object implementations. This process is popular because JavaScript has compact notations available for data types, such as arrays, and it allows for very flexible operations. Some AJAX frameworks use this ability to generate new client code from the server as needed, allowing the framework to provide a more centralized view of the development instead of the normal client/server dichotomy.

A mixed XML/JavaScript example could easily be built for the RPC XML in Listings 3-12 and 3-13. On the client side, you would send XML to the server, as is the case with the current code, but for the results, the server would return JavaScript and the client would `eval` it directly. To accomplish this, we need to make some small edits to Listings 3-12 and 3-13. For Listing 3-12, we need to replace lines 12–24 with a simple three-line callback that will run `eval` on the results from the server. This new callback is shown in Listing 3-14. The server URL on line 6 is updated to point to a new PHP script, which will be an edited version of Listing 3-13. This update is shown here:

```
var serverUrl = 'rpc-xml-javascript.php';
```

On the server side, lines 4–23 of Listing 3-13 are removed and replaced with the eight lines shown in Listing 3-15. The content type on line 34 of Listing 3-13 was also changed to `text/plain`.

Listing 3-14

Changes to `Make Rpc-xml-javascript.html`

```
12 client.callback = function(result) {
13     eval(result);
14 }
```

Listing 3-15

More changes to `Make Rpc-xml-javascript.html`

```
4  // functions that can be called remotely
5  function rot13($string) {
6      return "replace('target','".addslashes(str_rot13($string))."')";
7  }
8
9  function reverse($string) {
10     return "append('target','".addslashes(strrev($string))."')";
11 }
```

These small changes give you a simpler code base with which to work, and their use entails sending a much smaller amount of data back to the client. It also allows for simpler, more flexible coding because you can send back any JavaScript instead of only what your XML schema allows.

Taking this approach one step further and sending JavaScript in both directions would be nice because of the data savings, but that's a much harder task to do for a couple reasons. Most server languages don't contain a JavaScript interpreter, so they can't evaluate JavaScript code, but even if they did, you wouldn't want to allow arbitrary client-created code to run on your server. Running code from the client on the server would be a huge security problem. The solution to both of these problems is a subset of JavaScript called JSON, which is the literal syntax for JavaScript objects. It can be run by `eval()` on the JavaScript side. This allows for any JavaScript data types to be transferred, and it's much faster than an XML-based solution because the compact encoding allows for a much smaller amount of data to be transferred. On the server side, JSON is simple enough for a small parser to be built to serialize native data types into JSON and to create native data types from JSON.

While JSON is powerful and supports all JavaScript data types, it also has the drawback of being a more complex solution. A library is needed on the server to handle moving to and from the JSON strings, and a library is needed on the JavaScript side to create JSON strings—although `eval()` can be used to turn JSON into JavaScript objects. This makes a JSON example more complex than the examples shown in the other sections, which means if you want to use JSON, you'll need to find some external libraries to do the actual parsing. Appendix A contains a list of libraries that provide JSON processing. In Chapter 9, "Libraries Used in Part II: HTML_AJAX," a complete JSON RPC library for PHP HTML_AJAX is shown.

3.3 How to Decide on a Request Type

There are two main request types used in AJAX communication: POST and GET. These are the identical choices you have with forms in HTML, and the same rules apply. GET requests can be used when the URL performs no action. (For example, a URL such as `index.php?section=main` that displays the main section of a Web site is a good use for GET.) A URL such as `index.php?action=delete&id=1` should never be used with GET. The main reasons for this go back to the HTTP standard, which suggests that GET requests should not perform permanent actions and are not allowed to be cached by proxies and other infrastructure. Some Web accelerator products also prefetch GET URLs from pages, which causes huge problems when they hit a URL that deletes a record. GET requests also have the drawback of potentially limiting the amount of data that the client can send to the server; current HTTP specs don't limit size, but many servers and browsers limit the size to around 2,000 characters. POST requests aren't allowed to be cached by proxies or prefetched, and thus are much safer than GET requests.

In most AJAX setups, especially any using an RPC approach, only POST requests should be used. While some of the requests might be just to load new data, it's generally too hard to keep track of which type of request is which. In a document-centric approach, GET requests might be useful, especially when you're using AJAX to load in chunks of static HTML or XML content. If you go with an approach like that, you'll want to use a good naming convention to help keep track of which type of request is needed for each URL.

3.4 Summary

The examples in this chapter cover the basic ways to consume the data we learned to transfer in Chapter 2. Although fully working, their simple implementation is not the best choice for most production environments, because their simple style does not provide the robustness and feature set that a larger library would provide. In Chapters 9–12, many of these same patterns will be implemented using various libraries. These libraries offer better error handling and various helper functions to remove some of the repetitive code in the example. The more complex libraries also allow you to mix and match RPC serialization types, letting you use whatever serialization format is most efficient for the data in question.

You have two main choices when working with AJAX data:

- Document-centric approaches easily fit into current server-side modules and allow for a loose coupling between the client and the server.

- RPC-based approaches produce a tight coupling with the server side but offer the ability to write simpler server-side code.

Either approach will allow you to successfully build AJAX applications, but neither choice will guarantee it. Successful AJAX applications are not created because of implementation choices (although a good implementation always helps). They are created by good, user-centered design; the AJAX addition improves usability and gives the user the ability to do things he or she never imagined.

Chapter 4

Adding AJAX to Your Web Development Process

In this chapter

AJAX is not really a new technology, but because it involves new skills and ideas in creating Web pages, it introduces many new difficulties for Web, developers. There are three basic sets of problems:

- Technical aspects of implementing AJAX (covered in Chapters 2, "Getting Started," and 3, "Consuming the Sent Data")

- Overall problems that are a result of the nature of AJAX as a whole

- Deciding how to integrate a new set of third-party tools

This chapter covers the second and third problems. We'll first explore the changes AJAX brings to the development cycle and then cover what changes using JavaScript as a primary development language brings. Then we will look at how AJAX libraries fit into the overall development process and how you should decide which one to use, or even when the best solution is to build your own.

4.1 Changes to the Development Cycle

There are a variety of ways to use AJAX when integrating it into Web applications. On one end of the spectrum, you can use it to enhance a current site, making small noninvasive changes to an already completed application. On the other end of the spectrum, you have applications that are heavily driven by JavaScript and won't work at all if the user's browser doesn't support AJAX.

Moving to a 100% AJAX application usually isn't an option for a mass-market Web site because browser compatibility issues will cut out too many possible users, but it can be a successful choice for internal projects in which limiting support to one or two browsers is possible. Although browser compatibility can limit the possible choices, it's not the most important factor when deciding how AJAX will be implemented. Developer familiarity with JavaScript and the willingness of developers to make changes to the way they normally develop will usually play a larger role in how AJAX is used.

The more you rely on AJAX, the larger the changes will be. In an enhancement-only scenario, the largest impact will be the additional testing that is needed, whereas in a 100% AJAX application, all aspects of development—including design, implementation, and testing—will be affected. The amount of testing needed in any scenario is also affected by the number of browsers that need to be supported. In single-browser scenarios, testing can be focused solely on the new AJAX widgets and user interactions, whereas in a multiple-browser scenario, differences between browsers need to be tested as well; if older browsers are supported, then fallback scenarios also need to be tested.

4.1.1 Enhancement-Driven Changes

AJAX is typically used to enhance a current Web site after the site has been developed to a fully functional state. Specific areas where AJAX could improve user experience are chosen and then optional code is used to add AJAX to those areas. Examples include adding an AJAX-driven pull-down element to a search box that shows matching options as the user types or providing a way to validate that a username isn't already in use without submitting an entire form. Many AJAX libraries encapsulate all the functionality needed for features like these, making the only implementation and design challenge the integration of a new library. While this can be difficult depending on the framework in use, it's not really any different from supporting any other third-party library. If an AJAX library is not used, any implementation will make some major changes to your normal application development cycle; be sure to set time aside to create the needed infrastructure pieces.

Large amounts of JavaScript development can be especially disruptive for groups using unit testing or other automated testing tools. The disruption is caused by the lack of JavaScript support in normal testing tools. Unit testing of JavaScript is possible, but it may be hard to integrate into existing testing frameworks because it needs to run in a browser. In addition, it may need to run in different browsers to cover differences between them. Although getting JavaScript unit tests integrated into an existing framework can be a difficult task, it does have a large payoff because it helps hide many of the debugging differences that AJAX adds.

You'll find that even bringing in a small amount of AJAX leads to huge differences in debugging. These changes are caused by two main items:

- A larger amount of logic is encapsulated in JavaScript, which creates a second area to test code for problems. This testing process can be further complicated by the need to learn new tools because few Integrated Development Environments (IDEs) support JavaScript. This leads developers to rely more heavily on debugging tools that are built into browsers.

- The communication process is hidden. When you are loading a normal page, logic errors and debugging messages can be immediately shown, but with AJAX communication, these errors need to be caught in the JavaScript code and handled before they are visible. This makes logging problems at the server level more important and removes the direct feedback that most Web development languages provide.

When adding any amount of AJAX to a Web application, you can expect longer development and testing cycles. If AJAX libraries are used, the amount of additional time needed is about the same as adding any other feature. If all the development is new, then testing time will be increased, as more testing of basic functionality will be needed. Because more features are being added, implementation time is increased, but no other large changes are introduced. (These bolt-on features require little JavaScript to be coded once the basic infrastructure is in place.)

4.1.2 AJAX in Action: Removing a Popup User Search

A common task in many Web sites is selecting a user on which to perform an action. This task is especially common when dealing with permissions systems, where you can spend a large amount of time selecting users to add to groups or to update the permissions on. If the site contains only a small number of users, this can be accomplished by an HTML select box, but after a hundred or so users, this becomes less useful. It becomes less useful because of the time it takes to scroll through the list and find the item in question and because of the large amounts of data that need to be transferred for each box. One solution is to provide a link that opens a new page where the search can be done; the new page would then return the selected user. Although this scales to large numbers of users, it does have the disadvantage of taking a long time to select each user. An easy solution to this problem is to allow users to search directly on the page using AJAX.

AJAX searching can be achieved by putting an entire search form right on the page and submitting it over AJAX, or it can be done by building a combo box-style search box. As the user types, AJAX search requests are sent and the results are used to build a dynamic pull-down list below the text-input box. An example of this is shown in Figure 4-1. If this is the only AJAX you're adding to an application, it will require the following actions:

- Addition of an AJAX communication layer (usually provided by a library)
- Additional JavaScript and HTML code for building the drop-down elements
- New entry point to the application for getting unformatted search results
- Testing of the new feature
- Testing of the fallback to the old pop-up in non-AJAX browsers

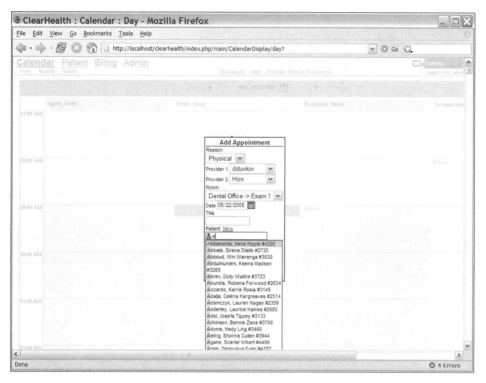

FIGURE 4-1
AJAX-driven user selection

As you can see from the list of actions, there are no wildly different additions to the development cycle. You just need some extra time to add in this AJAX feature. The biggest changes caused by this addition are the new entry point for your AJAX search and any debugging hassles caused by it.

4.1.3 Changes Caused by Creating an AJAX-Driven Application

AJAX can be useful when used as an enhancement tool that is targeted at specific tasks that are slow or hard to do within the normal Web environment. However, AJAX is most powerful when you rethink how you build Web sites and design it into the application from the ground up. This allows you to move from a design built on full-page reloads to an event-driven application where events drive small areas of the application to update. Requiring AJAX for your application does limit which browsers you can support, but in many circumstances, the tradeoff is worth it, because it allows you to create applications that are not possible in a normal Web application model.

Creating an AJAX-driven application is a much larger shift than just sprucing up a site with AJAX. One of the most invasive changes you'll find is the removal of the page concept from the application. In a normal Web application, you would go to the `/list/users.php` URL, and that page would generate HTML to show a table of users. In our AJAX-driven application, an event will be fired (maybe by clicking a button) that will cause JavaScript to load user data using AJAX and then update an existing table using the JavaScript Document Object Model (DOM). Depending on your design, the `/list/users.php` page on the server might still exist. However, it would now just output the data needed, not an entire page. The main shift here is moving the logic that puts together the different data sources from your server to the client.

This shift will have a number of effects on your server-side development efforts. Because you will no longer be generating HTML at each URL, you'll find yourself in a model where you're building an API instead of a bunch of pages. This will have a large effect on most development frameworks, because the front controller will lose command over the actual HTML-generation aspects of the page and instead will focus on data aggregation and security. By the same token, security handling will move to different parts of the application. Because much of the HTML generation will now be handled on the client, you will no longer rely on it to filter out records the user shouldn't be able to access. Although most people won't edit the JavaScript code that drives your application, there is nothing stopping them from doing so; therefore, security checks and filters that are implemented in JavaScript could be removed easily by a determined foe.

The heavy focus on JavaScript will also be a change for many developers; reusable widgets that were created in a template language before will now need to be moved to JavaScript constructs. You'll also find it harder to stay away from JavaScript functions that have inconsistencies between browsers. This is especially true of JavaScript events, because they are at the heart of any event-driven application. Events do work well in all new browsers, but there are some differences, especially with change events that make them unreliable when used by themselves. In most cases, a bit of research will find workarounds to these cross-browser problems, but this aspect will likely be an annoyance during development and will surely increase the amount of testing that needs to be done.

Testing needs will increase as you make a more complex user interface (UI), but this process is relatively straightforward; if you already implement a detailed testing plan, this won't be much of a change. The biggest difference is that more interaction is needed with the elements on the page to test their interactivity. The JavaScript-to-server communication layer also becomes a new point of testing. You will need to make sure that your application handles communication errors properly because you'll be handling them now (instead of leaving them to the browser). The actual testing of the server side will also be a change for developers who are not currently using some type of unit testing processes. In an AJAX application, it is important to be able to test the server separately from the client because this greatly reduces complexity during the debugging process.

An AJAX-Driven Application Use Case: Mp3act

Mp3act is an open source music management system; it allows you to search, browse, and stream music stored on a server. Although it's not as popular as client-side music management systems, such as iTunes, server-side music management does have a thriving niche, and there are many implementations of this same process using a normal Web development model.

Mp3act fully removes the page concept from the application; the application is divided into two independent sections. One section is the navigation bar, which contains links between major aspects of the application, such as search and playlists. The other section is the content area that is updated as needed, either from links in the navigation area or from an action performed inside the content.

Mp3act provides feedback while waiting for data to load so that the user knows something is happening. (This feedback is useful because the Web browser's loading throbber never moves.) This status message is shown in Figure 4-2; this consistent messaging is used throughout the application and is one of the interface touches that any good AJAX-driven application needs.

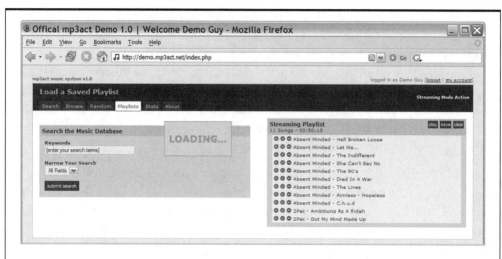

FIGURE 4-2
Mp3act—loading status shown switching to Playlists view

Mp3act performs two major types of AJAX actions: loading new application sections where large amounts of HTML are replaced, and dynamically updating tables. Figure 4-3 shows a table being dynamically updated; the plus button (on the right) is clicked, which adds the songs in the table to the playlist. The new songs are highlighted in green, showing the user that an action has been performed. (The highlight fades away in a couple seconds.) Items can also be deleted from the playlist and can be reordered using the arrow buttons. (Similar highlights with fade affects are used throughout the application.)

When compared to a similar application developed without AJAX, Mp3act requires a large number of development changes, such as the following:

- Addition of an AJAX communication layer
- Creation of a JavaScript playlist widget
- Visual-effect JavaScript code for fading highlights and loading messages
- Creation of a data-driven API on the server
- Increased testing of rich UI features, such as reordering
- Cross-browser testing
- Loss of support on browsers that do not support AJAX

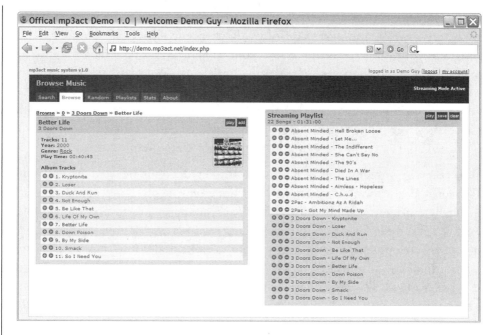

FIGURE 4-3
Mp3act—adding an album to a playlist

Although AJAX causes development changes, Mp3act's overall development timescale isn't necessarily longer than a non-AJAX version would require. Because Mp3act was conceived as an AJAX application from the start of its development and because its developers never planned for it to support non-AJAX capable browsers, its development process can skip normal Web-development work, such as building forms to reorder lists.

The one area that might still be overly time-consuming is the processing of developing good cross-browser support. In fact, in the original Mp3act release, Internet Explorer (IE) didn't work at all. Resolving these cross-browser issues, which involved items from XMLHttpRequest differences to various ways to create visual effects, could have been easily accomplished by using a library. However, some cross-browser issues, such as CSS layout, have no easy solution. Even if the overall development time is longer than for a non-AJAX version, the end result— a usable, attractive application that works the way a user expects—seems well worth it.

4.2 Integrating AJAX into a Framework

Whether you're planning to add only a few simple AJAX features or use AJAX throughout your site, integrating it into your current Web site design is a must. The more formal the framework, the harder the process is—especially if your framework provides a front controller that is heavily optimized for generating HTML. Frameworks without a front controller have an easier time incorporating AJAX because they can add a new entry point just for AJAX; many AJAX Remote Procedure Call (RPC) implementations provide code to help do this.

The way you integrate with a front controller depends heavily on the style of AJAX you're performing. If you're taking a document-centric approach, integration is generally easy; you just need the ability to create pages in the needed output format. (The controller's normal name spacing will work just fine.) This may take some new development, depending on your current design, because you'll need to generate small chunks of HTML (or other data formats, such as XML) instead of full pages. You will also need to make some naming decisions, such as whether you are going to put your AJAX pages next to normal pages or into their own distinct namespace. A distinct namespace makes it easy to locate your AJAX code, but it divides the code by usage instead of by function, so you can't see the AJAX code's relation to its non-AJAX version. Adding in AJAX pages next to your normal code lets you see the relation, but it makes it much harder to identify all of an application's AJAX-entry points. Either option can work well; the most important point is to use a consistent approach.

RPC AJAX implementations have the hardest time integrating with a front controller. This difficulty occurs because most RPC implementations are focused on exporting classes to JavaScript and have their own mini-controller implementation, which maps incoming calls to these classes. Many also generate JavaScript, which should be added to the page using a JavaScript `include`, which again needs its own basic controller logic. There are three main tasks you want to accomplish when performing this integration: managing what functions are exported to JavaScript, managing the permissions on those functions, and creating a clean entry point that fits the style of the current application.

The last task is generally the easiest to achieve. With most RPC libraries, you'll be passing information specifying which class and which function to call to the server. This information is similar to the section and page information that most controllers already manage; it allows for a pass-through or mapping system to be created easily. The problem comes with the first two tasks: If you enforce permissions at the controller level of your application, you may find yourself with no other choice but to create tons of stub functions to create the namespace needed for permission enforcement. The final task is deciding which functions to export. The simplest solution is to create classes that are used specifically for AJAX integration, but you may find that mapping functions on your current controllers is a better solution for you. If you need to perform complex permission or partial controller mapping, make sure to choose your library with that in mind. Some enforce strict name mapping between the server and JavaScript side, and most approaches like this will need a virtual mapping of the methods instead.

If you start using large amounts of AJAX in your application, you'll also want to look at ways to standardize your management of JavaScript code. Your framework will need a way to map the JavaScript that is needed to power each HTML page. In a small application, it can all be stored in a single file, but in most frameworks, you'll have various chunks of reusable JavaScript to manage. One way to manage this is to output all the needed JavaScript for a page through a dynamic page on the server, sending headers to allow the client to cache the JavaScript as if it were static. Another option is to build packages of prebuilt JavaScript files and then include the set you need for the page in question. Large amounts of JavaScript development will affect your framework in other ways as well, because JavaScript can become just as important as your server-side language.

4.3 JavaScript as a Primary Development Language

JavaScript is a powerful scripting language, but deserved or undeserved, it has gained a bad reputation. If you take some time to look at JavaScript with a fresh eye, you will notice that most of its problems no longer exist. The core language is now standardized with the European Computer Manufacturer's Association (ECMA) standards group and is supported on all modern browsers. Of course, these browsers also support older proprietary syntaxes, and you should avoid these as much as possible. Keeping to the standardized interfaces, JavaScript is portable with a minimal amount of testing and browser-specific code. Because of this standardization, writing complex JavaScript, which was close to impossible in the Netscape 4 days, is now an easy task, although each browser will still need its own testing.

High-quality libraries help reduce the amount of JavaScript you need to write. Many libraries, both open source and commercial, are immature, but the more popular ones are already usable tools, even though it can be harder to find documentation and examples for them than for server-side libraries. JavaScript libraries are especially useful for complicated user-interface elements, such as drag and drop. However, with less-complex elements, such as AJAX communications or visual effects (such as fading an element out), they are less useful because you still have to write all the glue, and that's a large part of the overall code. As AJAX becomes more popular and libraries mature, more and more solutions will be created that will generate all the JavaScript for you, allowing you to handle all the details from your primary development language.

JavaScript's greatest advantage is that it runs directly on the client, so it can react immediately to the user's actions. This interaction allows a JavaScript-driven Web application to offer a highly interactive user experience. The experience is interactive because tasks such as reordering a record no longer take an entire page reload. This direct interaction has driven the development of the language, focusing it on interacting with the HTML DOM. JavaScript's ability to add functions to elements of the page at runtime provides a different programming experience than most other languages. However, its position in the browser gives it the unique opportunity to provide compelling user experience opportunities, especially when teamed with the server communication opportunities that AJAX provides.

Just as with any new language, JavaScript will seem more familiar once you've used it on a couple of different projects. In most cases, the biggest problem isn't dealing with the language, or even the differences in its implementation between browsers, but dealing with the new development paradigm that AJAX brings. Splitting your application into two parts—one written in JavaScript and the other written in your normal server language—isn't without costs or problems.

4.4 Problems Created by the New Development Paradigm

Most of the problems with AJAX are caused by its added complexity. Because the communication with the server happens in an opaque manner, it is easy to lose error messages or learn that there is an error without also getting all the additional details you relied on before using AJAX. These aspects force you to rely on server-side logging, which is something most casual developers seldom do. The complexity is also increased by the more frequent use of JavaScript. No matter how comfortable you are with it, you still have two main development languages (JavaScript and whatever you run on your server) and cross-browser compatibility to worry about.

There are a number of ways to manage this added complexity. One of the simplest solutions is to create test constructs that allow you to test your server components without connecting them to the front end. The additional complexity created by adding a new language is harder to manage, but it can be done, either by using developers with lots of JavaScript experience or by limiting the scope of your JavaScript development to only those features that have the biggest payoff.

Developing with AJAX can also create new usability and design problems. As you add more interactive features to a Web site, it moves further away from the model your users have used. One way to avoid this is to make the site look and feel more like an application; this gives the users a clue that the site will be working like an application and not like the Web site to which they are accustomed. However, in many cases, there is no easy way to mimic native applications, especially in areas where no similar native application exists. In these cases, you'll have to use other cues to create appropriate usability expectations from your users. Following the usability guidelines provided in Chapter 6, "Usability Guidelines," can help solve many of these basic usability problems.

AJAX can also cause problems because it is new and because it's a prime candidate for overuse. AJAX is powerful and can create some great solutions, but that doesn't mean it can solve every problem. For instance, you may have a general usability problem that can be solved only by updating the user interface. Throwing AJAX at the problem isn't going to solve anything. In other words, keep in mind that AJAX isn't a magic bullet; to use it effectively, you must keep your goals and overall usability in mind when adding it to an application's design.

4.5 Advantages to Using a Library

As with any other technology, you can grab off-the-shelf components to handle implementing AJAX instead of writing all the code yourself. This can help reduce the changes to your overall development cycle, or it can cause more changes than starting everything from scratch. This effect depends not only on the quality of the library, but also on its fit into your current processes and development style. If you can find a library that fits your needs, it will help reduce the changes wrought by adding AJAX to your toolbox. The largest advantage comes from the library's ability to hide the hard parts of JavaScript development (cross-browser support, communications between different languages, and visual effects), but you can also make gains just from following the best practices of someone else instead of having to spend time figuring out all the new rules on your own.

When developers first take a look at AJAX, they may think it's a simple technology with enough support from major browsers that they can take off coding from scratch. This approach ignores the fact that even the major browsers have implementation differences around which you're going to need to work. If your approach is too simplistic, you can end up in a position where it's impossible to work around various browser bugs without recoding large amounts of your application or Web site. The better that the basic browser primitives are hidden, the easier it is to plug in new compatibility techniques. These techniques range from using IFrames on older browsers to implementing new JavaScript API elements that haven't yet been added to browsers.

An AJAX library needs to cover basic communications aspects, allowing you to make asynchronous requests to your server from all the browsers you need to support. Depending on your choices, you will also need some other features; if you need eXtensible Stylesheet Language Transformation (XSLT) support, you'll need a library that hides the differences between the Firefox and IE implementations. You may need code that encodes data in a specific type to be sent to your server; this can be any format, from JavaScript Object Notation (JSON) to Extensible Markup Language (XML). It is also useful to support the tasks often used in conjunction with basic AJAX development, including drag-and-drop, visual effects, dynamic positioning, and DOM manipulation.

A good library helps hide the problematic areas of JavaScript, adding in compatibility between different browsers while offering a clean, easy-to-use API. It also exposes its feature set without making you learn every inch of its API. Drag-and-drop is a great feature, but if it gets in the way of something more basic, then it's making tradeoffs that aren't useful to a developer. No matter the source of your AJAX library, make sure it meets your needs in a clean well-encapsulated manner. Don't be afraid to mix and match libraries, taking the best features from each one, but remember that each library has a cost in download size, and not every environment will be a high-bandwidth local network.

4.6 Reasons to Build Your Own Library

There are two reasons to build your own library: control and lack of a good alternative.

Control is the most common reason to build your own library; you want things to work in a specific way. Usually this is a matter of making AJAX fit into the ideas of a current Web development framework. You might also build a library to get a specific set of features, although this need generally presents itself only when minimizing library size is also a goal. This lack of feature want occurs because many of the large open source libraries already have such a large feature set. The need for control is often centered on intellectual property. There are cases when owning the copyrights to all your development is more important than cutting down the amount of work you need to do. In these cases, you're forced to start from scratch, although generally it is a good idea to look at libraries with liberal licenses because they offer many of the same intellectual property benefits as writing the code yourself.

Sometimes, you may also find that no AJAX library meets your needs. This is more likely to happen if you're developing a project on a nomainstream language. It can also happen if your project needs low overhead in terms of code size and has limited feature needs. Few AJAX libraries go the minimalist route because it's hard to meet a large number of people's needs in this fashion. Most single-purpose AJAX code supports only a single type of request and has little to no configuration. This is great if the code is written for a single application, but it generally isn't useful for a wide range of development tasks. Building your own AJAX library makes sense for many projects, but don't underestimate the amount of work that building a library takes. While the initial development may be easy, tracking down browser bugs in older browsers, or browsers with a small market share, is a time-consuming process, and it's this widespread compatibility provided by these workarounds that maximizes the cases where you can use AJAX.

4.7 How Open Source Fits into the Mix

As you look for an AJAX library, you will notice that many of the most mature options are open source libraries. In fact, most of the first libraries were open source, and an ecosystem has grown up around them; this has made it much harder for high-priced commercial libraries to gain a following because they have to offer more than their free open source counterparts to get people's attention. Open source

AJAX has also been driven by its match with open source scripting languages. These languages include Python, Ruby, and PHP. These languages often pick up new technologies faster than vendor-driven languages, such as ASP.Net or Java, because there is more competition at the tool level. This has allowed for quick integration of AJAX, although the implementation isn't always mature.

4.7.1 Evaluating an Open Source Library

When picking an open source AJAX library, keep in mind three main items: license compatibility, feature set, and maturity/community size.

License compatibility is simply a matter of picking a license that meets your needs; if your software will be released as open source, then the licenses need to work together. The simplest solution in this case is to pick a library with the same license as your currently chosen code or one that is very liberal, such as Berkeley Software Distribution (BSD) or Massachusetts Institute of Technology (MIT) software licenses. If you're using the library for internal development, licensing isn't generally an issue because most licenses apply to distribution, and you're the only user. If you're selling the software, you'll need to be more careful because you'll need to pick a license that has redistribution rules you can deal with. Open source licensing can be complex, but not necessarily more so than managing licensing from commercial vendors.

As with any library, picking one with an appropriate feature set is of vital importance. You may be quick to pick one that offers the biggest checklist, but it's generally a good idea to look at a couple options and pick one that fits your coding style and that can be easily combined with other libraries. As with any development, there is always a tradeoff between large monolithic libraries and smaller components. In addition, be sure to pay attention to how well the library integrates into any Web-development framework you might be using; an AJAX library designed with your framework in mind can, in many cases, provide a simpler development experience than a more general library.

The last item to look at when picking an open source library is the maturity of the project and the size of the community around it. The community offers support, testing, and documentation. The larger the community, the easier time you'll have getting started with the project. A large community also reduces risk because there are more people to share development in case the project's original developers abandon it. Because the barrier to entry in starting a new project is low, you'll want to pick a project in which the developers have proven they know how to support their users over more than one release. Libraries associated with larger projects, such as the PHP PEAR project (HTML_AJAX), or a framework like Ruby on Rails (Prototype), are also good picks because they have a large infrastructure and knowledge base from past larger projects.

4.7.2 Open Source Libraries in Relation to Commercial Libraries

Open source is popular in the AJAX world because it offers low cost, ease of customization, and widespread support in every possible language. Mainstream mature projects offer a quick route to AJAX deployment and a large community that is a great source for support. Smaller, more experimental projects can also offer great value if they meet your unique needs, but you need to be careful because many small projects will never generate a large enough community to gain support beyond their original developers.

Commercial languages developers, such as Microsoft, have also started developing AJAX libraries. These libraries have many of the same distribution advantages as open source libraries because they are not tied to per-server licenses. However, they don't offer the same customization possibilities that an open source library does. They also lack the ease of developer interaction that most open source projects have. This lack of ease occurs because there are fewer lines of communication with the developers of the actual library. The biggest advantage that libraries from major vendors have is the resources behind them. This leads to widespread testing and thorough documentation, even in early releases.

How I Decide Which Open Source AJAX Library to Use

The company I work for, Uversa Inc., is based around General Public License (GPL) software, so when I pick any library, it first needs to be compatible with the GPL. Because the GPL is so widespread, many licenses are compatible with it. (See www.fsf.org/licensing/licenses/index_html#GPLCompatibleLicenses for more information.) However, because licensing is a hard rule, you should always start your search by limiting it to the ones that meet your needs. After getting my license guidelines, I look at major features that are required. In my case, this includes good compatibility with PHP, including the ability to map data types between PHP and JavaScript. I also want to be able to easily combine the library with other JavaScript libraries, so well-name-spaced functions and variables are a plus. Finally, I want a focused design, so I'm looking just for an AJAX library; I don't need a large JavaScript framework that takes weeks to learn. Multiple developers will be using it, so the less they have to learn, the better.

During most of 2005, these requirements—and a bit of searching—would have left me with a small list of libraries from which to choose. I could investigate them and find one that fit the rest of my Web development framework without too much hassle. Today, though, these requirements leave me with a large list, so I need to enter some other items to narrow the list of items I'll investigate thoroughly. I can further limit my list by picking projects that are actively being developed, so I'll look in depth only at those with releases in the past few months and that seem to be developed by more than one person. You don't want to remove every single-developer project (after all, that's where many of the most innovative ideas come from); you just want to make sure that enough releases have been made that the library is not a one-time code drop of unfocused ideas. These criteria will help weed out the unsuitable projects and will keep me from wasting time on a project that will never gain the community needed to sustain it over the long run.

Once I have a short list of libraries, I'll do a quick review. Everyone has different goals, but I like libraries with at least basic documentation and an object-oriented (OO) design. (OO design is especially important to me on the PHP side because it will need to mesh with my existing code.) A good way to test any library is to do a basic install and to build a basic "hello world" application with it. If you can't easily complete a basic task, then the library probably isn't a good fit. AJAX isn't such a complicated technology that the basics can't be made easy while still making the difficult items possible.

Hopefully, after some basic use, one of the libraries will stand out from the pack and end my search. If a few libraries seem really good, I'll dig further into their documentation and user forums and make a final decision based on how easy learning all the details will be. If none of the libraries looks like it will work, then I'm left back at the starting gate. I can expand my search and look for less popular and hence harder-to-find libraries, or I can look into developing my own solution.

In my earlier searches, I had very few options when I was selecting a library; my first foray into AJAX was before the term had been defined. I picked the JPSpan library for its good PHP integration and object-oriented design. Although JPSpan was a decent solution, it didn't end up meeting all my needs. Over time, I decided to develop my own library, HTML_AJAX, for PHP's PEAR project. The reasons for building my own library relate more with wanting to help the PEAR community than in meeting my needs, but once you have your own library, it's an easy front-runner for future use.

As you make a decision on what library to use, you can apply much of this process. First, decide on your licensing needs; your needs can be as simple as a specific open source license or as complicated as a commercial solution. After that, look at your feature requirements, especially server-side language support, and build a list of possible solutions. If the list is large, looking only at more active projects is a great way to pare down the list. Then, take some time to investigate the libraries. I find it's always worth my time to actually write a small amount of test code. After that, it's just a matter of picking a library that seems like a good fit. Don't forget to take into account everything into which you'll be integrating this library; some solutions that might be easy in a standalone situation become a bear when integrated into your server-side Web development framework.

4.8 Use Case for Building: The Firefox Counter

After the Firefox 1.0 release, the Mozilla project added a number of grass-root marketing approaches to their marketing effort. One of these was asking people to add a counter to their Web sites showing the number of Firefox downloads. This data was provided by a Really Simple Syndication (RSS) feed; some implementations read this data at the server and then rendered it during the normal page generation process. Building on this basic approach, Matthew Levine built a small AJAX odometer-style counter that updates continuously. An example of this is shown in Figure 4-4. In this figure, an AJAX request is made on a regular interval, with rate information being used between updates to continually update the displayed count.

This is a very basic use case for AJAX. To implement the counter, you need to do a GET request to a single page and then grab three data points from an XML file. Because you're only going to be making a single type of request, you don't need the full-blown AJAX support that most libraries provide. It's also a small feature you are adding, so lots of error handling or other status feedback isn't really useful. The concept behind the counter is that it's an informative marketing technique, and while it's more active than a mere image, it's not the major draw of any page it's on. To accomplish this design goal, all you need is an implementation that updates in a smooth fashion or that dies silently when there are problems.

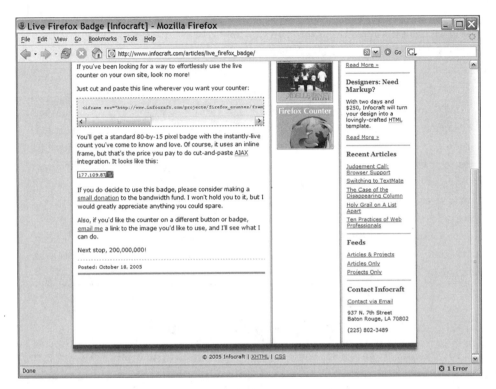

FIGURE 4-4
Version 2.0 of the Firefox counter

Simple functionality, combined with the goal of widespread installation on many different Web sites, makes building custom AJAX implementation a good choice. In the case of the actual counter, there is a small PHP script that produces the feed data; a small bit of JavaScript code; and a small HTML page that can be used as an IFrame to tie the pieces together. This makes for easy installation and a small amount of additional weight for the target page. The ease of installation and the small size are important features for any code you're hoping to widely deploy in a marketing effort.

In this case, building custom AJAX code was beneficial because ease of deployment and small size were more useful than the quick development time that a pre-built library might have offered. The simplicity of the AJAX code also removed much of the need for a library because in this basic case, we needed to focus on only one type of request. If we were combining the counter onto a site already using

AJAX, we might want to swap out the communication component to increase consistency, but because a counter by itself needs no other features, it makes little sense to bring along other features that will never be used.

4.9 Use Case for Downloading: An Intranet Web Site

A large amount of Web development is focused inward and is used to power company portals, content management systems, and myriad other applications. These applications are perfect places to deploy AJAX because they usually provide a high-bandwidth, homogeneous environment. The homogeneous environment aids in testing because you have fewer browsers to test against. In addition, the high bandwidth allows you to pull in any tool you need without much fear of increasing download times to an unacceptable level. These characteristics open up a huge number of possibilities when choosing an AJAX library; you may even choose to combine several to get the mix of features and the APIs that best suit your needs.

Internal sites generally have high levels of interactivity and may be the main application used by large numbers of employees. This is especially true within many content-management systems. They have many areas that can be enhanced through the use of AJAX, especially in the editing process. Commonly, content-management systems add in AJAX-based autosaves to keep authors from losing content. AJAX-based editing that allows for quick processing is also useful. Any powerful application will have many different places where AJAX makes sense, and these areas will have a variety of different communication patterns. The applications may also be enhanced by a variety of additional features. For instance, a content-management system may find drag-and-drop ordering of articles to be especially useful. Any application may also benefit from graphical fade effects that notify users that an action has taken place.

As you can see, an intranet Web site needs an AJAX library or multiple libraries that provide many types of features. The library needs to provide a communications layer that tightly couples with the backend programming language and framework while also covering different development patterns. These patterns range from buffering search requests on a find-as-you-type system to providing timed updates on an autosave system. Then, the library needs to provide graphical effects that can enhance ease of use; these can include features ranging from a visual effects library for fading in new HTML elements to a drag-and-drop ordering system. Writing a library that provides all these features can be a huge undertaking; this makes looking to prebuilt libraries a great solution.

4.10 Summary

Adding AJAX to an application isn't a magical cure-all. It's a great solution when you need to increase interactivity, but it's not without cost. For many developers, these costs will be higher than just the time it takes to do the basic implementation; AJAX development adds a number of new, higher-level challenges. These challenges include dealing with application logic divided into two parts: managing cross-browser compatibility and using JavaScript as a primary development language. The best way to mitigate these new problems is to keep AJAX's additional complexity as low as possible: Use well-tested libraries whenever possible, test your own code in its component parts whenever possible, and use AJAX only when you have an actual goal, not just when you want to add the newest technology. Keeping these items in mind won't prevent the inevitable changes, but it will keep them from becoming problems.

The easiest way to quickly integrate AJAX into your development is to bring in a library to do the heavy lifting for you. Of course, this brings in a new set of problems because you need to pick a library that meets your needs. Mature libraries are available from multiple sources, including many open source groups, commercial library developers, and large tool builders such as Microsoft. These libraries offer you the ability to immediately take advantage of AJAX instead of starting at the ground floor. They also offer myriad associated features, such as drag-and-drop support, animations, and visual effects, which are time-consuming to build when supporting multiple browsers is required. Remember that even a well-designed AJAX library can cause problems if it doesn't fit your needs and development style; spending extra time in the selection process will pay off down the road when you skip the painful processes of rewriting all your code to work with something else.

Chapter 5

Getting the Most from AJAX

In this chapter

AJAX offers a whole world of new possibilities, but to reap the benefits, you must keep focused on your primary goals. In this chapter, we will cover some of the general objectives people have when implementing AJAX, as well as how to measure whether these objectives are ultimately met. To that end, we must also explore how these objectives enhance current applications. (To do so, Web applications built with standard techniques would need to be compared to applications built using AJAX.) Some tradeoffs may be necessary to use AJAX in conjunction with other technologies, because AJAX by itself won't meet every application's needs. Let's get started!

5.1 Goals of AJAX

First and foremost, AJAX is about improving user experience; user experience improvements fall into two categories: making current tasks easier and making previously impossible tasks possible. Obviously, it is easier to focus on making current tasks easier. In Web development environments, this can be further broken down into two main goals: increasing interactivity and decreasing the time required to perform a task. In nonintranet cases, you may also have a related technical goal of reducing bandwidth use; by transferring less data to the browser, you can reduce page load times and improve the user's overall experience.

5.1.1 Increasing Interactivity

One of the overall goals of adding any amount of JavaScript to a Web site is to increase its interactivity. Even without AJAX, you can provide content-sensitive information when the user moves over a link or validates a form without reloading the page. This extra interactivity provides more information to the users without overwhelming them. Using AJAX, we can build on this general process instead of focusing on adding extra static information; in other words, we can add extra information dynamically.

A good example of increasing interactivity is using AJAX to add a real-time search to a normal search form on your Web site. An example of real-time search is the Google Suggest application (www.google.com/webhp?complete=1&hl=en),

which suggests possible search terms in a drop-down widget as you type your query; the widget would also indicate the number of results the search would return. Using Google Suggest to search for AJAX is shown Figure 5-1. Similar approaches can be used for any search application. The possibilities range from selecting a user on which to change permissions to picking a city to which to send a package.

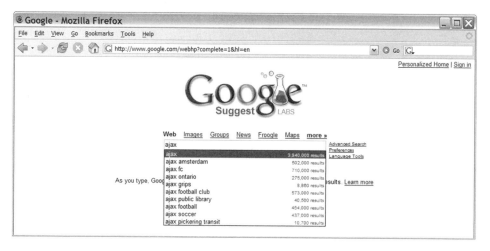

FIGURE 5-1
Using Google Suggest to search for AJAX

You can also use AJAX to increase interactivity in ways other than search methods. One way is to use a scrollbar to move through a page of results instead of using the Web method of next page links. AJAX works well for items such as these because data is still loaded only as needed, just as with a normal table, but the later rows can be accessed much more quickly. Figure 5-2 shows a standard table paging widget, whereas Figure 5-3 shows a table using an AJAX scrollbar instead. The example in Figure 5-3 also allows columns to be sorted without loading the page. AJAX-based filtering could also be added to the table, making for a quick and natural data-browsing experience.

AJAX opens up lots of new ways to increase interactivity because the extra data you're showing can be loaded as needed. This becomes especially useful when working with medium-sized data sets, because you can see all the data without increasing the original page-load time or needing another reload to see the data. The biggest problem with increasing interactivity is that it is hard to measure, so increasing interactivity becomes most useful when looked at when addressing our secondary goal—decreasing the time required to perform the actions.

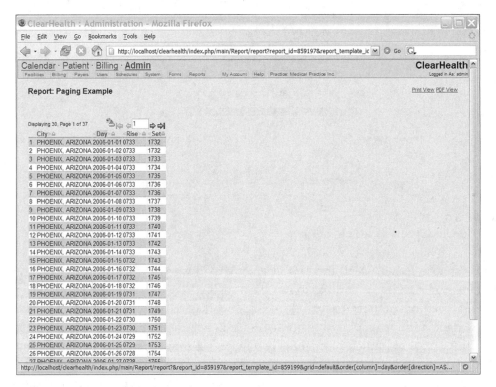

FIGURE 5-2
A standard table paging widget for a Web site, with each link causing a page reload

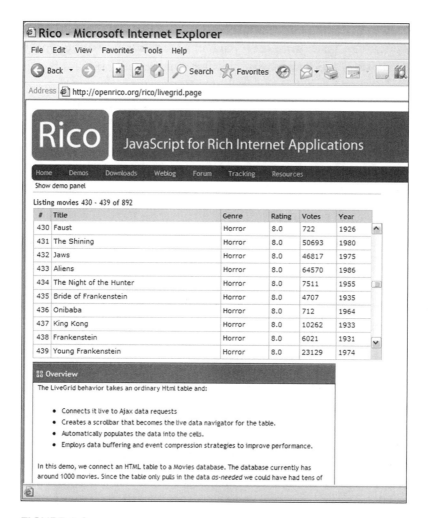

FIGURE 5-3
AJAX-based scroll table with new data being loaded by moving the scroll bar

5.1.2 Decreasing the Time Required to Perform Actions

One of the biggest disadvantages of Web applications is that any multistep process becomes a multiminute process. On a fast connection, each page-reload connection adds two to five seconds of pure wait time as the next page is generated and downloaded by the browser, and on a slow connection, the waits can be double or triple that. Using AJAX to load in the new data allows us to remove these page reloads, making for a seamless experience with only a small one- or two-second wait for extra data.

There are lots of other cases where AJAX can be used to decease process times. They include using multistep wizards and reviewing and updating online content. Once you've found a task that takes a long time, such as moderating posts on a customer support forum, you look for the specific subtasks that take up the most time. In forum moderation, the problem is that each page reload takes a long time because you may be looking at 20 or 100 posts at once. Moderating posts requires one reload to start editing and then one reload to save your edit—a painful process. Other tasks, such as moving a post, are also slow because each page reload can make you lose your place in the list of posts.

For example, consider a conference-room booking system at a large company. After a room is chosen, each participant needs to be searched for and added to the booking so that he or she can receive a notification email. Because the company has over 100 employees, a select drop-down widget isn't a good choice. Using it would greatly increase page load times because so much data would need to be preloaded. An extremely large drop-down widget would also be unwieldy to use.

The solution to this selection problem prior to AJAX was to add a search system to find each employee; the search system might even be put in a popup window to lower the amount of data to be reloaded, but no matter how it is implemented, adding each person becomes a 5- to 30-second process. This clunky interface isn't a problem when adding 1 or 2 people, but it becomes unbearable when adding 20 or more. An AJAX approach allows the search to happen using a real-time search. The interface would look much like Google Suggest in Figure 5-1, displaying employees' names instead of search terms. In this case, by using AJAX, we make adding 20 employees a 1-minute process instead of a 5-minute process.

Using AJAX, you speed up the process by adding in-place editing and by using drag-and-drop to move a post. In-place editing works by creating a text editing box without reloading the page. Because the content is already displayed, no request needs to be sent to the server to start an edit. At the end of the process, the changes are transparently saved while the user moves on to editing the next post. An example of using inline editing is shown in Figure 5-4. Drag-and-drop moving of posts is also a large time-saver, mainly because it's much easier to see the target location on your normal post-browsing screen than it is to see it in a list of post titles that a non-AJAX process would be forced to use.

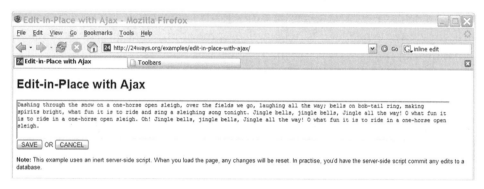

FIGURE 5-4
In-place editing

One of the things that make reducing task time such a great AJAX implementation goal is that it is easily measurable. All you need to do is sit down and perform some of the tasks and track the amount of time they take to complete. Depending on the tasks, you can even add timers to the application to record normal-use data. Once you have these baseline numbers, you can create specific targets for your AJAX implementation. Combined with further tracking after you've created an AJAX implementation, you can obtain data to decide how effective your enhancements have been. With a real and repeatable measurement, the effectiveness of AJAX moves from guesswork to simple math. You can even use this process-time measurement to improve on your current AJAX use, swapping out techniques or adding in prefetching to make a process take less time.

5.1.3 Reducing Bandwidth Use

Reducing bandwidth use can be a useful goal in some AJAX implementations because a smaller amount of data takes less time to transfer, providing the user a more seamless experience. If you're paying for hosting, reducing bandwidth use can also be an effective way to save money. However, if you're using your application on an internal network, this may be a goal that doesn't matter at all because the fast network keeps load times low no matter how much data you transfer.

Bandwidth use is easy to measure; the related metrics are always easier to use than subjective comparisons. Of course, unlike the measurement of time to perform a task, bandwidth use isn't a number that you always want to see decrease as a whole. Reducing the amount of data loaded in the initial page load can be useful, especially if that data is seldom used and can be easily loaded as needed. However, in some cases, the best user experience is achieved by preloading data and increasing the overall bandwidth use.

You can preload data directly during the initial page load or by using AJAX call, but you'll find that using AJAX is beneficial as long as the data isn't needed immediately. AJAX preloading can happen after the page is loaded, making it less noticeable to the user. It can also be tied to the beginning of a task that will use it. This is especially true when browsing large data sets because they generally have consistent access patterns that can be discerned by monitoring the users of the applications.

AJAX doesn't have guaranteed bandwidth reductions and, in some access patterns, it will likely use more bandwidth. This is especially true when you're performing event-driven AJAX requests. Each request may be small, but a search for each keystroke can quickly add up. These effects may be reduced by limiting the number of events to one per time period, but the effects will still build up over time. Your goal should be to make each request as small as possible, while realizing that these bandwidth reductions may be eaten up by the greater quantity of requests and by using prefetching to make a highly interactive interface.

5.1.4 Creating Rich Applications

Our first three goals focused mainly on making enhancements to current Web applications; however, AJAX also gives us the possibility to create an entirely new class of Web applications. When creating rich applications, developers have the goal of making them work as much like native applications as possible, while trying to keep Web development's advantages in ease of deployment and implementation. In addition, rich applications development still has the goal of increasing the interactivity of the application and decreasing the time needed to perform actions, although the design and implementation of these goals may be different.

Because you're not taking a current application and fixing slow spots, you don't have the baseline metric of a standard Web application. Instead, you have to compare your application against its native equivalent. This can be challenging because native applications can use large persistent data stores to reduce the number of slow interactions, whereas AJAX applications are limited to smaller session-based caches. Depending on how data-intensive the task is, you may be unable to match the performance of a native application, so you'll need to focus on different usage patterns that will hide this problem. The easiest native applications to mimic are those that deal with a large dataset that isn't stored fully on the local client; because the data-access speeds are similar, the Web application needs to compete only on the quality of its user interface.

Many rich applications use more bandwidth than their standard Web application counterparts because they rely heavily on prefetching data to give a seamless user experience. This makes rich applications better suited for internal deployments where a fast network and the lack of bandwidth charges remove bandwidth reduction as a necessary goal.

The decision to build a rich application instead of an enhanced Web site should not be taken lightly. Rich applications work best when they are targeting the tasks performed by a native application. Email clients, RSS readers, and reporting applications are good examples of native applications that are easy to mimic. That being said, services normally provided by Web sites, such as shopping at an online store or displaying product information, don't translate well to rich applications. These tasks are better suited to an enhanced Web site where only the slow, complex tasks are replaced with AJAX versions.

5.2 Measuring Improvements

Measuring the time it takes to complete a task is one of the most useful metrics when looking at the success of an AJAX implementation. The actual measurement process is broken down into three simple steps:

1. Identifying a task's starting and ending points

2. Adding instrumentation to measure the starting and ending times

3. Combining multiple data points into useful information

Deciding which tasks to measure is generally a simple process; you need only find the areas in the application about which users always complain. If a process is slow and clunky, it's a good target for AJAX and therefore a good target for measurement. After choosing the task you need to measure, identify its starting and ending points.

It's important that you measure the entire process. You don't want to focus on page loads or the technical pieces, but actual steps taken by the user. If the process is complex, you may find it useful to watch users in action to see how things are actually done.

Once you've identified the start and end points, you need to add instrumentation. In most cases, you can do this by making some simple AJAX requests to a recording script. One call marks the beginning of the process, and a second records the ending. In our example case, we'll be recording the time it takes to select a user to edit, as shown in Figure 5-5. This example is extremely artificial, but useful, because the goal is to show how to instrument a process, not how to build an AJAX user editor.

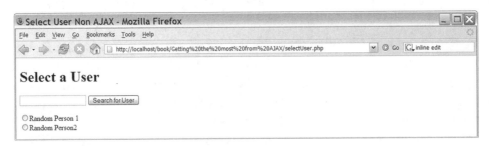

FIGURE 5-5
Selecting a user

The breakdown of this task is as follows: Load the page, search for a user, and then select the user from the results. The start of this task could be considered the loading of the page or the clicking of the Search for User button. In our example, we use the clicking of the Search for User button because it will help reduce the amount of variance in our measurement. The end of the process occurs when the `selectUser` JavaScript function runs; in an actual implementation, this would either redirect us to a user editor or populate an editing form below the selection section. A unique ID will also need to be created so that the start and end times can be matched together, but as long as the client is making only one request at a time, this ID can be created and stored in our data-storing script.

To implement the instrumentation, we will be using our basic `HttpClient` `XMLHttpRequest` wrapper. We will be making an AJAX call to `process.php` at the beginning and the end of the process. `process.php` will store this data in the session, and then `process.php`'s endProcess function will match it with a second end request that happens when the process is complete. A simple report (see Figure 5-6) can then be run to see how long each attempt to select a user took. The data storage is basic in this implementation and would need to be replaced with a database if you wanted to collect data from multiple machines.

The reusable parts of the measurement process are the `process.php` storage script shown in Listing 5-1 and the `Monitor` JavaScript class shown in Listing 5-2.

Listing 5-1

process.php

```php
1   <?php
2   session_start();
3
4   if (!isset($_SESSION['data'])) {
5       $_SESSION['data'] = array();
6   }
7   if (!isset($_SESSION['id'])) {
8       $_SESSION['id'] = false;
9   }
10
11
12  function startProcess() {
13      if (!$_SESSION['id']) {
14          $now = time();
15          $id = uniqid('m');
16              $_SESSION['id'] = $id;
17          $_SESSION['data'][$id]['start'] = $now;
18          $_SESSION['data'][$id]['name'] = $_GET['process'];
19      }
20  }
21
22  function endProcess() {
23      $now = time();
24      $_SESSION['data'][$_SESSION['id']]['end'] = $now;
25      $_SESSION['id'] = false;
26  }
27
28  function printStats() {
29      echo "<table border=1><tr><th>Name</th><th>Start Time</th>
30          <th>Run   time (seconds)</th></tr>";
31      foreach($_SESSION['data'] as $process) {
32          echo "<tr><td>$process[name]</td><td>".
33              date('Y-m-d H:i:s',$process['start']) .
```

```
34          '</td><td>';
35        if (isset($process['end'])) {
36          echo ($process['end'] - $process['start']);
37        }
38        echo '</td></tr>';
39      }
40      echo "</table>";
41  }
42
43  switch($_GET['action']) {
44    case 'start':
45      startProcess();
46      break;
47    case 'end':
48      endProcess();
49      break;
50    case 'data':
51      printStats();
52      break;
53  }
54  ?>
```

Listing 5-1 uses a PHP session to store its data, so the script starts out by setting this up. We start the session on line 2 and then set some default values on lines 4–9. Lines 12–41 define three functions, one for each of the actions the script can take. The startProcess function (lines 12–20) first checks if we have a current ID stored in the session; this check allows us to ignore multiple start requests for the same process. If there isn't a stored ID, startProcess stores the current time, creates a new random ID, and then puts this data, along with the process name, into the session. The endProcess function (lines 22–26) stores the current time as the end time and then clears out the ID to allow another process to start. These two functions provide the basic data-gathering capabilities of the script.

The third function, printStats (lines 28–41), creates a table that provides basic reporting. It loops over the data stored in the session and creates an HTML table. While doing this, it uses the start and end times to calculate how long each process took. The output from this function is shown in Figure 5-6. Lines 43–53 control which of the functions is called. The function to call is selected by the GET variable action. On the HTML side, JavaScript monitoring code makes AJAX requests to process.php to store the usage data.

FIGURE 5-6

A simple report of how long attempts to select a user took

Listing 5-2

```
Monitor.js
```

```
1   // Class for monitoring time users spend performing actions
2
3   function Monitor() {
4       this.httpclient = new HttpClient();
5       this.httpclient.isAsync = true;
6       this.httpclient.callback = function() {};
7   }
8   Monitor.prototype = {
9       startProcess: function(name) {
10          this.httpclient.makeRequest(
11          'process.php?action=start&process='+name);
12      },
13      endProcess: function(name) {
14          this.httpclient.makeRequest(
15          'process.php?action=end&process='+name);
16      }
17  }
```

The monitor class is quite simple; it sets up an instance of `HttpClient` for asynchronous operation in its constructor (lines 3–7) and then defines two functions. The first `startProcess` sends a request to `process.php`, which triggers its `startProcess` function. The second function, `endProcess` (lines 13–16), sends a similar request to `process.php`, but this time, the AJAX request triggers the matching `endProcess` PHP function. The main purpose of this class is to make it easier to instrument application pages, so it takes care of the boilerplate code for you. It is also a good place to add other methods if you find yourself needing to collect other data, such as which actions a user performs.

Now that we have a basic instrumentation framework set up to collect process times, we need to add it to a script. The process-time data can be useful in AJAX-driven pages to collect data that is generated by changes you are making. It is also useful in non-AJAX pages to help measure slow processes and to find ones that should be updated. Data collection like this can also be useful in making decisions on what data to prefetch, but normally, more data than simple timings is necessary because you need to identify which actions the user is most likely to perform. Listing 5-3 shows a simple user-selection script that uses the `Monitor` JavaScript class from Listing 5-2 to record how long each selection takes.

Listing 5-3

`selectUser.class.php`

```
1   <?php
2   /**
3    * This is an example class, which searches for a user from an array
4    * In most cases this class would actually query a database
5    */
6   class selectUser {
7
8       var $users = array(
9              1 => 'Joshua Eichorn',
10             2 => 'Travis Swicegood',
11             3 => 'Random Person 1',
12             4 => 'Random Person 2',
13             );
14
15      function search($input) {
16             $ret = array();
17
18             foreach($this->users as $key => $name) {
19                    if (stristr($name,$input)) {
20                           $ret[$key] = $name;
21                    }
22             }
23             return $ret;
24      }
25  }
26  ?>
```

The actual searching takes place in a related class, `selectUser`. This class does all its searching against an array to keep the example as simple as possible, but in most cases, this process would be database-driven. The class has a single method `search` (lines 15–24), which takes an input. The method then case-insensitively checks this input to see if it exists in the array of any of the users stored in the class. Last, the method builds an array from the matching results and then returns this array. The HTML user interface is built in Listing 5-4, which uses the `selectUser` class to handle POST requests to the page.

Listing 5-4

selectUser.php

```
1   <html>
2   <head>
3     <title>Select User Non AJAX</title>
4
5
6   <script type="text/javascript" src="HttpClient.js"></script>
7   <script type="text/javascript" src="Monitor.js"></script>
8   <script type="text/javascript">
9   var monitor = new Monitor();
10   function selectUser(el) {
11      alert('Selected User with an id of: '+el.value);
12      monitor.endProcess('Select User');
13   }
14   </script>
15   </head>
16   <body>
17
18  <div id="HttpClientStatus"></div>
19
20  <h1>Select a User</h1>
21
22  <form action="selectUser.php" method='post'>
23     <input name="name" onclick="monitor.startProcess('Select User')">
24     <input type="submit" value="Search for User">
25  </form>
26
27  <?php
28  require_once 'selectUser.class.php';
29
30   if (isset($_POST['name']) && !empty($_POST['name'])) {
31     $users = new selectUser();
32     $results = $users->search($_POST['name']);
33
34     foreach($results as $key => $val) {
35       echo "<input type='radio' name='user' value='$key'".
36                 "id='user_$key' onclick='selectUser(this)'>".
37         "<label for='user_$key'>$val</label><br>\n";
38     }
39  }
40 ?>
```

The script starts with some basic setup; then, line 6 includes the XMLHttpRequest wrapper, and line 7 includes the JavaScript Monitor class. Line 9 creates an instance of the Monitor class so that we can easily call startProcess and endProcess throughout the page. Lines 10–13 define the JavaScript function that is called at the end of the user-selection process; this function just outputs a selected message and then runs endProcess. Lines 20–25 provide the basic HTML UI of the page; this is a form that POSTs its results to the current page. The search input box runs a start process when you click it to start entering your search term.

Lines 27–40 perform the search after the form is POSTed to the page. An instance of the selectUser class does the actual searching. The results from this search are then looped over, creating a radio button for each result. An onclick action is added to each radio button, which calls the selectUser function defined in lines 10–13.

The basic workflow of this page is shown in Figure 5-7.

1. The user clicks the Search input box, sending a startProcess request.

2. The user clicks the Search for User button, POSTing the form.

3. The script uses the name sent in the POST request to build a list of radio buttons from which the user can select a specific user.

4. The user clicks a radio button, sending an endProcess request.

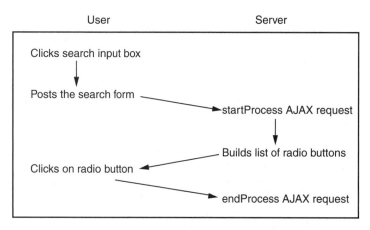

FIGURE 5-7
Workflow measuring how long it takes to select a user

Data collection is an important first step to making good decisions about how and when to implement AJAX. If the user-selection process is already fast, it doesn't make sense to spend time adding AJAX to it; instead, you'll want to find a different process to upgrade. If the process is slow, you can build an AJAX version that adds instrumentation to it and then obtain real numbers on how effective the process is. Ultimately, you may find that an AJAX version of the form won't give you the increased speed that you need, because searching by name doesn't scale to the number of users in your system; instead, your best results might be accomplished by limiting the search results using other criteria, such as department or job title.

5.3 Promises and Problems of Combining AJAX with Other New Technologies

As you work with AJAX, you may hear of related technologies that you can use with AJAX. They fit into two main groups: mature technologies that are widely available in many browsers today, and new technologies that are available only on a specific browser. The mature technologies include Java and Flash. (Flash is the most important because its plug-in is widely installed, and its design is optimized for providing interactive elements and animations to Web sites.) Java can also be used to add interactivity to sites, but its popularity has waned over the past five years, and it's no longer installed by default everywhere.

5.3.1 Combining AJAX with Flash

Flash makes a good partner with other AJAX techniques because it provides a number of features that are not available with pure JavaScript. These include a canvas on which images can be added and positioned and a drawing API that can be used for creating graphics. In addition, Flash has the ability to stream video and sound, and it includes support for vector animations. The biggest drawback of Flash is that it adds a new, separate development environment, and although you can make calls between the JavaScript on your page and the ActionScript of your Flash movie, it's not tightly integrated with the rest of your page. Flash also has a different look than the rest of the elements on an HTML page, which makes it hard to deliver a consistent feel and operation when using it for small elements within a bigger picture.

The drawbacks of Flash—poor JavaScript integration and a different look and feel—are not insurmountable, but they do lead many people to pick a complete

Flash solution when they need to do anything complicated. This helps control complexity, but it leaves you fully tied to a single vendor and means that you have to use Flash remoting for your communications layer instead of AJAX. Adding Flash to your AJAX application gives you the ability to support many graphical tasks that would be impossible without it, but be prepared for a more complex design and debugging process.

5.3.2 Scalable Vector Graphics (SVG)

The new technologies in the browser world are not as widely deployed as Flash, and some, like Microsoft's Extensible Application Markup Language (XAML), have had only beta releases. They do have the benefit of being fully integrated into the browser, making them fully scriptable with JavaScript and available as first-class elements on Web pages. Scalable Vector Graphics (SVG) is a new W3C standardized language for creating vector graphics. It has many of the same features as Flash, allowing for animations and interactive graphical elements to be added to the page. SVG avoids many of Flash's problems because it uses JavaScript for scripting; in addition, it can be embedded directly into an HTML page and modified just like any other element.

SVG's biggest problem is that browser support has been slow to develop; a plug-in from Adobe currently supports many of its features, but it leaves some of the same integration problems as Flash. The next versions of both Firefox and Opera browsers will have built-in support for SVG, but that still leaves it as a niche technology that can be used only on internal projects.

SVG is also missing a canvas element, so there is no way for users to draw on elements, as can be done with Flash. To address this, a bitmap canvas was created by Apple for its Safari browser. This effort has since been codified by the Web Hypertext Application Technology Working Group (WHATWG). This group is supported by many browser developers, including Mozilla and Opera, so support will be forthcoming in new releases of these browsers; however, support by Internet Explorer seems less certain.

5.3.3 XML User Interface Languages

Many of the new technologies are missing widespread browser support, and XML-based user interface languages are no exception. These languages, which include Mozilla's XML User Interface Language (XUL) and XAML, add the ability to describe normal application elements (such as menus, scrollbars, text boxes, and buttons) in an easy-to-use XML markup. Microsoft and Mozilla built their XML languages to allow for the creation of highly interactive rich applications that look and feel much like native applications right out of the box. However, because they are supported only by a single vendor, they do create problems of lock-in and tie you to a specific browser. This lock-in makes for a much less compelling solution than widely compatible solutions built on top of JavaScript and HTML.

XUL was created to define the user interface of Mozilla's browser and has been available for a number of years. Recently, it has begun to gain momentum as Firefox has increased in popularity, but it will never be able to move beyond niche products until other browsers support the language. XAML was created by Microsoft as part of its .NET effort, and it is scheduled to be released as part of Windows Vista. It's hard to know what its effect will be until it's widely released and until we know how accessible it will be to Web developers.

The rise of popular new Web browsers has led to the creation of exciting new Web technologies. The biggest problem is that most haven't made it beyond being implemented in a single browser. As support for these new technologies increases, they may become larger players, adding in the technology needed to increase inter-activity beyond the level that AJAX and dynamic HTML (DHTML) can reach on their own.

5.4 Summary

To get the most out of AJAX, you need to identify and target the areas where it will have the most effect and then take steps to monitor that effect. AJAX can be used in most any Web site design, but it's most effective when used to speed up searching and multistep processes. For solving simple problems, just picking appropriate areas to apply AJAX will give good results. However, as complexity increases, you'll want to add instrumentation to your applications to get hard data on the changes AJAX is causing. Using this data, you can fine-tune your approach and start down the path to effective AJAX. The final step in using AJAX effectively comes from looking at the usability of the graphical interfaces you're creating; we'll cover this process in the next chapter.

Chapter 6

Usability Guidelines

In this chapter

119

As shown in previous chapters, AJAX offers an exciting new set of possibilities, but it also creates new challenges. A big part of those challenges is creating a new interaction model that works not only from a technology standpoint, but also from the users' perspective. Your new designs need to work and to be easy to discover. In addition, they need to allow for productive, regular use. This chapter looks at usability, provides a set of principles that help you create highly usable interfaces, and shows real examples to illustrate some common mistakes and ways to avoid them.

6.1 Defining Usability

Usability is defined by the International Organization for Standardization (ISO) in document 9241 as "the extent to which a product can be used by specified users to achieve specified goals with effectiveness, efficiency and satisfaction in a specified context of use." For our purposes, this broad definition boils down to this: Can people easily understand and use your Web site?

Usability expert Jakob Nielson has a framework for looking at the usability of a Web site. It breaks down usability into five components: learnability, efficiency, memorability, errors, and satisfaction. By using this framework, we can identify usability problems in AJAX designs and identify ways to solve them:

- **Learnability** looks at how easy it is to accomplish tasks the first time the user visits the site. Learnability can be a problem in many AJAX designs because the site no longer acts like a standard Web site to which the user is accustomed. These problems are most common when the results of standard actions are changed. Creating new widgets can also be a problem, although this can be alleviated by making the new widgets look like their counterparts in the standard application world. Simplicity and consistency are keys to making an interface learnable. The goal isn't to make a flashy unique interface; it's to create one that new users can instantly recognize.

- **Efficiency** refers to how quickly the user can perform a task once it has been learned. This component sometimes stands in juxtaposition against learnability because the most efficient interfaces may require a large amount of knowledge to use. (A text-based data entry system is one example of an efficient interface.) Efficiency is the area of usability where AJAX can make a huge difference. AJAX can combine multistep processes into one quick screen to greatly reduce the time required to complete a task. This savings is most obvious in item-selection cases where multistep popup search screens can be replaced with search-as-you-type AJAX widgets.

- **Memorability** looks at how easily a user can regain proficiency in the use of the interface after not using it for a period of time. In such situations, the use of AJAX might not have a large effect, but it still can make a difference. AJAX can be used to streamline processes, which reduces the amount of steps that the user has to remember. It can also be used to create unique interface widgets that may hurt memorability because the user has no points of reference for them.

- The **errors** component focuses on having a system with few errors. It also focuses on how easy it is to recover from errors that are received. Web development as a whole is prone to network-related errors, but these errors are seldom fatal because users can just reload their browsers. In an AJAX application, network errors will need to be trapped in application code because the browser's Reload button won't resend the AJAX action. The greater use of JavaScript can also create more errors if developers aren't used to the language. One way to help alleviate these problems is to use an AJAX library that simplifies cross-browser development.

- The final component is a subjective measurement of **satisfaction**. Does the user enjoy using the design? This component is affected by many items, especially visual design, but AJAX can still play a part. A highly efficient AJAX interface that provides good feedback about what it's doing will be more satisfying than a standard, slow Web interface that requires tons of page reloads.

6.2 Usability Guidelines

Many usability experts have criticized AJAX by pointing out cases where it hurts usability. Although it is possible for AJAX to have that effect, I don't think AJAX inherently hurts usability; it's just that many developers have the wrong focus when adding AJAX to their sites. Focus on buzzwords and the latest technology results in nice demos but not necessarily in easy-to-use sites. Web development should always be user focused; adding AJAX to the mix shouldn't change that.

As you use AJAX, keep the following guidelines in mind, and you'll end up with a highly usable site or Web application:

- Keep the user's expectations in mind
- Provide feedback to actions
- Maintain the user's focus when adding content
- Keep the ability to undo actions
- Know if you are developing an application or a Web site
- Only use AJAX where it has the greatest effect
- Have a plan for those users without `XMLHttpRequest`

The following subsections cover each of the points in more detail.

6.2.1 Keep the User's Expectations in Mind

Keeping the user's expectations in mind is a broad guideline, but it is also an important one. At the simplest level, it means not changing how things operate without letting the user know. In most Web pages, buttons are used to submit forms, so having some other action, such as the clicking of a hyperlink, to submit a form can be confusing to users. This rule comes into play in any place where you redefine the standard way a Web site works.

One area in which you'll have a hard time meeting expectations is with bookmarking and the Back/Forward button operations; in many cases, these will no longer work, and you'll need new ways to support bookmarking within your application. This guideline doesn't mean that you have to change how the user interacts with your site; it just means that you need to work to provide the user with enough feedback so that he or she knows what is going on.

6.2.2 Provide Feedback to Actions

The next guideline focuses on providing feedback that an AJAX action has taken place. With this feedback, users know that some action has happened—even if it doesn't work as expected. In a basic Web application, the page reload shows that something is happening. In an AJAX application, we remove the reload, so we need to replace this feedback. This feedback mechanism ranges from a loading message in the corner of the screen that is similar to the waving flag that Internet Explorer uses to visually highlight the sections of the page that have changed. In many cases, you'll want to use multiple approaches, such as showing a standard loading box while the new content is being transmitted and then highlighting the part of the page that was updated. Providing feedback keeps your application from feeling broken. When someone clicks a link, he or she expects something to change; without the feedback, it's easy to miss what happened.

6.2.3 Maintain the User's Focus When Adding Content

As you add feedback to your AJAX application, avoid disturbing the user's focus. This usability guideline is especially important when using popup messages; they should never be used except in areas where immediate action is required.

Here are some items to watch out for when thinking about maintaining a user's focus on one area:

- **Actions that move the focus of a cursor.** Such actions will cause the user to type in the wrong input box or have to take the time to figure out the current cursor location.

- **Actions that cause page reflows.** If a user fills out a form and an error message causes the form to move down half an inch, the effect can be disorienting.

- **Distracting message styles.** Blinking red text can steal the user's focus just as easily as a popup can.

As a user interacts with your site, remember that he or she controls the interaction, not you; if your message isn't important enough to require immediate action, don't push it into the user's focus prematurely.

6.2.4 Keep the Ability to Undo Actions

Many AJAX applications try to outthink their users by automatically saving data as needed or submitting a form without clicking a button. When this is done well, it can be effective, but you must keep the user's expectations in mind when applying these techniques. Users are used to a forgiving Web environment where they can simply reset a form if the current input is incorrect. As you add AJAX, you must keep that level of forgiveness; operations should always be undoable. Autosave is one of the worst offenders in this area, but it is easily fixable by adding a Reset button on an autosave form or exposing the history of the saves.

6.2.5 Know If You Are Developing an Application or a Web Site

As you develop with AJAX, it is important to know if you are creating an application or a Web site. If you are developing an application, focus on having it act like a native application; following the human-interface guidelines of the target operating system is often a good idea. If you are developing a Web site, strive to have your work fit the standard feel and interaction model. This focus helps set the user's expectations and will make your interface more learnable because the user will have a correct frame of reference against which to compare it.

6.2.6 Only Use AJAX Where It Has the Greatest Effect

AJAX is a powerful tool, but it should be only a part of your Web development arsenal. Always make sure not to overuse AJAX. It should be used in areas where its extra capabilities provide enough benefits to overcome its drawbacks. An example of such an area is the breaking of bookmarking within a page. AJAX is a great tool to update part of a page—just load the changed content—but it should not be used to load an entire page. Normal pages work just fine and are going to be just as fast as reloading the page with AJAX. When you are deciding on using AJAX, look for a problem that needs solving, not just for places where it might be possible to use AJAX.

6.2.7 Have a Plan for Those Users Without `XMLHttpRequest`

The last usability guideline is to have a plan for users whose browsers can't perform AJAX operations. No matter how usable an application is, if the user can't run it, it's useless. For internal applications, this is seldom an issue because a specific browser can be required, but that's not always a great idea for a mass market Web site. If you're using AJAX just to enhance slow tasks, an easy solution is to keep support for the slower non-AJAX operation. However, if much of your site depends on AJAX, you will need either to create a non-AJAX version or to keep non-AJAX users out of your site. Users who use browsers that don't support AJAX should always at least get messages that some actions won't work for them. As you add AJAX, make sure to understand your audience. Although AJAX is widely supported, it won't work in all browsers (especially mobile ones), and you don't want to lock out any part of your audience without addressing the consequences.

6.3 Common Usability Problems

Although AJAX has the ability to create a more usable and efficient interface, it doesn't always achieve this goal. Usability problems can steal away any gains created from the use of new technology. This section discusses some common usability problems and then gives examples on how to fix them. Many of these problems can happen without the help of AJAX, but they are prevalent in AJAX applications, which are more active by nature.

6.3.1 Stealing Focus with Validation Messages

A common use of AJAX is to perform complex validation before the user has submitted a form. This is especially useful on large forms where large amounts of data are input before validation can take place. Simplistic attempts at continuous validation are often worse than waiting until the form is submitted to perform the validation, because they continuously steal the user's focus.

Figure 6-1 contains a basic registration form. AJAX is used to validate that the username hasn't already been taken and that the zip code matches the city/state information. The problem here is that validation steals the user's focus because it uses popup alerts to give validation errors as the user tabs to the next field.

One solution to this problem is to change from a popup error message to an inline one. In some cases, this is an acceptable solution, but it still causes problems.

(In this case, the problem is that the more useful error message will cause the form to move down quite a bit in the user's view.) Although usable, this approach pushes most of the form off the user's page after a couple error messages are shown. It's also not clear which fields need to be updated. Figure 6-2 shows an inline validation message.

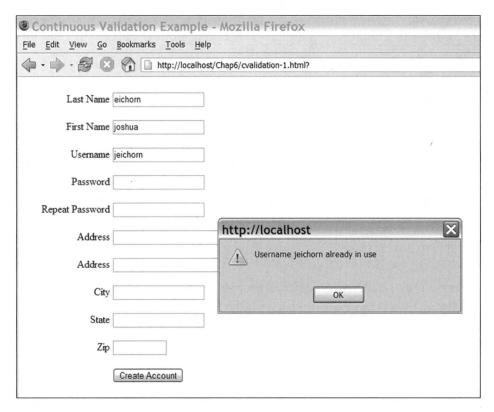

FIGURE 6-1
A validation message stealing focus on a user registration page

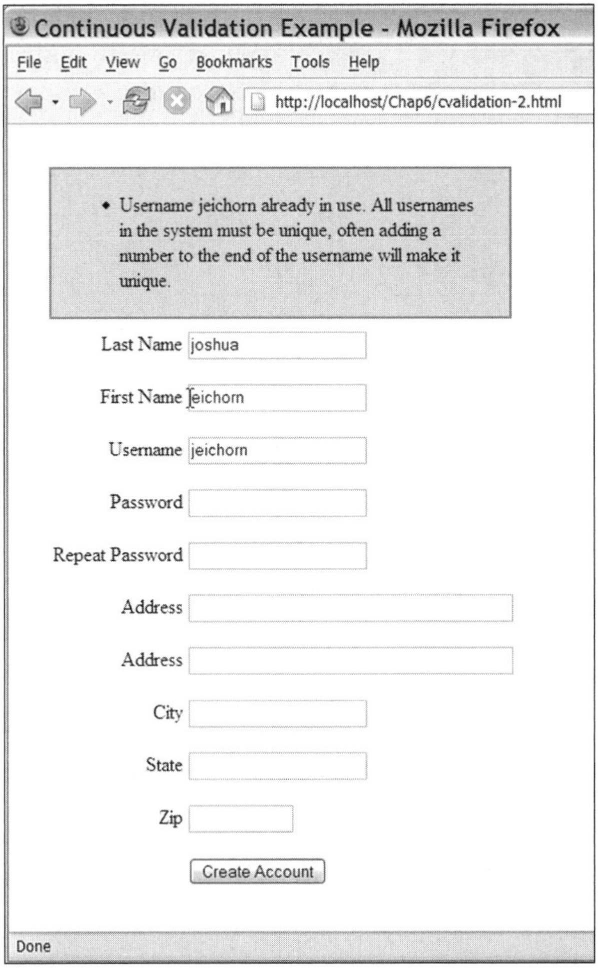

FIGURE 6-2
A validation message that pushes the rest of the form down

Figure 6-3 shows a possible solution to these problems. The size of the error messages was reduced to a single line, and the use of a "More Info" link now provides information on how to solve the error. The fields with errors were also highlighted to show what needed to be updated.

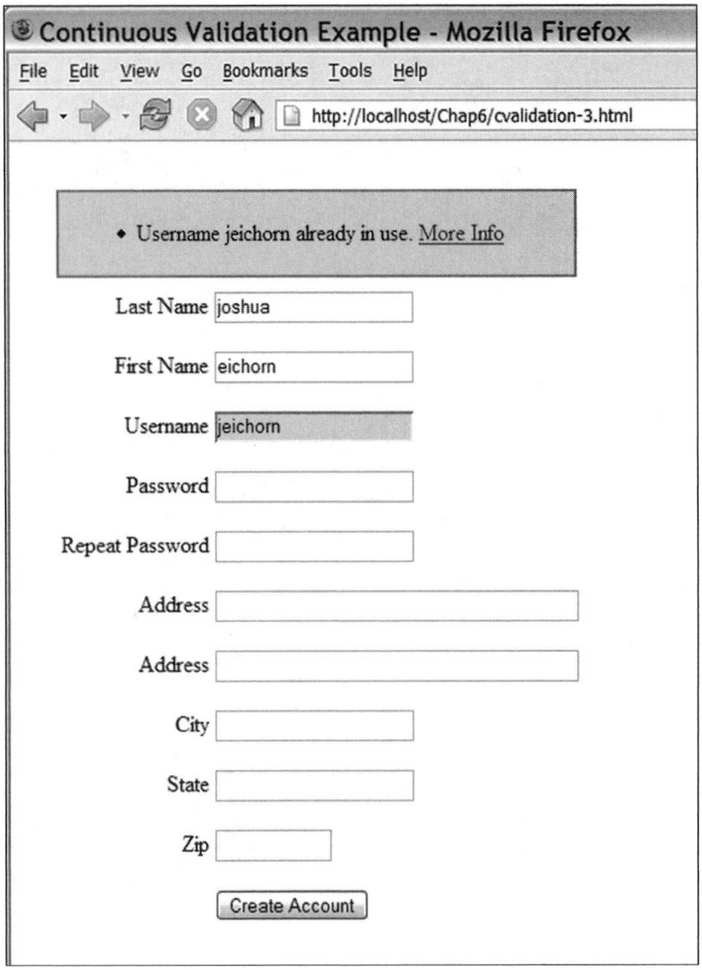

FIGURE 6-3
Validation messages with the usability problems fixed

Stealing focus problems often happen when trying to meet the guideline of providing user feedback. Although user feedback is important, it should not prevent the user from completing his or her current task. This is especially important when feedback is combined with automatic actions, because the user has no reason to expect the feedback to happen.

6.3.2 Preventing Undo with Autosave

In conventional Web applications, large forms can be dangerous because they are impossible to save automatically, and submitting the form on a regular basis depends on the user clicking a button. Plus, such saving interrupts the user's workflow. Here's an example: A content management system was upgraded with AJAX to save an article automatically every five minutes. This seemed like a great solution because then only five minutes of work could be lost by a browser crash or an accidental closing; however, after more use, a couple of problems with this approach were found.

One problem occurred when an author opened an article to edit it. He or she would make some changes and then decide, perhaps, that he or she didn't like the approach taken. In other words, the author ended up wanting to revert to the old version, but couldn't; during the editing process, the autosave process had already overwritten the original. This was not good.

As you can see from the previous scenario, editing couldn't be done on live articles because the autosave process would push out changes before they were complete. This problem can be solved easily by creating a separate autosave area to store the data from this process. This autosave area can keep anywhere from one to an unlimited number of autosaves. An interface is then added to let users load an autosave and save it as a normal version.

In some content management systems, documents are versioned so that the original problem of overwriting data doesn't happen. However, saving each autosave as a new version can also be problematic because it makes for a clumsy document history and can cause data-storage needs to explode. In a versioned content management system, a separate autosave area would also work, but it may be more useful to use a subtree in your version history to which autosaves are written. The application can then remove the old autosaves when each normal save is complete. This allows autosaved articles to be accessed by the normal article-management process without causing an explosion in version history.

Preventing undo operations often happens when AJAX implements autosave. This prevention results in data-loss situations from a process that was supposed to prevent them. Whether you are using time-based saving while editing an article or autosaving a form by detecting what field is edited, you are changing the way a Web form normally operates. Because you are moving the save decisions out of the user's hands, you need to provide a way for the user to revert his or her changes.

6.3.3 Updating Sections of a Page Without the User Realizing It

One way to use AJAX is to update parts of the page with new content in response to a user's action. This AJAX updating process could be used in technical documentation to load definitions or related information. A basic example of this is shown in Figure 6-4. When you click any term with a dashed link, its definition is loaded into the sidebar on the right.

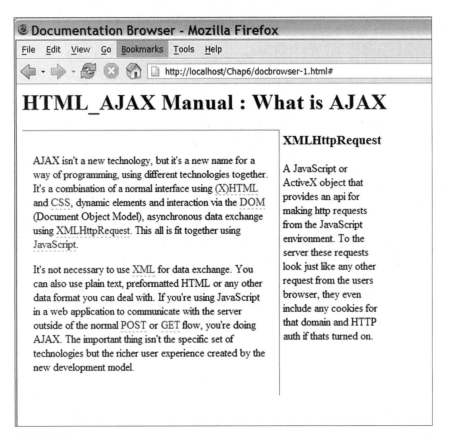

FIGURE 6-4
Documentation Browser with no feedback

The page in the preceding figure is already taking some usability steps, such as using a different link style for definition links, but it still has one problem: No feedback is given to the user regarding the fact that something has changed. Feedback is important in this case because we are redefining a standard browser action.

Normally, when you click a link, it loads a new page. If the user were expecting a new page to load and didn't notice the change on the right, he or she might think the link was just broken.

Providing feedback is about finding the right balance; we want to show that something has changed without annoying the user with effects that are overly flashy and distracting. There are a number of different techniques we can use in this case. One technique is to show a loading message while the browser is waiting for the server to respond. At this same time, we can fade out the current content and then fade it back in after the new content has arrived. Figure 6-5 shows this approach in progress.

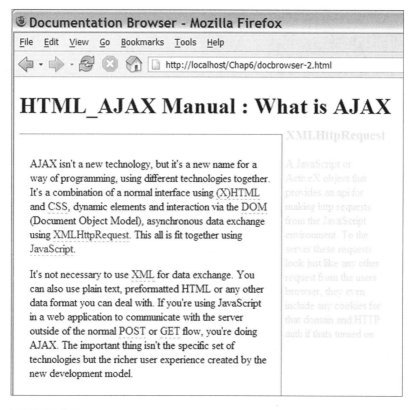

FIGURE 6-5
Documentation Browser while loading new content

An alternative to providing loading feedback is to wait until the new content is loaded and then highlight it in a pale yellow background. Over a period of three to five seconds, this yellow then fades to the white background color. Figure 6-6 shows the beginning of this process. In a documentation browser, I would recommend this approach because it doesn't distract the user until there is actually something to see. However, in another application where the content may take a while to load, immediate feedback would also be needed. You could combine both approaches, but in most cases, a more subtle approach is just as effective and is more aesthetically pleasing.

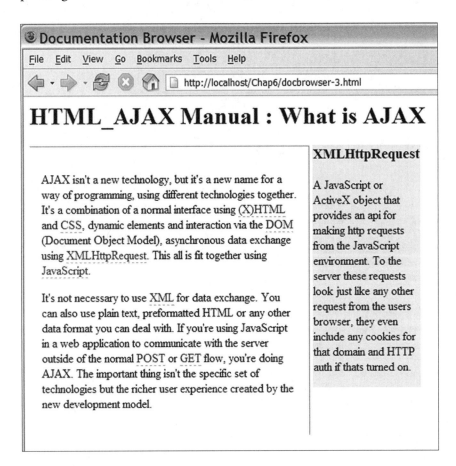

FIGURE 6-6
Highlighting content to provide feedback that the content has been updated

6.3.4 Breaking Bookmarking by Using AJAX to Load Entire Pages

Many times, when developers adopt a new technology, they see it as the solution to every problem they have. One area where AJAX can be overused is as a replacement for HTML framesets. This AJAX usage allows you to skip the loading of the navigation sections and just update the main body of the document. However, unless you take steps to make bookmarking work, you have the same problems as using frames—plus a more complicated development process. Figure 6-7 shows an example of this mistake; here, everything below the navigation bar is loaded using AJAX.

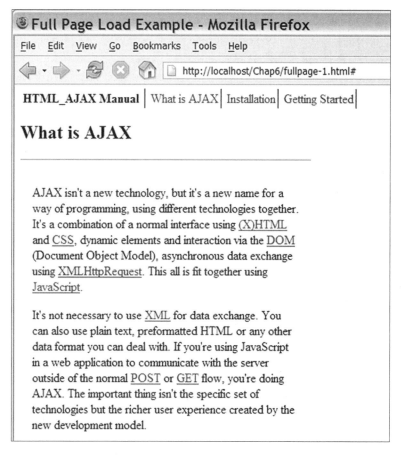

FIGURE 6-7
Loading an entire page using AJAX

In most of these cases, the simple solution is to use only normal pages; because navigation is seldom a large part of a page's loading time, these approaches save little in load times. In other cases, you may find that trying to load entire pages using AJAX is just a symptom of larger design issues, and you'll need to start at the beginning and focus on how users will interact with your information. AJAX is a great tool, but it is not the solution to every problem. Design and development should always keep the user in mind. The end result might not use every technology you would like, but it will make for the best user experience.

6.3.5 Making AJAX Required on a Web Store

Although AJAX adds great capabilities to a Web site, it's not always worth the cost. The biggest cost is preventing users from using a site because they're not using an advanced-enough Web browser. While it's easy to say "Please upgrade," doing so is not always possible, especially if the user is using a mobile device, such as a PDA or cell phone. Let's look at a fictional scenario to see some of the problems that might be caused by requiring AJAX. A Web-based store updated its shopping cart to use AJAX; it then tested AJAX on all the major browsers, and everything worked fine. Because the store was supporting all major browsers, it decided to drop its non-AJAX version. After rolling out the new shopping cart, a large number of complaints came into the company's support email. After some research, the store noticed that all the complaints were from users using Pocket IE on smart phones or PDAs.

This is a fictional example, but it shows important points. Although no new computer will come with a browser that can't be used with AJAX, lots of mobile devices still will. If your site has a broad user base, requiring AJAX may shut out a sizable part of your audience.

6.4 Summary

AJAX can create great interfaces that have much higher usability than current Web development techniques. However, using AJAX doesn't guarantee that the end result will be highly usable. Usability requires the solid presence of many different aspects of the user interface. AJAX has the ability help some aspects, but it has a tendency to hurt others. This chapter's usability guidelines can help keep you on the right track. While developing with AJAX, remember the following:

- Think about the user's expectations

- Provide feedback when performing actions

- Avoid breaking the user's focus

- Give the user the ability to undo every action

- Follow the style of a Web site or an application, not a mixture of both

- Use AJAX to improve usability, not to add new technology

- Plan for users whose browsers don't support `XMLHttpRequest`

AJAX can help you to produce great applications that use the latest technology and to perform tasks you didn't think were possible. However, there is more to success than implementation. An AJAX application is compared not only to other Web applications, but also to native applications. This comparison raises the bar higher, because we're moving into a more mature development space. A highly capable site with poor usability is no success; great development has usability as a major focus and offers the new features in a highly usable package.

AJAX Debugging Guide

One of the biggest difficulties of developing in AJAX is figuring out how to put your code back together when your applications go wrong. You don't know if the problem is code on the server or code on the client, or if it's caused by a cascade of problems between the two. Debugging server-side problems can be especially difficult because the client-side JavaScript code has a tendency to hide the errors, but there is a solution. This chapter covers a number of tools and techniques that let you see exactly what is happening. Once you have information, solving the actual problem becomes easy.

7.1 Two Sides to Debugging

When you look at an AJAX application, it is important to remember that there are two sides to the equation: the server, which interacts with the back end, and the client, which adds interactivity to the user's environment. Although this two-sided model has always existed, what has changed dramatically with the rise of AJAX is the complexity of the code running on the client. A secondary complexity is the number of interaction points between the two sides. Added complexity always makes debugging harder, so your focus when debugging an AJAX application needs to be on the various ways you can reduce that complexity.

The first step to debugging any problems is to separate the two sides as much as possible. This is generally an easy process on the server side; if you are generating HTML page chunks, you can go to the URL and inspect the output, looking for errors generated by the server code. If you're using a JSON or other RPC-based approach, it's slightly harder. However, you can always check the code that is being run by the RPC call, using normal development tools to look at its state before it's encoded. Many people find unit tests to be especially helpful in verifying the operation of the server-side code. It's especially useful for applications that expose chunks of functionality as services to the client. Unit tests work well on the server side because every major language has mature tools for managing these processes, and it narrows the type of problems you'll see on the data-production side.

On the JavaScript side, unit tests have a harder time being effective. This is due both to the lack of tools and the difficulty of testing an environment that relies on user-created events. There are a number of jUnit ports to JavaScript, and by using these testing frameworks and working hard, you can successfully use unit tests on the JavaScript side as well. Unit tests are a tool, and in AJAX development, they can be powerful because they provide a framework to test both sides of the equation

138

separately. Note, however, that they are not your only option. The most important item to remember is to debug the easy stuff first. If you get an error, always verify that your server-side code is working properly before moving on to the JavaScript.

7.2 Looking at AJAX Communications

Commonly, when you get an error, it's caused by a small problem, and all you need to do to solve it is to look at what the client sent to the server and then look at the server's response. Some libraries provide logging mechanisms to record this information, and you can easily create a generic request logger using PHP, but I find tools that directly interact with my browser to be more effective. However, you don't always have access to these tools, or you may need to debug in a nondevelopment environment. In such cases, you'll want to know how to build a logger.

7.2.1 Building an AJAX Logger

To build an AJAX logger, you first need to identify the information that is sent from the client. This information includes three types of information: query parameters, HTTP headers, and possibly a POST payload. In PHP, the query parameters are automatically parsed and made available in the $_GET variable; if the data sent to the server is a form submission, the POST variables are made available under a similar variable, which is $_POST. You can also read the raw POST submission by reading from php://input; this raw access is required to see the information if the client sent a JSON or XML payload. Finally, you can access the headers through the $_SERVER variable. Listing 7-1 shows an example of reading this information.

Listing 7-1

read.php

```php
1  <?php
2
3  echo "Query (GET) parameters<br>";
4  var_dump($_SERVER['QUERY_STRING']); // raw
5  var_dump($_GET); // parsed
6
7  echo "POST parameters<br>";
8  var_dump(file_get_contents('php://input')); // raw
9  var_dump($_POST); // parsed
10
11 echo "HTTP Headers<br>";
12 $headers = array();
```

```
13 foreach($_SERVER as $name => $val) {
14    if (preg_match('/HTTP_(.+)/',$name, $m)) {
15      $headers[$m[1]] = $val;
16    }
17 }
18 $other = array('CONTENT_TYPE','CONTENT_LENGTH');
19 foreach($other as $o) {
20    if (isset($_SERVER[$o])) {
21      $headers[$o] = $_SERVER[$o];
22    }
23 }
24 var_dump($headers);
25 ?>
```

The query parameters are the easiest inputs with which to work; the raw version is available as an index in the $_SERVER array (line 4), and that same data turned into an array is available through $_GET (line 5). POST data is available only when a POST HTTP request has been made. This can be done by using either a form or XMLHttpRequest. The raw POST header is read from php://input (line 8), and the parsed version is on line 9. $_POST is populated only when the POST has a Content-type of application/www-form-urlencoded or multipart/form-data.

Reading the headers is a little harder because they are stored in $_SERVER along with a bunch of other data. The majority of the HTTP headers are prefixed with HTTP_, so we can display them by looping over $_SERVER and doing a regular expression match (lines 13–17). This match will store the matching headers into an array. A couple of important HTTP headers don't have an HTTP prefix, so we look for the Content-type and Content-length headers using a secondary check (lines 18–23).

The examples for this chapter, which can be downloaded from the book's Web site, include a small test page (test.php) so that you can see the output of this script. The output for a GET request with a query, a form POST, and a POST from XMLHttpRequest are shown in Figures 7-1 through 7-3.

FIGURE 7-1
A GET request with a query string

FIGURE 7-2
A form POST

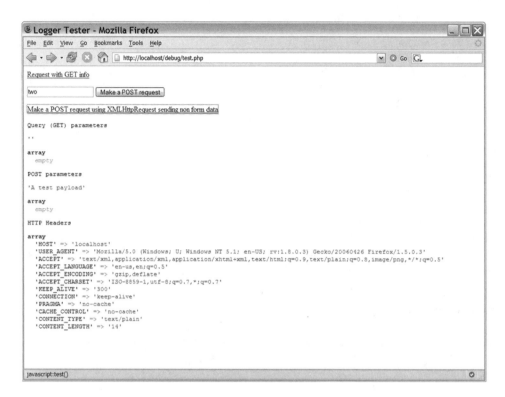

FIGURE 7-3
A POST **request from** XMLHttpRequest

To make this code usable for AJAX logging, we just need to format the output and add the ability to write it to a file. It's also useful to let the server code log what data it is going to send to the client. The final setup is a class called `logger`. It has two methods: `storeServer`, which sets the content we're going to send to the client, and `write`, which puts the information in a file. Listing 7-2 shows an example of a page that generates HTML chunks for an AJAX page.

Listing 7-2

pageChunk.php

```
1   <?php
2   require_once 'logger.class.php';
3
4   $logger = new logger();
5
6   // create some content
7   // use an output buffer so we can log it
8   ob_start();
```

```
9   ?>
10  <p>
11  Some random content
12  It could be anything generated from PHP
13  or static like this
14  </p>
15  <?php
16  echo $_GET['input'];
17
18  // page is done
19  $logger->storeServer(ob_get_contents());
20  $logger->write();
21
22  ob_flush();
23  ?>
```

7.2.2 Using the Logger

Adding our logger is a fairly simple process. We include the `logger` class (line 2) and then create a new instance of it (line 4). When the `logger` instance is created, it automatically grabs the information from the client, so if the `$_GET`, `$_POST`, or `$_SERVER` variables are changed by other parts of the code, our logging is not messed up. Then, we start an output buffer (line 8). This will allow us to log what is being sent back to the client without changing any of our existing code. Lines 10–16 contain some example input, and then we finish our logging process. Line 19 uses the `ob_get_contents` method to read all the output that has been created and to set it on our logger. Then, on line 20, we write out a log entry. The script ends by calling `ob_flush` (line 22), which sends out all the generated content we've been buffering. This simple logging process stores most of the details of an example entry from the log file, as Listing 7-3 shows.

Listing 7-3

Log Entry

```
################################################################################
Request to: /debug/pageChunk.php
Time: 2006-02-25 11:45:13

RAW Query String: input=test
_GET:
array (
  'input' => 'test',
)

RAW POST:
```

```
_POST:
array (
)

HTTP Headers:
HOST:localhost
USER_AGENT:Mozilla/5.0 (Windows; U; Windows NT 5.1; en-US; rv:1.8.0.1)
Gecko/20060111 Firefox/1.5.0.1
ACCEPT:text/xml,application/xml,application/xhtml+xml,text/html;q=0.9,te
xt/plain;q=0.8,image/png,*/*;q=0.5
ACCEPT_LANGUAGE:en-us,en;q=0.5
ACCEPT_ENCODING:gzip,deflate
ACCEPT_CHARSET:ISO-8859-1,utf-8;q=0.7,*;q=0.7
KEEP_ALIVE:300
CONNECTION:keep-alive
COOKIE:clearhealth=fcf23cdc7394e71b5c83a9929f0fdb7e
CACHE_CONTROL:max-age=0

Sent to client
<p>

Some random content

It could be anything generated from PHP

or static like this

</p>

test
```

Logging like this is easy to build into the AJAX library that you are using (if it doesn't already have its own). It's easy because the process happens automatically. If you're using an HTML page chunk approach, you could also build it right into your framework; in that case, the logging could be done on a preconfigured set of pages, or it could be turned on by sending a custom header when you make a request using XMLHttpRequest. Logging like this is especially useful in large-scale testing or production environments in which you don't have access to the browser to see error messages.

7.2.3 Firebug: A Firefox Debugging Extension

While logging provides you with a lot of information, it's not the most efficient way to get the information you need. It means keeping another file open and parsing through large text entries for the required information. Logging also doesn't have access to what is happening to the JavaScript on the browser, so it doesn't contain the full picture. Tools that can be added to the browser can get around most of these problems and have the ability to offer you a rich user interface.

If you're using Mozilla Firefox, extra functionality can be added to your browser through the use of an extension. The Firebug extension (www.joehewitt.com/software/firebug/) adds a popup bar at the bottom of the browser that lets you see JavaScript errors. With it, you can also view details of each XMLHttpRequest request, inspect DOM elements, and run JavaScript commands against the current page. An installation link is available from the project's Web site. The basic interface is shown in Figure 7-4.

FIGURE 7-4
Firebug: a Firefox debugging extension

Firebug attacks the debugging process from the JavaScript side. Whenever a JavaScript error happens, an error icon is shown in the lower-right corner (see Figure 7-5). Clicking this icon will bring up the console, showing you the errors. In its default configuration, these errors include errors generated by CSS, the browser, and its extensions (see Figure 7-6). To limit the displayed errors to just JavaScript ones, use the Errors drop-down box to deselect Show Errors From Chrome and Show CSS Errors. You can also get to the dialog box even when an error hasn't happened by clicking the error icon in the lower-right corner (see Figure 7-7). Doing this gives you an easy way to get to the XMLHttpRequest inspector.

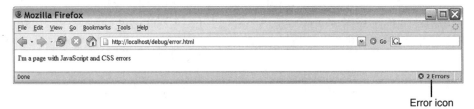

Error icon

FIGURE 7-5
Firebug error icon

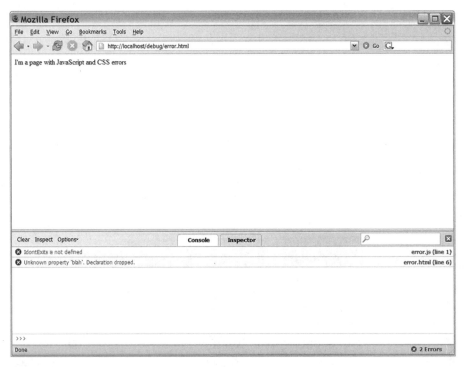

FIGURE 7-6
Firebug error selector

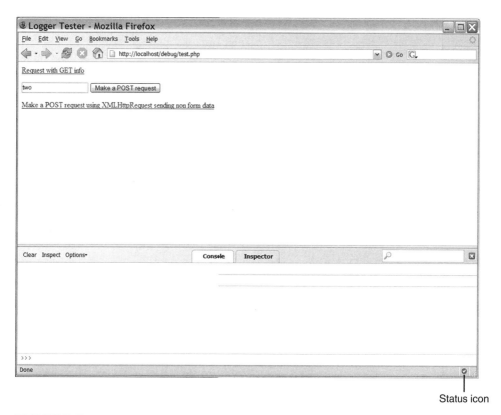

FIGURE 7-7
Firebug status icon

The XMLHttpRequest inspector lets you see the POST payload that was sent to the server, the response from the server, and the properties of the XMLHttpRequest object that sent it. A new row is added to the Firebug pane each time a request is made using XMLHttpRequest, so you can also use it as an overview of your AJAX activity. Each request entry includes the HTTP request type (generally GET or POST) and the URL to which the request was made. Figure 7-8 shows Firebug with several requests in it.

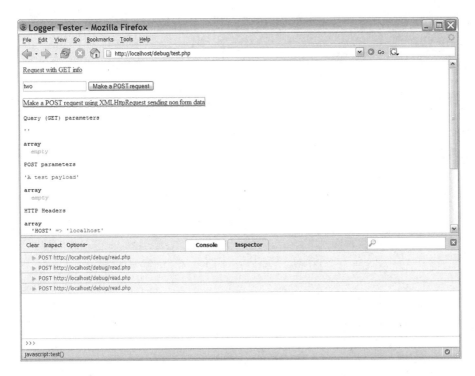

FIGURE 7-8
Firebug with multiple XMLHttpRequest entries

Now if you have a request that isn't working as expected, you can start the debugging process by doing the following:

1. Open Firebug and find the request in the pane. Requests are added to the bottom of the list, so scroll down to the most recent one. Selecting the request expands it, giving you three tabs from which to choose.

2. Select the Post tab on the right side to see the POST payload that you sent to the server.

3. Select the Response tab to see the data that the server returned.

4. Select the Headers tab to see the HTTP headers that the server returned.

Depending on the configuration of the server, you may see a large number of headers returned with the data, as in Figure 7-9. The most important ones are Content-type and Set-Cookie. Content-type has to be set to `text/xml` for XML-based requests to work. Many libraries also use this header to determine if the server is sending JSON that the library needs to decode, or if the content is just plain HTML. The Set-Cookie headers mark which cookies were set on this request; you can use them to verify that new authentication or other cookies were set as needed.

FIGURE 7-9
Firebug showing the Headers tab of an **XMLHttpRequest** entry; the important fields are outlined

Firebug also has the capability to run any JavaScript command against the current page. To do this, type a JavaScript command such as `document. getElementByName('test').style.color = 'red';` into the field at the bottom of the page (see Figure 7-10). You can also inspect page elements, get layout information, and view all elements, DOM properties, and events (see Figure 7-11). These features are useful in the overall development processes, but the biggest aid to debugging AJAX requests is the XMLHttpRequest inspector.

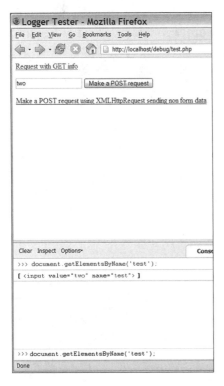

FIGURE 7-10
Running a JavaScript command in Firebug

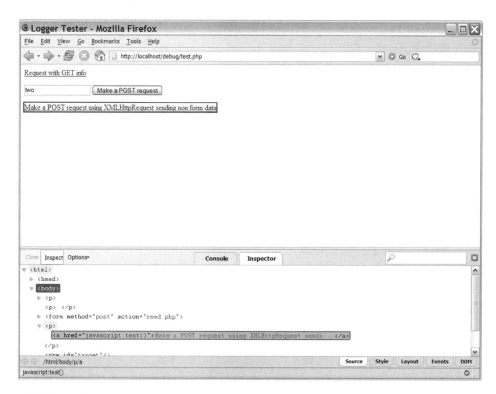

FIGURE 7-11
Inspecting a DOM element with Firebug

7.2.4 Fiddler

If you develop in Internet Explorer or just need to track down an Internet Explorer-specific bug, you obviously won't be able to use Firebug, but there still are a number of useful tools to help you. One tool is Fiddler, which is an HTTP debugging proxy that lets you see each request made by Internet Explorer and the response it receives from the server. Because it is an external tool, it can't look at the JavaScript the way Firebug can, but it does have an easy-to-use interface and it does give you an easy-to-use view of each request.

You can download Fiddler from www.fiddlertool.com/; this Web site also includes a wealth of information on how to use its advanced scripting and transformation features. Once you have it installed, you just need to run it, and Internet Explorer will automatically be set up to use it. You can also use it with other browsers by setting them up to use Fiddler as an HTTP proxy. You just set the proxy host to `localhost` and the port to `8888`. An example of setting up the proxy in Firefox is shown in Figure 7-12.

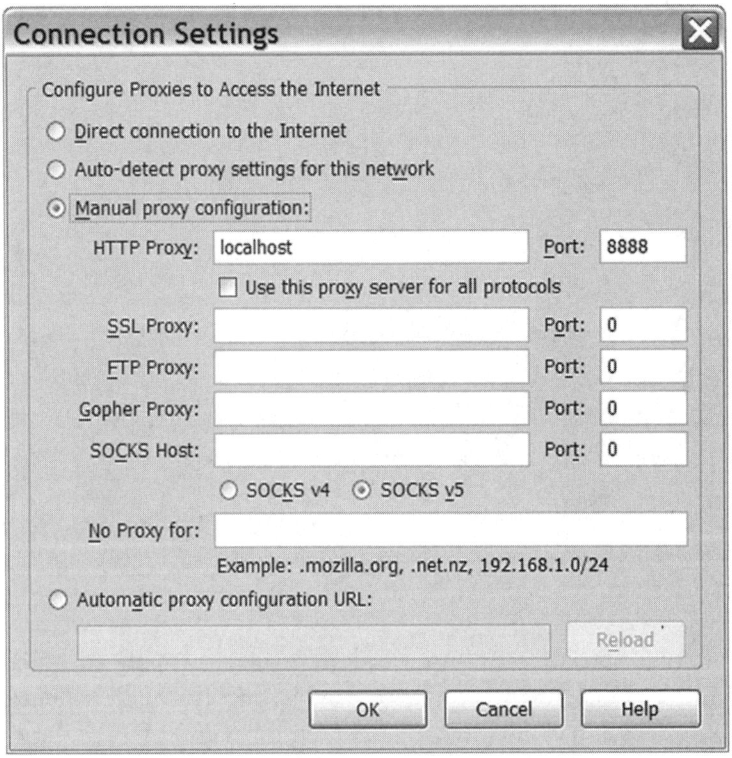

FIGURE 7-12
Setting up Firefox to use Fiddler as its proxy

Once you've run Fiddler, open your browser and perform the request that is giving you problems. Each HTTP request is shown as an entry in the main pane; secondary requests for images and CSS files will be shown with gray text, and the two HTML pages will be shown in blue. You can clear entries from the pane by right-clicking them and selecting remove. The basic session browsing interface is shown in Figure 7-13.

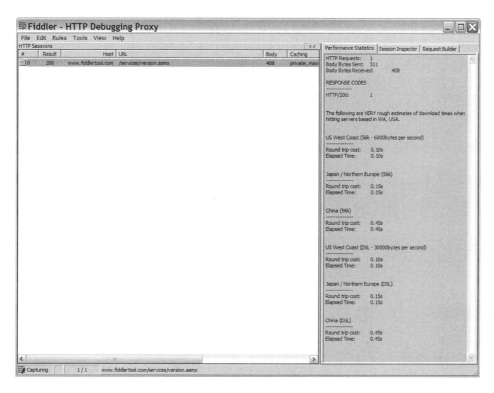

FIGURE 7-13
Main Fiddler interface

Once you've identified the HTTP request you want to inspect, select it in the sessions pane on the left side and then look at the pane on the right side. This pane has three main tabs. For debugging purposes, the most useful tab is the Session Inspector. After you select the Session Inspector tab, the pane will be split into two sections: the top showing the information that was sent to the server and the bottom showing the server's response (see Figure 7-14). For both the request and the response, you can view the request in a number of different formats, the most useful being the Headers and TextView views. If you're using XML to move data between the client and the server, you will also find the XML view to be useful because it will show the XML data in a formatted display.

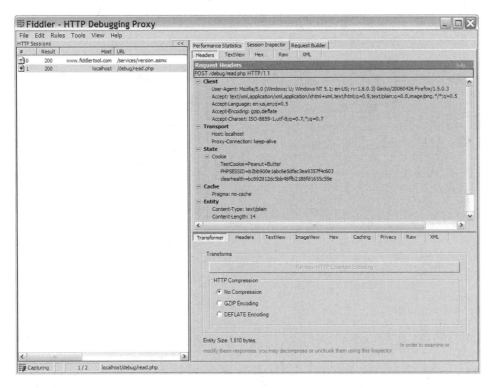

FIGURE 7-14
Fiddler session Inspector interface

The Headers view shows you a formatted version of the HTTP headers used in the request (see Figure 7-15). You can use this view to verify cookies are being sent, to see the Content-type of the data, and to view any HTTP status codes. The online help gives more details, but outside of verifying expected Content-types, you shouldn't need to spend much time here. The TextView view shows you the content that was sent to the server in a POST request and the results that the server sent back. The view offers the ability to search the content inline (the blue Find bar) and to open another program, such as your favorite text editor. (The open with command is the button to the right of the blue Find bar). You can see an example of the

TextView in Figure 7-16. Fiddler offers a number of other features, which are useful for transforming the request and responses, but they are not all that useful in basic AJAX debugging situations.

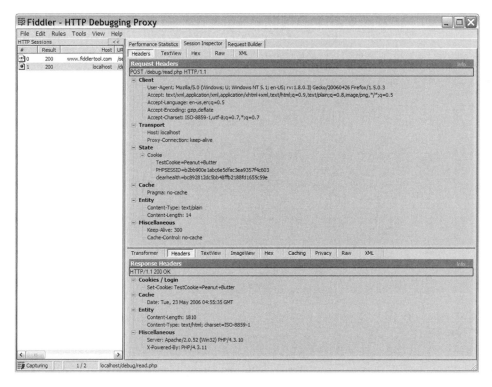

FIGURE 7-15
Fiddler Headers view

7.2.5 General Debugging Scenarios

Firebug, Fiddler, and custom logging code all provide extra information about an AJAX request. These types of tools are useful in scenarios in which you make an AJAX request and the request dies without giving useful information to your JavaScript code. In most cases, looking at the response from the server will quickly point out the problem. It could be an error in your server code or just some unexpected data being returned.

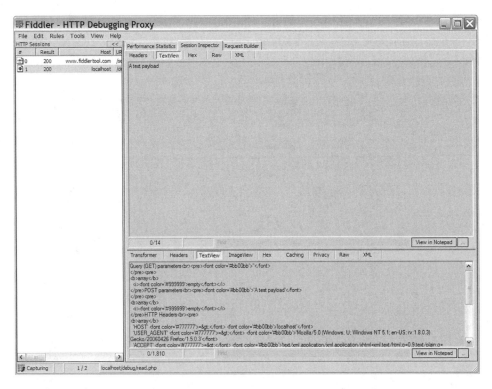

FIGURE 7-16
Fiddler TextView view

Debugging tools such as Fiddler or Firebug can help you figure out what data you're sending to the server. This can be especially useful once you start using more complex JavaScript widgets and AJAX libraries. These libraries offer a lot of functionality, but they move the AJAX operations far away from the actual event. This can make it hard to see what is really happening, so by using a tool like Firebug or Fiddler, you can see the HTTP request that was sent to the server and know what is really going on.

7.3 JavaScript Debugging Tools

The tools we've looked at so far are good at giving you a picture of the communication between the client and the server, but they're not a huge help if the bug is somewhere in your JavaScript code. JavaScript isn't known for having a large number of tools to help the developer, and if you're working with Internet Explorer, that lack of tools is still true; however, Firefox (and other browsers) gives you a lot of tools that are helpful with debugging and developing JavaScript. For instance, the most basic Firefox development tool is the JavaScript console (see Figure 7-17). Any JavaScript errors are shown in it, and clicking one of them will show you the line in your code where the error happened. You can view the console by selecting it from the Tools menu; it's labeled either JavaScript Console or Error Console, depending on your Firefox version. (Note that a number of Firefox extensions, including Firebug, provide quicker access to this information.)

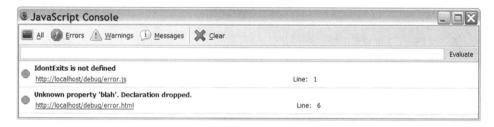

FIGURE 7-17
Firefox JavaScript Console

Out of the box, Internet Explorer gives you a particularly hard time debugging JavaScript because it doesn't provide correct lines numbers when external files are used. The solution to this is to install the Microsoft Script Debugger (www.microsoft. com/downloads/details.aspx?FamilyID=2f465be0-94fd-4569-b3c4-dffdf19ccd99&DisplayLang=en). After you install the debugger, you need to turn it on. To do so, follow these steps:

1. Open Internet Explorer and go to Tools -> Internet Options.

2. Select the Advanced tab.

3. In the Advanced tab, you see an option labeled Disabled Script Debugging (Internet Explorer). Uncheck this option to enable the debugger. This debugger dialog box is shown in Figure 7-18.

4. Once you have the debugger enabled, you receive a dialog box for each JavaScript error. The dialog box asks if you want to debug your error (see Figure 7-19). Selecting Yes will open the debugger and show you the line in the file where the error occurred.

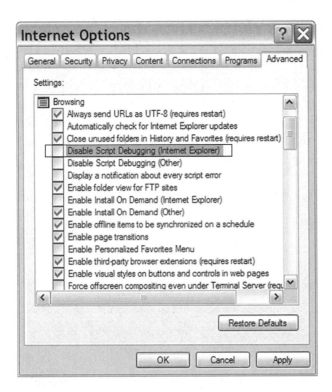

FIGURE 7-18
Enabling the Microsoft Script Debugger

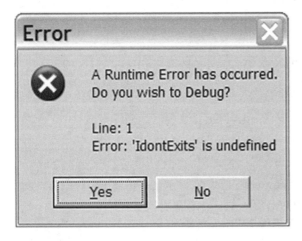

FIGURE 7-19
Script Debugger Error dialog box

The basic debugger interface is shown in Figure 7-20. From this screen, you can step through the code using the Debug menu, just as with any other debugger. The debugger has two main drawbacks: It creates a popup dialog box for each JavaScript error that has to be dealt with, and it tends to become unstable when actually using it for debugging. That being said, the Script Debugger quickly gives you the actual line where JavaScript errors happen, which is a big advantage over the normal IE error message.

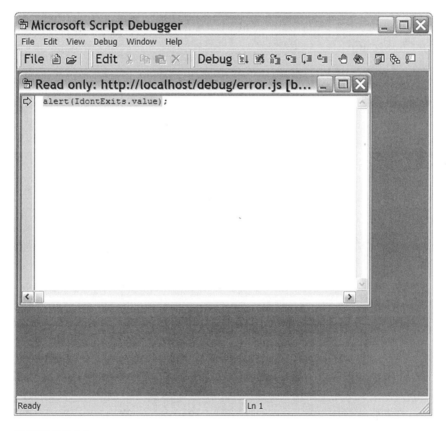

FIGURE 7-20
Basic Script Debugger interface

7.4 JavaScript Exceptions

JavaScript has a number of language features that are useful in the debugging process. The biggest one of these is the ability to catch any JavaScript error as an exception. This is done by wrapping code that can cause errors inside of a try block followed by a `catch` block. In the `catch` block, you have access to an `Error` object, which contains additional information about the error. This `Error` object contains the name of the error and a message. On Firefox, it also includes the file in which the error happened, the line on which it happened, and a call stack. Listing 7-4 shows an example of catching an error. Listings 7-5 and 7-6 show the output of the `catch` block in Firefox and IE.

Listing 7-4

`exception.html`

```
1   <html>
2   <body>
3       <div id="error">
4       </div>
5
6   <script type="text/javascript">
7   try {
8       alert(IDontExist);
9   }
10  catch (e) {
11      var msg = '';
12      for(var i in e) {
13        msg += i+':'+e[i]+"<br>\n";
14
15      }
16      document.getElementById('error').innerHTML = msg;
17  }
18  </script>
19  </body>
20  </html>
```

Listing 7-4 is simple. It contains a basic HTML page with a JavaScript block that creates the error and then prints out the resulting error object. Lines 3–4 give us an element to which to write an error message. Line 7 starts the try block; it's ended by the bracket on line 9. All JavaScript errors that happen in the try block will cause the catch block to be run. If no error happens, the code in the catch block is ignored. The catch block on lines 10–17 takes the error object and prints out each property. This text is then added to the error element, showing the value of the error object.

Listing 7-5

Output of `exception.html` *in Firefox*

```
message:IDontExist is not defined
fileName:http://localhost/debug/exception.html
lineNumber:8
stack:@http://localhost/debug/exception.html:8
name:ReferenceError
```

Listing 7-6

Output of `exception.html` *in Internet Explorer*

```
name:TypeError
message:'IDontExist' is undefined
number:-2146823279
description:'IDontExist' is undefined
```

Looking at the error messages, you can see that exceptions in Firefox are more useful for general debugging, but exceptions are still useful even without line properties because you end up knowing which block of code caused the error. They also allow you to handle the error programmatically, letting you give the user an error message or even perform a workaround instead of having your code silently break.

7.5 Dumping Variables

As shown in lines 10–17 of Listing 7-4, there are lots of cases in JavaScript in which you have an object but don't know what properties it contains. This is especially common when you are passing JSON-encoded data from the server to the client. JavaScript provides the "for in" loop for looping over the properties of any object. Using this loop, you can construct a basic dump function that allows you to quickly see the properties of an object. Listing 7-7 shows an example function.

Listing 7-7

A JavaScript Property Dumping Function

```
function dump(input) {
  var msg = '';
  for(var i in input) {
    msg += i+':'+input[i]+"\n";
  }
  return msg;

}
```

You can then use this function to alert the contents of the object or assign the debug output to a debug element on a page. A simple function like this can save a great deal of time in the debugging and development processes. Building on this same concept, the HTML AJAX library provides a utility function called varDump that provides additional information. This method is based on the var_dump function in PHP and provides the type of each element as well as its value. It also supports recursion, giving you the output of any child objects. Listings 7-8 and 7-9 show the output of varDump against different inputs. Sample usage is shown in the following code:

```
alert(HTML_AJAX_Util.varDump(input));
```

Listing 7-8

Sample varDump *Output (an Array with Another Nested Inside It)*

```
array(3) {
  [0]=>
  number(1)
  [1]=>
  array(3) {
    [0]=>
    number(1)
    [1]=>
    number(2)
    [2]=>
    number(3)
  }
  [2]=>
  number(3)
}
```

Listing 7-9

Sample varDump *Output (an Object)*

```
object(Object) (2) {
  ["bar"]=>
  string(3) "baz"
  ["bat"]=>
  number(5)
}
```

7.6 Summary

One of the biggest risks in adding AJAX to an application is the increased complexity of debugging. Using the tools covered in this chapter, you can help reduce that risk. The following tools and techniques offer a solution to many of the problems you will hit when debugging AJAX:

- **Server-side logging.** This logs AJAX requests and results, allowing you to debug AJAX communications without additional tools. It also allows you to collect debugging data from multiple clients.

- **Firebug.** This is the Firefox extension that adds a viewer for AJAX requests and results. It also provides DOM viewing and JavaScript console improvements.

- **Fiddler.** This is the debugging proxy, cross-browser way to view AJAX requests and results.

- **Script Debugger.** This adds basic JavaScript debugging to IE and is the only way to find a line of JavaScript that caused the error in IE.

- **JavaScript exceptions.** The use of these is the programmatic way of managing JavaScript errors, and they allow you to isolate problematic sections of JavaScript code.

- **Dumping variables.** With these, you can build JavaScript functions to see the contents of an object on the fly.

The most important item to remember in the debugging processes is to test the server side and the client side separately whenever possible. When that's not an option, you'll find that looking at the data sent between the server and the browser is helpful. Most importantly, like debugging in any language, strive for a clean simple design. AJAX is already adding the complexity of client/server communications; if you add tons of complexity in your design, debugging your application will quickly become unworkable.

PART II

Libraries Used in Part II: Sarissa, Scriptaculous

In this chapter

Part I of this book gives you a good understanding of the basics of AJAX, but it doesn't give you a complete understanding of how you would implement it. Part II fills in that gap, solving real-world problems by using libraries that would be a good choice for any AJAX implementation you choose. Chapter 8 provides an introduction to two of the libraries, with Chapter 9, "Libraries Used in Part II: HTML_AJAX," following up with a third library that we will be using in the use cases.

A total of three use cases are presented in this section of the book, showing how AJAX can be used in realistic situations. The cases strive to show not only how to use specific techniques, but also how each one improves the user's experience over a standard site. They also show how you can use various open source libraries to add AJAX without a lot of hard work on your part. The libraries used throughout these use cases are covered in the rest of this chapter.

8.1 Overview of the Use Cases

The three use cases presented in this book are as follows:

- The first case is focused on improving data display. It takes a large amount of data and displays it in an interactive grid that shows how AJAX can remove a common cause of "click and wait."

- The second case looks at using AJAX to build login systems. Updating the standard process allows for quicker feedback and makes it easier to add logins to applications like the comment systems on blogs.

- The final case is a Web-based trouble ticketing system used to provide technical support. This case focuses on building a complete AJAX application. It shows various techniques that can be used to manage an application that is written primarily in JavaScript. It also shows what a lightweight server back end would look like.

8.2 Libraries Used in Part II of This Book

Many powerful libraries exist in the AJAX world, especially if you're looking for one available under an open source license. Most are focused on one area or were developed with a specific Web development framework in mind. This section covers the basic usage of these libraries:

- **Sarissa:** XML usage, including XSLT

- **scriptaculous:** Visual effects and drag-and-drop

- **HTML_AJAX:** Communications with tight PHP integration

8.3 Sarissa

Sarissa is a GPL license library focusing on providing a cross-browser wrapper for the native JavaScript XML APIs. It provides an ECMA style API on all browsers it supports, which allows you to write to the standard no matter what browser you might be using. Its major features are AJAX communications, XPath, and XSLT support. Sarissa supports most major browsers, including Firefox and other Mozilla-based browsers, Internet Explorer (MSXML 3.0+), Konqueror (KDE 3.3+), Safari, and Opera. The code has reached a stable level and no longer has frequent releases, but the forums are busy and the developers respond to questions. Sarissa can be downloaded from http://sourceforge.net/projects/sarissa, and it has online documentation available at http://sarissa.sourceforge.net/.

8.3.1 Installation

Sarissa is a pure JavaScript library, so it's quite easy to install. Download the zip file from the SourceForge.net download page, and extract its contents to an accessible location on your Web server. The examples in this chapter use Sarissa version 0.9.6.1 installed at http://localhost/sarissa/; the Sarissa code is extracted into a subdirectory below that.

The release includes API documentation, including a basic tutorial located in the `doc` directory. It also includes unit tests that can be run by loading `testsarissa.html` and a sample application, minesweeper, in the `sample-apps/minesweeper` directory.

8.3.2 Making an AJAX Request

Sarissa gives you the ability to access `XMLHttpRequest` directly (or on IE6, a wrapper classes that looks the same), but that's not how you usually want to use it to make AJAX requests. Sarissa is designed around loading XML documents, so you can easily use the `load` command on its DOM documents to make a remote request.

Listing 8-1 does three main tasks: It includes the Sarissa library, creates a `loadDoc` function (which does an AJAX load of an XML file), and provides a simple UI for running the `loadDoc` function. The Sarissa library is included on line 5; in this example, the library is installed in the `Sarissa` subdirectory. Lines 9–21 define the `loadDoc` function; it's made up of a number of subtasks. Line 10 gets an empty Sarissa `DomDocument`. Lines 12–17 define a handler function that is called each time the ready state of the `DomDocument` is called. This ready state handler is just like the one on `XMLHttpRequest`; state 4 is reached when the document is fully loaded. When this state is reached (line 13), we use the `Sarissa.serialize` method to turn the loaded document back into its textual XML representation and then turn < into its entity form so that we can show the XML document in an HTML document (lines 14–15). Line 19 attaches the handler we defined to the `DomDocument`, and line 20 loads the `sarissaNews.xml` file from the server. In most cases, this XML file would be a dynamically generated file, but to keep this example simple, a static file is used.

Listing 8-1

SarissaMakingAnAJAXRequest.html

```
1   <html>
2   <head>
3   <title>Making an AJAX Request with Sarissa</title>
4
5   <script type="text/javascript" src="sarissa/sarissa.js">
6   </script>
7
8   <script type="text/javascript">
9     function loadDoc() {
10    var oDomDoc = Sarissa.getDomDocument();
11
12    var rHandler = function() {
13      if(oDomDoc.readyState == 4) {
14        document.getElementById('target').innerHTML =
15        Sarissa.serialize(oDomDoc).replace(/</g,'&lt;');
16      }
17    }
18
19    oDomDoc.onreadystatechange = rHandler;
20    oDomDoc.load("sarissaNews.xml");
21 }
```

```
22 </script>
23 </head>
24 <body>
25   <a href="javascript:loadDoc()">Load news.xml</a>
26   <pre id="target"></pre>
27 </body>
28 </html>
```

8.3.3 Basic XML Features

The Sarissa library focuses on providing good cross-browser XML support. To provide this, it creates a standardized interface to DOM documents loaded from any source. Most of this work is providing compatibility methods for Internet Explorer, hiding the fact that the XML capabilities are provided by the MSXML ActiveX control instead of by native JavaScript objects.

8.3.4 Working with DOM Documents

DOM documents are created in Sarissa through the use of the `Sarissa.getDomDocument()` method. Once you have a document, you can load content into it using three different methods. You can load remote data using AJAX (as shown in Listing 8-1), you can parse a string that contains XML data, or you can create the elements using standard DOM functions. Sarissa also includes a utility method, `Sarissa.serialize()`, for working with DOM documents. This prints out the document as its XML output, which is useful for debugging or in cases in which you want to send XML payloads to the server. To use the `serialize` method, just send the method a DOM document; a basic example is shown here:

```
Sarissa.serialize(domDoc);
```

8.3.4.1 Loading DOM Documents from a String

Loading DOM documents from a string gives you the ability to load a number of XML documents in a single request and then parse them into DOM documents to work with them. This can be a useful strategy for preloading XML during the normal page load, or it can be used with `XMLHttpRequests` that return data other than XML. (An example of such data is JSON.) A small example HTML page, which loads a short XML string into a Sarissa DOM document, is shown in Listing 8-2.

Listing 8-2

SarissaDOMDocumentString.html

```
1   <head>
2   <title>Loading a DOM document with an XML string</title>
3
4   <script type="text/javascript" src="sarissa/sarissa.js">
5   </script>
6
7   <script type="text/javascript">
8       var xmlData = '<rss version="2.0"></rss>';
9
10      function loadDoc() {
11          var parser = new DOMParser();
12          var domDoc = parser.parseFromString(
13              xmlData, "text/xml");
14
15          document.getElementById('target').innerHTML =
16              Sarissa.serialize(domDoc).replace(/</g,'&lt;');
17      }
18  </script>
19  </head>
20  <body>
21      <a href="javascript:loadDoc()">Load XML String</a>
22      <pre id="target"></pre>
23  </body>
24  </html>
```

In Listing 8-2, all the Sarissa interaction takes place within the `loadDoc` function, which is defined on lines 10–17. The Sarissa library is loaded on lines 4–5, and an example XML string is defined on line 8. In practice, this string would be generated from a server-side language like PHP, allowing XML data to be accessed without an extra HTTP request. Line 10 starts our worker `loadDoc` functions. First we create a `DOMParser` (line 11), and then we use its `parseFromString` method to parse our XML string data contained in the `xmlData` var (lines 12–13). `parseFromString` takes two parameters: the XML string and its content-type. Content-type is usually `text/xml`, but `application/xml` and `application/xhtml+xml` can also be used. The `parseFromString` method returns a DOM document, which can be used just like the one from `Sarissa.getDomDocument()`.

On lines 15–16, we print out the document using some basic entity replacement so that we can see the output in the browser. The rest of the XML is a link to run the example, line 21, and a pre-element that we use as a target for the printed-out DOM node.

8.3.4.2 Creating a DOM Document Manually

Because Sarissa works with DOM documents, all the normal DOM methods and properties are available. This allows you to create a DOM document with just its root node specified and then append additional nodes to it. In most cases, you won't use this functionality to create a complete DOM document; instead, you will use it to update a document loaded by one of the other methods. When creating a document manually, you'll want to specify the root node to create to the getDomDocument method; this is done by filling in getDomDocument's optional parameters. Sarissa.getDomDocument takes two parameters: the namespace of the root and the local name of the root node. Listing 8-3 shows a small example using this method.

Listing 8-3

SarissaCreateNodesWithDom.html

```
1   <html>
2   <head>
3   <title>Sarissa: Create elements on a DomDocument</title>
4
5   <script type="text/javascript" src="sarissa/sarissa.js">
6   </script>
7
8   <script type="text/javascript">
9       function loadDoc() {
10            var domDoc = Sarissa.getDomDocument(null,'foo');
11
12          var elBar = domDoc.createElement('bar');
13           domDoc.firstChild.appendChild(elBar);
14
15           var elBaz = domDoc.createElement('baz');
16           var text = domDoc.createTextNode('Some Text');
17           elBaz.appendChild(text);
18
19           domDoc.firstChild.appendChild(elBaz);
20
21          document.getElementById('target').innerHTML =
22          Sarissa.serialize(domDoc).replace(/</g,'&lt;');
23      }
24  </script>
25  </head>
26  <body>
27     <a href="javascript:loadDoc()">Create an
28                 XML document manually</a>
29     <pre id="target"></pre>
30  </body>
31  </html>
```

Listing 8-3 follows the same pattern as the previous examples: A `loadDoc` function is called by a small HTML interface. On lines 5–6, we include the Sarissa library, followed by the main JavaScript block, which defines `loadDoc` (lines 8–24). Line 10 creates the empty DOM document; we're not setting the XML namespace, so we pass `null` into that property, and the root node has a value of `foo`. Line 12 creates a new element with a tag name of `bar`; this is appended to the document on line 13. The `bar` element is appended to the `firstChild` of the DOM document, not directly to the document. This appending is done because an XML document can have only a single root element.

Lines 15–19 repeat the same process for an element with the tag name of "baz". This time, however, the difference is that we add a child node to "baz". In this case, it is a DOM text node with the value of "Some Text", but it could also be any other XML element. There are two main types of nodes you work with in XPath: element nodes, which represent the XML tags, and text nodes, which hold the content within tags. This distinction also exists in HTML, but you don't see it as often because you can use the `innerHTML` property to grab the text content without worrying about DOM notes. Lines 21–22 use `Sarissa.serialize` to output the generated document to the target element.

8.3.5 Using XPath to Find Nodes in a Document

Many times, when you're displaying data from an XML document, you'll want to look only at specific portions of the document. This is especially true for formats such as RSS that contain a number of news entries. XPath is an XML technology that allows you to select specific nodes within a document. A basic XPath follows the nodes from the root of the document to the element you're specifying. Each element can be directly addressed by a path; these paths start with a / and contain a / between each node (`/rss/item`). Further specificity can be provided by adding a bracketed number after the node name (`/rss/item[1]`). This path selects a particular occurrence of the node when there are multiple instances of a tag in this particular branch of the document. XPath can also query a document by starting with a double slash (//); these paths return any matching nodes (`//item`). Listing 8-4 shows an XML document that is used in some subsequent examples in this chapter.

Listing 8-4

An Example XML File

```
1  <rss>
2      <item>
3              <title>AJAX Defined</title>
4      </item>
5      <item new="true">
6              <title>Web 2.0 News</title>
7      </item>
8  </rss>
```

You can refer to the nodes of this document in a number of different ways. First, there are absolute paths. The path `/rss/item[1]` refers to the `item` node that starts on line 2 and ends on line 4. The path `/rss/item[2]/title` refers to the `title` node on line 6. You can also query style paths; the path `//item` refers to both the `item` node on lines 2–4 and the `item` node on lines 5–6. These queries can also look at attributes by using an "@"; the path `//item[@new="true"]/title` refers to the `title` node on line 6.

XPath is able to do more complex queries than what is shown in this simple overview. If you're dealing with XML documents in the browser, you will find XPath to be an important tool. XPath is a W3C standard, so you can easily find more information to move past the basics.

Sarissa provides the IE XPath API to all the browsers it supports, which provides an easy to use cross-browser API. The API consists of two methods on a DOM document: the `selectSingleNode` method and the `selectNodes` method. Each method takes an XPath, with `selectSingleNode` returning a single DOM node and `selectNodes` returning a node collection that you can iterate over to access all the nodes. Listing 8-5 is a small example page that shows how to use these XPath methods.

Listing 8-5

SarissaSearchingWithXpath.html

```
1  <html>
2  <head>
3  <title>Sarissa: Searching XML with XPath</title>
4
5  <script type="text/javascript" src="sarissa/sarissa.js">
6  </script>
```

```
7  <script type="text/javascript"
8  src="sarissa/sarissa_ieemu_xpath.js"></script>
9
10 <script type="text/javascript">
11 var domDoc;
12 function loadDoc() {
13     domDoc = Sarissa.getDomDocument();
14
15     var rHandler = function() {
16         if(domDoc.readyState == 4) {
17             document.getElementById('target').innerHTML =
18             "Document Loaded, ready to Search";
19
20             document.getElementById('afterLoad'
21             ).style.display = 'block';
22         }
23     }
24
25     domDoc.onreadystatechange = rHandler;
26     domDoc.load("sarissaNews.xml");
27 }
28
```

Lines 1–8 perform the basic HTML setup. Besides including the main Sarissa library file, we also include the `sarissa_ieeme_xpath.js` file. This file provides the IE XPath API to other browsers, and it is how Sarissa provides cross-browser XPath support. Lines 12–27 define a `loadDoc` function, which loads the remote XML document we will be searching in this example. This code is identical to the earlier AJAX XML loading examples. The only exception is that now, we're defining the `domDoc` variable outside of the function so that it can be used elsewhere. In addition, we're showing a DIV element, which contains more links when the document is loaded instead of just printing it out. This file is continued in Listing 8-6 where the logic appears for searching the DOM using XPath.

Listing 8-6

`SarissaSearchingWithXpath.html` ***Continued***

```
29 function searchBuildDate() {
30     var el = domDoc.selectSingleNode('//lastBuildDate');
31     document.getElementById('target').innerHTML =
32     "Build date = " + el.firstChild.nodeValue;
33 }
34
35 function searchItems() {
36     var list = domDoc.selectNodes('//item/title');
37
```

```
38      var target = document.getElementById('target');
39      target.innerHTML = "Number of Items = "+ list.length+
40          "<br>Titles:<br>";
41
42      for(var i = 0; i < list.length; i++) {
43          target.innerHTML +=
44                  list[i].firstChild.nodeValue + "<br>";
45      }
46 }
47 </script>
48 </head>
49 <body>
50    <a href="javascript:loadDoc()">Load news.xml</a>
51      <div id="afterLoad" style="display: none">
52        <a href="javascript:searchBuildDate()">Last build date</a>
53        <a href="javascript:searchItems()">List item titles</a>
54      </div>
55    <pre id="target"></pre>
56 </body>
57 </html>
```

Lines 29–33 define the searchBuildDate function; this function performs an XPath query against the loaded document to find the last build date of the document. This information is provided in a single tag called lastBuildDate, so the XPath to get the information is //lastBuildDate. The XPath query happens on line 30 when we call selectSingleNode. The value of the resulting node is then displayed in the target element. Because the lastBuildNode is from an XML document, we can't just use the innerHTML attribute. Instead, we access the text node inside the returned element and get its value (line 32).

Lines 35–45 define the searchItems function; this function performs an XPath query that selects all the title nodes that are inside item nodes from the document and then outputs their value in the target element. The XPath query takes place on line 36; it returns a node collection to the list variable. On line 39, we use the collection's length attribute to output the number of items in the loaded RSS document. Lines 42–45 loop over the returned nodes, outputting the value of the nodes to the target; this lists the title of each item in the RSS feed.

Lines 50–55 create the document's basic user interface. Links are provided to run each JavaScript function with the search links that are accessible only after the RSS document is loaded. This delay is accomplished by putting them inside a DIV that is hidden until the document's onreadystatechange change callback shows it on line 21.

8.3.6 Transforming XML with XSLT

XSLT is a powerful XML-based template language. XPaths are used inside the template, which allows you to easily apply multiple subtemplates to different XML templates. Describing how to create an XSLT template could take a book as long as this one, so we focus only on the API that Sarissa provides to transform documents. The API is easy to use; you create a new XSLTProcessor, load a stylesheet that contains the transformation rules, and then transform the document using the processor's transformToDocument method. You'll usually want to import the resulting document into the main HTML document using its importNode method so that you can add it to the DOM and display the results. A short example is shown in Listing 8-7. The data is the same RSS feed of the Sarissa news used earlier; the only exception is that the stylesheet is shown in Listing 8-7.

Listing 8-7

transform.xsl

```
1   <?xml version="1.0"?>
2   <xsl:stylesheet version="1.0"
3      xmlns:xsl="http://www.w3.org/1999/XSL/Transform">
4
5   <xsl:output method="html" />
6      <xsl:template match="/rss">
7         <div>
8            <xsl:for-each select="//item">
9               <h2><xsl:value-of select="title"/></h2>
10           </xsl:for-each>
11        </div>
12     </xsl:template>
13  </xsl:stylesheet>
```

This is a really basic stylesheet with a single template that matches the root rss element in the document (lines 5–11). Inside this template, we output a DIV container so that we have an HTML element encasing the rest of the output, which will make it easy to add to the main document. Lines 8–10 loop over the results from an XPath query. The query //item selects each item node in the document. The code then displays the value of the title of each item inside an h2 tag (line 9). The rest of the file is basic XSLT boilerplate. This XSLT stylesheet is used by an HTML and JavaScript page to transform an XML document; this page is shown in Listing 8-8.

Listing 8-8

SarissaTransformWithXSLT.html

```
1  <html>
2  <head>
3  <title>Sarissa: Transforming Documents with XSLT</title>
4
5  <script type="text/javascript" src="sarissa/sarissa.js">
6  </script>
7  <script type="text/javascript"
8  src="sarissa/sarissa_ieemu_xslt.js"></script>
9
10 <script type="text/javascript">
11 var domDoc = Sarissa.getDomDocument();
12 var styleSheet = Sarissa.getDomDocument();
13 styleSheet.load("transform.xsl");
14 var processor = new XSLTProcessor();
15
16 function loadDoc() {
17     var rHandler = function() {
18         if (domDoc.readyState == 4) {
19
20             document.getElementById('target').innerHTML =
21             "Document Loaded, ready to transform";
22
23             document.getElementById('afterLoad'
24             ).style.display = 'block';
25         }
26     }
27
28     domDoc.onreadystatechange = rHandler;
29     domDoc.load("sarissaNews.xml");
30 }
31
32 function transform() {
33     processor.importStylesheet(styleSheet);
34     var output = processor.transformToDocument(domDoc);
35
36     var target = document.getElementById('target');
37     target.appendChild(document.importNode(
38                 output.firstChild,true));
39 }
40 </script>
41 </head>
42 <body>
43    <a href="javascript:loadDoc()">Load news.xml</a>
44    <div id="afterLoad" style="display: none">
45    <a href="javascript:transform()">Display Items</a>
```

```
46      </div>
47      <div id="target"></div>
48   </body>
49   </html>
```

Listing 8-8 takes the `sarissaNews.xml` file, transforms it with the `transform.xsl` XSLT stylesheet, and then adds its results to the main document's DOM. The Sarissa library is included on lines 5–8. Notice that we're including the cross-browser XSLT support files as well as the main library file. On lines 11–14, we set up the objects we will use on the rest of the transformation process. On line 5, we set up an empty `DomDocument` into which we will load our RSS feed; then, on line 6, we create a similar object into which to load the stylesheet. On line 13, we load `transform.xsl` into the `styleSheet` document; you could also use the string parser to load `transform.xsl`. This would be accomplished by loading the contents of `transform.xsl` into a JavaScript variable and then creating the `DomDocument` using the `DOMParser`. Doing this would let you reduce the number of HTTP requests needed to load the document, which is helpful from a performance standpoint as long as the stylesheet is small. Finishing the basic setup, we create a new `XSLTProcessor` on line 14.

Lines 16–30 define the `loadDoc` function, which loads `sarissaNews.xml` so that it can later be transformed. This works the same as the earlier examples; we're just adding a few more actions to perform after the document is loaded. On lines 20–21, we output a message saying the document is loaded, giving the user feedback that something has happened. Then, on lines 23–24, we show a DIV in the main HTML document. This DIV contains the links that do the actual transformation; by keeping it hidden until the document is loaded, we are able to prevent errors from happening. The rest of the method contains the simple Sarissa document loading processes; on line 28, we register the callback function, and on line 29, we load the `sarissaNews.xml` document.

Lines 32–39 define a JavaScript function that does the transformation. This is a three-part process. On line 33, we import the stylesheet we previously set up, and then on line 34, we transform the document assigning the result to a variable. We finish the processes on lines 36–38, selecting an output element and then appending the output to it after importing it to the HTML document. When importing the nodes, passing a Boolean value of `true` as the second parameter to `importNode` makes the method perform a deep import. A deep import imports the element passed in and all its children; without this flag, only the top-level element is imported.

The rest of the document is the basic HTML user interface. A link is provided on line 43 to load the `sarissaNews.xml` document, with the transform link enclosed in a hidden DIV so that it will be available only after the news document is loaded (lines 44–46). We finish up with a target DIV on line 47 that we use for giving messages to the user and for showing the transformed document.

8.3.7 Sarissa Development Tips

Sarissa is a highly focused library that provides an easy-to-use, cross-browser API to the major browsers' XML functionality. If you're looking to use XML technologies such as XSLT or XPath, then Sarissa is a perfect solution for you. While using Sarissa, keep in mind these tips:

- Be sure to include the `sarissa_ieemu_xpath.js` or `sarissa_ieemu_xslt.js` files if you're working with XPath or XSLT. Without them, your scripts will work only in Internet Explorer.

- Use the XML string-loading capabilities to cut down on the number of individual XML files that you need to load.

- Run the test cases in `testsarissa.html` to make sure your browser is supported if you're on a less commonly used browser.

- Mix Sarissa with other libraries if Sarissa meets only some of your needs; Sarissa is focused on XML.

- XPath is extremely effective at searching XML documents; try using it before creating custom solutions to search XML.

- If you have a question about what method to use, check out the project's Web site; it contains complete API documentation.

8.4 Scriptaculous

Scriptaculous is an MIT-licensed JavaScript library that provides visual effects, drag-and-drop support, and controls, such as sliders, to HTML pages. It is built on top of the Prototype JavaScript library, which provides AJAX support (and a number of other features) to the Ruby on Rail Web application framework. Because it's built on Prototype, scriptaculous has AJAX support, but its main focus is on providing highly interactive visual components that can take an AJAX application to the next level.

8.4.1 Installation

You can download scriptaculous from http://script.aculo.us. After extracting the archive, copy the contents of the `src` and `lib` subdirectories into a directory in the document root of your Web server. After doing that, you just need to include the prototype and scriptaculous libraries in your HTML files. The components of scriptaculous will be automatically included as needed as long as they are in the same directory as `scriptaculous.js`. An example of these includes is shown here:

```
<script src="/scriptaculous/prototype.js"
type="text/javascript"></script>
 <script src="/scriptaculous/scriptaculous.js"
type="text/javascript"></script>
```

8.4.2 Visual Effects

One of the most exciting features of scriptaculous is its visual effects. These effects can be used to notify the user that an event has happened or that some content is updated. The effects can be applied to any DOM element, making them very versatile, because they will work no matter what the display type of the element is. To apply an effect, you create a new instance of a method of the `Effects` class, passing in the element to update. This element can be an ID or a DOM element accessed directly in JavaScript.

A wide variety of effects are provided. They perform two main tasks: showing or hiding elements and drawing attention to an element. Some of the show/hide effects are available in pairs and can be used with the `Effect.toggle` method to hide or show an element, doing the opposite of the element's current status. The rest of the functions can be used individually, like the simple examples in the following list of effects. An effects tester is also included so that you can see what each effect looks like. Scriptaculous also includes the lower-level methods that can be used to build new effects; the API for these methods is included on its Web site.

8.4.3 Hide/Show Pairs

`BlindDown` hides the element, and `BlindUp` shows it:

```
new Effect.toggle(element,'blind');
new Effect.BlindDown(element);
new Effect.BlindUp(element);
```

`SlideDown` hides the element, and `SlideUp` shows it:

```
new Effect.toggle(element,'slide');
new Effect.SlideDown(element);
new Effect.SlideUp(element);
```

`Fade` hides the element, and `Appear` shows it:

```
new Effect.toggle(element,'appear');
new Effect.Fade(element);
new Effect.Appear(element);
```

A large number of nonpaired effects for hiding elements is also included:

```
new Effect.SwitchOff(element);
new Effect.DropOut(element);
new Effect.Squish(element);
new Effect.Shrink(element);
new Effect.Fold(element);
```

The `Grow` effect is the only unpaired effect for showing an element:

```
new Effect.Grow(element);
```

The `Effects` class also contains a number of methods for drawing attention to an element:

```
new Effect.Pulsate(element);
new Effect.Shake(element);
new Effect.Highlight(element);
```

The effects tester is located in the `scriptaculousViewAllEffects.html` file. Listing 8-9 shows a short example of how to apply various effects.

Listing 8-9

`ScriptaculousViewAllEffects.html`

```
1   <html>
2   <head>
3   <title>Script.aculo.us Visual Effects</title>
4   <script src="scriptaculous/prototype.js"
5      type="text/javascript"></script>
6   <script src="scriptaculous/scriptaculous.js"
7      type="text/javascript"></script>
8   </head>
9   <body>
10
11  <p>Reload the page to reset the effects.</p>
12
13  <div onclick="new Effect.Fade(this)">
14     Click Me to see a Fade Effect
```

```
15 </div>
16
17 <p>
18 <a href="#" onclick="new Effect.Puff(this)"
19    >Click to hide this link</a>
20 </p>
21
22 <p>
23 <a href="#" onclick="new Effect.Fold('cell')"
24    >Hide the table cell</a>
25 <a href="#" onclick="new Effect.Grow('cell')"
26    >Show the table cell</a>
27 </p>
28
29 <table border=1>
30    <tr>
31         <td>A cell</td>
32         <td id="cell">Cell to Hide</td>
33    </tr>
34 </table>
35
36 <p>
37 <a href="#" onclick=
38    "new Effect.toggle('box','blind')"
39    >Toggle the box below</a>
40 <div id="box"
41    style="border: solid 1px black;
42    width: 50px; height: 50px">
43    BOX
44 </div>
45 </p>
46 </body>
47 </html>
```

One way to attach an event is to tie it to the click event of a DOM element; this passes the element being clicked and performs the effect directly on the current element. This approach is easy to do and is shown on line 13 against a block-level element, and on line 18 against an inline element. There are few cases where this direct attachment is useful; in most cases, you'll want the effect to be performed against another element on the page because the point of the effect is to draw attention to the action that is happening. Line 23 hides the element with an ID of cell by using the Fold effect, whereas line 25 shows the same element using the Grow effect. Line 38 shows the toggle utility method, which alternately shows and hides an element. This method is useful for building interface elements that show optional information.

8.4.4 Drag-and-Drop

Drag-and-drop gives you the ability to visually drag elements around the page and have other elements that accept the drop. The scriptaculous implementation separates the drag-and-drop components into two parts, allowing you to make elements draggable without providing a place to drop them. This can be useful for adding palettes or note elements that can be moved anywhere within the window by the user. To create a draggable element, create a new instance of the `Draggable` class, passing in the element to drag and any options. A common option is `revert`; when it is set to `true`, the item returns to its original position when the user lets up on the mouse:

```
new Draggable(element,{revert:true});
```

In the second half of drag-and-drop, the drop target is provided by the `Droppables` class. Drop targets are useful in a number of cases, from building a visual shopping cart to allowing you to visually move mail to a new folder. Drop targets can be any element and can take a number of options, including an `accept` parameter that limits the elements that can dropped to those with a matching class. They can also include an `onDrop` handler, which is run when an element is added to the drop target:

```
Droppables.add(el, { onDrop: function(e) { alert(e); });
```

Listing 8-10 shows a small drag-and-drop application. In this listing, there are three draggable boxes and one drop target. Only the first two boxes can be dropped on the target because the third box has a class that isn't in the accept list of the drop target. This example also uses the `$()` alias function; it works the same way as `document.getElementById`. Formatting for this example is done with CSS, which is included in a separate file to decrease the amount of noise.

Listing 8-10

ScriptaculousDragNDrop.html

```
1   <html>
2   <head>
3   <title>Script.aculo.us Drag and Drop</title>
4   <script src=""scriptaculous/prototype.js"
5       type="text/javascript"></script>
6   <script src="scriptaculous/scriptaculous.js"
7       type="text/javascript"></script>
8
9   <link rel="stylesheet" href="dnd.css"
10      type="text/css">
```

```
11  </head>
12  <body>
13      <div id="box1" class="box">Box 1</div>
14      <div id="box2" class="box">Box 2</div>
15      <div id="box3" class="other">Box 3</div>
16
17      <br style="clear: both">
18      <div id="drop">Drop Target</div>
19
20
21  <script type="text/javascript">
22      new Draggable('box1',{revert:true});
23      new Draggable('box2',{revert:false});
24      new Draggable('box3',{revert:true});
25
26      Droppables.add('drop', {accept: 'box',
27          onDrop: function(el) {
28          $('drop').innerHTML =
29          'Dropped: '+el.id;
30      }
31      });
32  </script>
33
34  </body>
35  </html>
```

Most of this page is set up in HTML with a small amount of JavaScript code to activate the drag-and-drop functionality. The page starts with a basic setup. Lines 4–7 include the scriptaculous JavaScript library, and lines 9–10 include a CSS file to do some basic formatting. Lines 13–18 create the basic user interface; it is made up of three 200×200 pixel boxes that are floated next to each other. Below that is a 100×400 pixel drop target.

Lines 21–32 make these boxes draggable and create a drop target for them. Lines 22–24 create the draggable boxes; the first parameter is the ID of the box, and the second is a hash of options. On line 23, we set the `revert` property of the second box to `false`; this lets us drag it around the screen. This property isn't very useful for dragging to a drop target, but it can be useful for other use cases. Lines 26–30 create the drop target; the first parameter is the ID of the element, and its second parameter is a hash of options. Here we're setting two options. The first is the `accept` variable, which takes a class to accept; in this case, it's set to box, which allows box 1 and 2, but not box 3, to be dropped. The second option is the `onDrop` function; this is called when a draggable element is released while over the drop target. The function displays some simple feedback displaying the ID of the dropped element in the drop target.

8.4.5 Sortables

A *sortable* is a predefined component built from the drag-and-drop building blocks that scriptaculous provides. Sortables make it easy to build graphically reorderable lists and can even be used to let you move items between multiple lists. Sortables are usually used with HTML lists, but they can also be used with floated elements. To create a sortable list, you simply run `Sortable.create`, passing in an ID and any options you want to specify, like so:

```
Sortable.create("element",{ghosting:true});
```

Some of the more commonly used properties are `overlap`, `ghosting`, and `onChange`:

- The `overlap` property, which takes the values of `horizontal`, `vertical`, or `false`, limits how you can drag the elements around; the `false` setting has no limits.

- Setting the `ghosting` property to `true` leaves the element in its current position; the user then drags a faded version until it is dropped.

- The `onChange` property lets you set a callback function, which is called after an item has been moved.

If the elements in your sortable have the ID property set using the naming convention of `name_item`, you can use the `Sortable.serialize` method to quickly build a query string, which can be sent to the server and used to update the order on the server. An example output from the serialize method is this:

```
list[]=one&list[]=three&list[]=two&list[]=four
```

If you used this string as the query string on a request to a PHP page, `$_GET['list']` will be populated with an array that contains the updated positions of the list. The array is ordered in its new position, with the value being the specified ID. Listing 8-11 shows an example of this operation.

Listing 8-11

ScriptaculousSortable.php

```
1  <html>
2  <head>
3  <title>Script.aculo.us Sortables</title>
4  <script src="scriptaculous/prototype.js"
5     type="text/javascript"></script>
```

```
6  <script src="scriptaculous/scriptaculous.js"
7     type="text/javascript"></script>
8
9  <style type="text/css">
10 #list {
11    cursor: pointer;
12 }
13 </style>
14 </head>
15 <body>
16
17 <ul id="list">
18    <li id="i_one">One</li>
19    <li id="i_two">Two</li>
20    <li id="i_three">Three</li>
21    <li id="i_four">Four</li>
22 </ul>
23
24 <a href="javascript:updateList()"
25    >Send Changes to server</a>
26
27 <pre><?php
28 if (isset($_GET['list'])) {
29    var_dump($_GET['list']);
30 }
31 ?></pre>
32
33 <script type="text/javascript">
34 Sortable.create("list"});
35
36 function updateList() {
37    var update = Sortable.serialize('list');
38
39    window.location = '?'+update;
40 }
41 </script>
42
43 </body>
44 </html>
```

This page is mainly an HTML/JavaScript page with a small amount of PHP mixed in to show how a server-side language parses the output of `Sortable.serialize()`. The script starts with a basic setup, with lines 4–7 including the scriptaculous library. Then, on lines 9–12, we include a small amount of CSS, which gives all the sortable elements a pointer cursor. This is an important usability step; without it, the elements will have a text select cursor, and the user won't realize they are sortable. Lines 17–22 build the list that will be sorted; each item has an ID in it, which defines the value that will be returned to the server. Lines 24–25 complete the user interface, creating a link that reloads the page and sends the list's new order to the server.

Lines 27–31 contain the small amount of PHP code in this script. If the list variable has been passed in by the query string, its outputs are echoed out using a debugging function. PHP and many other Web development languages automatically turn the query string provided by `Sortable.serialize` into an array; from here you could update the database with the new order.

Lines 33–40 contain the JavaScript for this example. On line 34, we make the `list` element sortable, using most of the default options because they are optimized for use with HTML lists. Then, on lines 36–40, we build a small function that builds a query string using `Sortable.serialize` (line 37) and then reloads the page by setting `window.location`.

8.4.6 Slider Control

Scriptaculous also provides a slider control, which is useful for selecting values that are in a range. This control can be used in its basic state to build something like a color selector. It can also be used as a building block for more advanced elements, such as a JavaScript-powered scrollbar for an AJAX grid. An example of the slider control in both horizontal and vertical modes is shown in Figure 8-1.

Scriptaculous provides only the behavior of the slider, not its looks. As long as you follow the pattern of a container element with a slide handle inside of it, you can make the slider look any way you want. Because you control the look of the sliders, you also control their usability. One simple usability tip is to set the cursor of the slide handle to a value of `move`. This gives you the browser's standard cursor icon for items that can be moved around, which helps users understand how to move the control. The slider returns a value from 0 to 1 as you scroll across its range; to translate this to a more usable value, you simply multiply it by the maximum value of your target range, rounding it if you want an integer, like so:

```
var outputValue = Math.round(100*sliderValue);
```

FIGURE 8-1
The scriptaculous slider control shown in both horizontal and vertical modes

Listing 8-12 shows an example page that implements both a horizontal slider and a vertical slider.

Listing 8-12

ScriptaculousSlider.html

```
1   <html>
2   <head>
3   <title>Script.aculo.us Slider</title>
4   <script src="scriptaculous/prototype.jsv
5       type="text/javascript"></script>
6   <script src="scriptaculous/scriptaculous.js"
7       type="text/javascript"></script>
8   </head>
9   <body>
10
11  <h3>Horizontal Slider</h3>
12  <div id="track1" style="
13      width: 200px;
```

```
14     background-color: rgb(170, 170, 170);
15     height: 5px;">
16 <div id="handle1" style="
17     width: 5px;
18     height: 10px;
19     background-color: rgb(255, 0, 0);
20     cursor: move;
21     "> </div>
22 </div>
23  <div id="debug1"></div>
24
25 <h3>Vertical Slider</h3>
26 <div id="track2" style="
27     height: 100px;
28     background-color: rgb(170, 170, 170);
29     width: 5px;">
30 <div id="handle2" style="
31     width: 10px;
32     height: 5px;
33     background-color: rgb(255, 0, 0);
34     cursor: move;
35     "> </div>
36 </div>
37 <div id="debug2"></div>
38
39 <script type="text/javascript">
40 var d1 = document.getElementById('debug1');
41 var d2 = document.getElementById('debug2');
42
43 new Control.Slider('handle1','track1',{
44 onSlide:function(v){d1.innerHTML='slide: '+v},
45 onChange:function(v){d1.innerHTML='changed! '+v}
46 });
47
48 new Control.Slider('handle2','track2',{
49 axis:'vertical',
50 onSlide:function(v){d2.innerHTML=Math.round(100*v)},
51 onChange:function(v){d2.innerHTML=Math.round(100*v)}
52 });
53 </script>
55 </body>
56 </html>
```

Like the rest of the scriptaculous examples (Listings 8-9–8-11), this page includes the JavaScript library files in its header (lines 4–7). After that, the HTML for the sliders is laid out: first the horizontal slider (lines 11–23) and then the vertical slider (lines 25–37). Both sliders follow a similar pattern; first the slider track is defined, setting its ID, width, height, and color (lines 12–15 and 26–29). Then, the handles for the sliders are defined (lines 16–21 and 30–35). The handles set most of the same basic style elements as the track, adding a cursor of move for improved usability. The HTML definitions are finished by creating empty DIV elements to display the current value of the slider (lines 23 and 37).

The next section of the page is the JavaScript that turns these DIV groups into sliders. We start this process by assigning the debug DIV elements to variables so that we can easily reference them later (lines 40–41). Then we create a slider instance for the horizontal slider control (lines 43–46). The Control.Slider function takes three parameters: the track element, the handle element, and any options. In this case, we are setting two options: the onSlide and onChange event handlers. The onSlide handler is called as we move the handle around; the onChange handler is called when we're done dragging the handle. The onSlide handler is usually used to provide feedback, whereas the onChange handler is used to make the value of the slide accessible to other parts of the page, storing its value in an input box or JavaScript variable.

Lines 48–52 follow much of the same process for the vertical slider. In this case, we set an extra option, axis, to the value of vertical setting. This does what it suggests and makes the slider work in a vertical fashion. We also translate the value of the slider to a 0–100 scale in the onSlide and onChange handlers.

8.4.7 Scriptaculous Development Tips

Scriptaculous contains functionality for creating visually impressive Web sites. While using it, keep these tips in mind:

- Most scriptaculous functions have further documentation and examples at http://script.aculuo.us, so if you're not sure how to make a function operate, start there.

- Scriptaculous contains a variety of prepackaged effects and components, but if they don't meet your needs, it also provides the tools to build new ones.

- Besides the Web site, you can find more scriptaculous examples in the tests directory, in the scriptaculous download. The functional tests are very useful in this regard.

- Scriptaculous contains a number of additional controls that you should explore before building your own. These include the following:

  - **Autocompleter:** Provides Google Suggest style auto completing text fields

  - **InPlaceEditor:** Provides click-to-edit content with AJAX saving the changes

8.5 Summary

Sarissa and scriptaculous are powerful AJAX libraries. Sarissa is focused on XML, making it a great choice if you already heavily use XML throughout your tool chain. Its main features include the following:

- Cross-browser support

- The ability to create DOM documents from XML strings

- XSLT support for transforming XML documents

- XPath support for querying nodes within XML documents

Scriptaculous offers many of the exciting features that AJAX applications are known for. Using it, you can easily create highly interactive applications that are both visually appealing and easy to use. The main features of scriptaculous include the following:

- Visual effects, such as fade in/out elements

- Drag-and-drop support

- Sortable lists

- Slider controls

Both of these libraries make a good building block for an AJAX application. They offer clean API, useful functionality, and a tight enough focus that they are easy to combine with other libraries. In the next chapter, we look at HTML_AJAX. It is a JavaScript/PHP library that focuses on server interaction, simplifying using PHP as the back end for an AJAX application.

Chapter 9

Libraries Used in Part II: HTML_AJAX

In this chapter

The libraries shown in Chapter 8, "Libraries Used in Part II: Sarissa, Scriptaculous," consisted solely of JavaScript and so could be used with any server-side language; in this chapter, we're taking a look at a library that takes a language-specific approach. HTML_AJAX contains JavaScript code and PHP code; both are tightly integrated, making the process of communicating between the two sides easier. If PHP isn't your language of choice, but you still want to look at tightly integrated libraries, look in Appendix B, "AJAX Libraries with Server Ties"), which contains a list of AJAX libraries with tight server-side integration.

9.1 HTML_AJAX

HTML_AJAX is an AJAX library for PHP licensed under the Library General Public License (LGPL); it provides a JavaScript API and a PHP API. It supports a number of different communication strategies and use cases. It also provides the ability to pass data directly from PHP to JavaScript (and vice versa) using JSON. HTML_AJAX focuses on providing a complete communication layer and tight PHP integration, but it also provides a number of JavaScript utility functions that are useful for debugging and performing common actions in a cross-browser manner.

HTML_AJAX is part of the PHP Extension and Application Repository (PEAR), giving it wide infrastructure support. HTML_AJAX has a small development team, the leader of which is me, the author of this book. This, of course, makes me partial to HTML_AJAX, but HTML_AJAX is widely used and is a good example of an AJAX library that strives for tight language integration.

HTML_AJAX provides many choices in how you use it. This makes it usable for many styles of development but also makes it harder to see where to get started. The three main ways of using HTML_AJAX are as follows:

- The JavaScript API provides methods to perform general AJAX actions, such as replacing a DOM element with the results of an HTTP request or submitting a form using AJAX. It's targeted at developers who don't mind writing JavaScript code to tie everything together, and it is especially useful when used with behaviors, which allow you to tie JavaScript code to HTML using CSS selectors.

- The mapped PHP classes' API makes it easy for JavaScript code to call directly into PHP code and get results. It's most useful when you need raw data moved from PHP to JavaScript. It lets you format the data and control its interaction from the JavaScript side.

- The HTML_AJAX_Action code starts off using mapped PHP classes, but instead of returning raw data, it returns a set of actions to perform against the HTML page; this can include updating the content of nodes, changing the value of an attribute, or running some JavaScript code. This usage pattern allows for a minimal amount of JavaScript to be written and keeps the majority of the logic encapsulated within PHP code.

9.1.1 Installation

Because HTML_AJAX is part of the PEAR project, its installation process is the same as any other PEAR package. You simply need to use the `install` method of the PEAR package manager, like so:

```
pear install HTML_AJAX
```

If you already have HTML_AJAX installed, you can upgrade to the newest version by using this upgrade command:

```
pear upgrade HTML_AJAX
```

If you don't have the PEAR package manager installed, you can find installation information on the HTML_AJAX Web site (http://htmlajax.org) or on the PEAR Web site (http://pear.php.net). The HTML_AJAX Web site also provides information on how to install HTML_AJAX without using the PEAR installer, but it's not the recommended method because it makes keeping your installation up-to-date a much more time-consuming process.

To use an HTML_AJAX installation, you will need to provide a way for browsers to access its JavaScript library. The simplest way is to create a page that exposes an instance of the `HTML_AJAX_Server` class. This class will serve up the JavaScript library from its installation point in the PEAR `install` directory, which is normally located outside of your document root. This class supports combining multiple libraries and client-side caching to improve performance. Alternatively, you can copy the library from its installation location, the PEAR `data` directory, to

somewhere in your Web root. A single file version of the library named
HTML_AJAX.js is provided for this use. A version with comments and whitespace
stripped is also provided in HTML_AJAX_lite.js. An example PHP script that can
serve up the JavaScript library is shown in Listing 9-1.

Listing 9-1

server.php

```
<?php
require_once 'HTML/AJAX/Server.php';

$server = new HTML_AJAX_Server();

$server->handleRequest();
?>
```

You can include the library in an HTML page by loading the page with the
client=all query string set. You could also include just the parts of the library you
need; examples of both are shown here:

```
<script type="text/javascript
src="server.php?client=all"></script>

<script type="text/javascript
src="server.php?client=main,request,httpclient,json,loading"></script>
```

If you want to copy the library, you'll need to find the location of the files. You
first find the PEAR data directory by running the following command:

```
pear config-get data_dir
```

On most UNIX-like systems, this directory is /usr/share/pear/data. After
you find the directory, look in the HTML_AJAX/js directory underneath it. In this
directory, you'll see files for each individual part of the library and the combined
files as well. To use the library in an HTML file, just include it in the page, like so:

```
<script type="text/javascript src="pathtolibrary/HTML_AJAX.js"></script>
```

9.1.2 HTML_AJAX JavaScript API

HTML_AJAX's JavaScript API provides easy access to common AJAX operations. These operations are exposed through the HTML_AJAX static class. The
most important methods on this class are as follows:

9.1.2.1 `grab`

Method signature:

```
HTML_AJAX.grab(url,callback)
```

The `grab` method loads the content from the given URL and either returns it or gives it to a callback. The `grab` method provides a way to do trivial AJAX requests. The first parameter is the URL to load, and the second is a callback function. The second parameter is optional, and if it's not specified, a synchronous request is performed. Because synchronous requests lock the user interface, you'll usually want to pass in a callback function. The callback function takes a single parameter, which is the content of the loaded URL in string format.

9.1.2.2 `replace`

Method signature:

```
HTML_AJAX.replace(id,url)
```

or

```
HTML_AJAX.replace(id,className,methodName)
```

The `replace` method takes the content of a URL and updates the content of the specified element with the content that has been loaded. The `replace` method can load a URL directly (the first version of the method call), or it can be used with a PHP class that has been registered on a server calling one of its methods (the second version of the method signature).

9.1.2.3 `append`

Method signature:

```
HTML_AJAX.append(id,url)
```

or

```
HTML_AJAX.append(id,className,methodName)
```

The `append` method works like the `replace` method, except that instead of replacing all the content of the element specified, it appends the new content to the end of the HTML element. This method can be used to load a URL or against a registered PHP method.

9.1.2.4 `formSubmit`

Method signature:

```
HTML_AJAX.formSubmit(form,target,customRequest)
```

The `formSubmit` method provides an easy way to submit a form over AJAX. The `form` parameter is the form to submit over AJAX; it can be the ID of the form or a DOM element. The `target` parameter is the element whose `innerHTML` property will be replaced with the results. This can also be an ID or a DOM element, and it is optional; if not specified, the `form` element is also used as the target. `customRequest` is also optional and provides a way to pass in a custom `Request` object, which is useful for setting a custom loading message for this request. The method returns false on a successful submission, allowing it to be used in a form's `onsubmit` property to cancel the normal form submission because it has already happened in AJAX. This allows you to quickly make an AJAX form by adding an `onsubmit` handler, like so:

```
<form onsubmit="return HTML_AJAX.formSubmit(this)">
```

9.1.2.5 Properties

HTML_AJAX also contains methods that you can override to change the behavior of both the default loading notification and the error handling. In default operation, errors thrown by HTML_AJAX are left for the browser to handle; this usually means a message shows up in a JavaScript error console. You will normally want to handle this in a more informative way because common errors include page loading timeouts and "404 URL not found" messages. If you are making AJAX calls directly into PHP functions, these messages can also include errors from the PHP code that was called. To change the default behavior, you simply need to set a new function on `HTML_AJAX.onError`. This function can then show a message to the user or try to recover from the problem. Here is a basic custom error handler:

```
HTML_AJAX.onError = function(e) {
    document.getElementById('error').innerHTML =
        HTML_AJAX_Util.quickPrint(e);
}
```

Most of the methods in the JavaScript API can take either a URL to which to make a request or a class name and a method name. When a class name and method name are provided, the request is made to the default HTML_AJAX server, where the PHP class that matches the class name is called. To make a class available for an

AJAX request, it has to be registered with the server; you would update the `server.php` file from the installation example, adding a registerClass call before calling `handleRequest`. Listing 9-2 shows a basic server with a `Test` class.

Listing 9-2

testServer.php

```
1  <?php
2  require_once 'HTML/AJAX/Server.php';
3
4  class Test {
5    function serverTime() {
6      return date('Y-m-d H:i:s');
7    }
8
9    function echoString($str) {
10     return 'From Server'.$str;
11   }
12 }
13
14 $server = new HTML_AJAX_Server();
15
16 $server->registerClass(
17   new Test(),
18   'Test',
19   array('serverTime','echoString')
20 );
21 $server->handleRequest();
22 ?>
```

Like the HTML_AJAX server example in Listing 9-1, this page starts by requiring the HTML_AJAX_Server class. Then, it defines a trivial class called Test (lines 4–12); this class contains a function that returns the current date from the server and one that echoes a string back to the caller. On line 14, we create a new HTML_AJAX_Server instance, and then on lines 16–20, we register an instance of the Test class on the server instance. The first parameter to registerClass is the instance to register (line 17), the second parameter is the name to call it in JavaScript code (line 18), and the last parameter (line 19) is an array of methods to make available. Both the second and third parameters are case sensitive and optional. If they are not provided, PHP's introspection code is used to gather the information. You usually want to provide these options because it guarantees compatibility between PHP4 and PHP5; this compatibility problem exist because PHP4 doesn't keep the case of class/method names, and the later versions of PHP do.

Now that you have a server page that will accept AJAX requests, you're almost ready to use both URL and method uses of HTML_AJAX functions, such as `HTML_AJAX.replace`. You just set the server to make the class/method requests; this is done by setting `HTML_AJAX.defaultServerUrl`. Listing 9-3 shows an example of the JavaScript API usage. `testServer.php` is used to handle class/method calls, and `page.html` is used for URL calls.

Listing 9-3

HTML_AJAXBasicJSRequest.html

```
1   <html>
2   <head>
3   <title>HTML_AJAX: Basic Request JavaScript API</title>
4   <script type="text/javascript"
5     src="server.php?client=all"></script>
6
7   <style type="text/css">
8   .target {
9     width: 200px;
10     border: solid 1px black;
11  }
12  </style>
13
14  <script type="text/javascript">
15  HTML_AJAX.defaultServerUrl = 'testServer.php';
16
17  HTML_AJAX.onError = function(e) {
18     document.getElementById('error').innerHTML =
19     HTML_AJAX_Util.quickPrint(e);
20  }
21  </script>
22  </head>
23  <body>
24  <pre id="error">
25  </pre>
26
27  <h3>HTML_AJAX.formSubmit Basic</h3>
28  <form action="form.php"
29       onsubmit="HTML_AJAX.formSubmit(this,this);
30       return false;" method="post">
31
32    <input name="field">
33    <input type="submit">
34  </form>
35
36  <h3>HTML_AJAX.formSubmit Custom loading message</h3>
37  <script type="text/javascript">
```

```
38     function customForm(form) {
39       var r = {
40       Open: function() {
41         form.innerHTML = 'Loading Please Wait...';
42       }
43       }
44
45       HTML_AJAX.formSubmit(form,form,r);
46       return false;
47     }
48 </script>
49 <form action="form.php"
50     onsubmit="return customForm(this);"
51     method="post">
52
53   <input name="field">
54   <input type="submit">
55 </form>
56
57 <h3>HTML_AJAX.grab</h3>
58 <a href="#" onclick="
59     HTML_AJAX.grab('page.html',
60     function(r) { alert(r); });
61 ">Grab page.html</a>
62
63 <h3>HTML_AJAX.replace url</h3>
64 <div id="replaceTarget1" class="target"></div>
65 <a href="#" onclick="
66     HTML_AJAX.replace('replaceTarget1','page.html');
67 ">Replace target with page.html</a>
68
69 <h3>HTML_AJAX.replace class/method</h3>
70 <div id="replaceTarget2" class="target"></div>
71 <a href="#" onclick="
72     HTML_AJAX.replace('replaceTarget2',
73     'Test','serverTime');
74 ">Replace target with Test::serverTime</a>
75
76
77 <h3>HTML_AJAX.append url</h3>
78 <div id="appendTarget1" class="target">
79   Current Content: </div>
80 <a href="#" onclick="
81     HTML_AJAX.append('appendTarget1','page.html');
82 ">Append page.html to target</a>
83
84 <h3>HTML_AJAX.append class/method</h3>
85 <div id="appendTarget2" class="target">
86     Current Content: </div>
87 <a href="#" onclick="
```

```
88      HTML_AJAX.append('appendTarget2','Test',
89      'echoString','Some Text');
90 ">Append Test::echoString('Some Text') to target</a>
91 </body>
92 </html>
```

The first section of the listing does the basic setup. On lines 4–5, it includes the HTML_AJAX JavaScript library. Then on lines 7–12, it sets up a basic CSS style that will be used to mark elements that will be updated by the AJAX methods. Finally, it finishes the setup by adding the `defaultServerUrl` (line 15) and adding an error handler, which is useful for debugging problems during the development process.

The `defaultServerUrl` is used in requests to methods on PHP classes. Lines 27–34 set up a form and make it possible to submit it over AJAX. The form has a text box, which is defined on line 32, and a Submit button, which is defined on line 33, but only the input box on line 32 will be submitted. This is because only data from elements with name attributes are submitted. The AJAX activation of the form happens on line 29, which is where we send the `onsubmit` method to `HTML_AJAX.formSubmit`. The current form is used both for the form to submit and the element to update the `innerHTML` with the results. This means that the form tag will still exist, but all its children (lines 53–54) will be replaced. Also note that `false` is returned from the `onsubmit` method; this prevents the normal form submission from happening. The `method` and `action` attributes of the form are read by `formSubmit`, and they are used to determine where the form is submitted.

Lines 36–55 show a more advanced case of AJAX form submission. The form is set up the same way, but instead of calling `formSubmit` in the `onsubmit` method, we call a custom function instead. This function, which is defined on lines 38–47, defines some options for the form submission and then runs `HTML_AJAX.formSubmit` (line 45). These extra options are passed in as the third parameter; these options allow you to set any attribute on the `Request` object that will be built to submit this form. Some commonly overridden attributes are the `Open` and `Load` event handlers and the `RequestUrl`. In this example, we're setting only the `Open` event handler (lines 40–42). This is called when we open the HTTP connection to the server, and it is generally used to provide custom loading messages. Normally, this event handler is matched with the `Load` event handler, which is called at the end of the request, but that's not needed in this case, because the `Open` function replaces the contents of the form, and this message will then be replaced by the form's results.

Lines 57–61 show an example of the `HTML_AJAX.grab` function. This simple function is used when you want to make a `GET` request to a page and perform an action on its results. The second parameter (line 60) is the callback function; in this case, it just creates an alert box with the value of the page. If this parameter is left out, a synchronous request—instead of an asynchronous one—is made.

There are two examples of the `HTML_AJAX.replace` function. The first one is on lines 63–67 and loads a URL and then replaces the contents of a DIV with the new content from the server. The second example is on lines 69–74 and calls a PHP method and replaces the contents of a DIV with the results from the PHP method call. In URL mode, `replace` takes two parameters (line 66): the ID of the element to replace and the URL to which to make the request. In PHP method mode, `replace` takes three parameters: The first is the ID of the element to replace, the second is the PHP class, and the third is a method on that class. The URL to use for this request is determined by the `HTML_AJAX.defaultServerUrl` variable, which was set on line 15. If the class and method haven't been registered for AJAX access by the server, an error will be thrown; this error can then by handled by the `HTML_AJAX.onError` method.

The final sets of examples are for the `HTML_AJAX.append` method (lines 77–90). This method works exactly like the `HTML_AJAX.replace` method, except that instead of replacing the `innerHTML` of the specified element, the new content is appended to `innerHTML`. If you need more complicated replacement rules, use the `grab` method and provide a custom callback function with the needed logic.

9.1.3 Remote Stub AJAX

As was shown in `testServer.php` in Listing 9-2, HTML_AJAX has the ability to make PHP classes directly available to AJAX calls from JavaScript. By default, HTML_AJAX accomplishes this by passing JSON-encoded messages between the server and the client. This allows all serializable PHP and JavaScript data types (resources in PHP and DOM objects in JavaScript can't be sent) to be seamlessly sent between the client and the server. Although these PHP functions can be accessed through HTML_AJAX's JavaScript API, they also offer another possibility: generated JavaScript classes that mimic the API of their PHP counterparts.

This system allows you to have a JavaScript class with the same methods that were registered on the server. For example, `testServer.php` registered the `Test` class; this class has two methods, `serverTime` and `echoString`, so after including the generated JavaScript stub file, you now have a class called `Test` in JavaScript with `serverTime` and `echoString` methods. A call to either of these methods will automatically be sent over `XMLHttpRequest` to the PHP server; the matching PHP method will then be called, and its results will be sent back to JavaScript where they will be passed to a callback method.

To import the JavaScript stub class, you simply add `stub=className` to your inclusion of `testServer.php`. You can choose to combine this with the request you're already doing for the client libraries, or you can add a second JavaScript `include` to handle this. While including the JavaScript library and the stubs in one request is handy, it's not always the best approach from a caching standpoint. HTML_AJAX includes code that causes client Web browsers to cache JavaScript served up by the `HTML_AJAX_Server` class whenever possible, but for this to work, the content needs to remain consistent. If you are requesting a different stub class on each page load, you'll defeat this cache even though only a small part of the requested content is changing.

When you create an instance of the stub class, you pass in an object that provides the callback methods. Each method has its own callback named the same as the method that was called. These callback methods take a single parameter, which contains the results sent from the PHP code. The callback class can also provide custom handlers that work the same as the general handlers in the HTML_AJAX class. This allows handling errors and loading messages specifically for this class. Listing 9-4 shows an example that uses the `Test` class provided by `testServer.php`.

Listing 9-4

HTML_AJAXStubAJAX.html

```
1   <html>
2   <head>
3   <title>HTML_AJAX: Stub AJAX</title>
4   <script type="text/javascript"
5       src="testServer.php?client=all"></script>
6   <script type="text/javascript"
```

```
7        src="testServer.php?stub=Test"></script>
8
9  <style type="text/css">
10 .target {
11   width: 200px;
12   border: solid 1px black;
13 }
14 </style>
15
16 <script type="text/javascript">
17 var callback = {
18 serverTime: function(result) {
19     document.getElementById('target').innerHTML
20         = 'Server Time:<br>' + result;
21 },
22 echoString: function(result) {
23     document.getElementById('target').innerHTML
24         = 'Echo String:<br>' +result;
25     }
26 }
27
28 var remote = new Test(callback);
29 </script>
30 </head>
31 <body>
32
33 <a href="#" onclick="remote.serverTime()"
34     >Show Server Time</a><br>
35
36 <a href="#" onclick="remote.echoString('Test')"
37     >Echo a String</a><br>
38
39 <div class="target" id="target"></div>
40
41 </body>
42 </html>
```

Listing 9-4 allows you to run the serverTime method, which displays the formatted date and time from the server, and echoString, which returns the passed in string with From Server prepended to it. The page starts with a basic setup; lines 5–6 include the JavaScript client library; this library provides the automatically generated stub class, which is included on lines 6 and 7. The parameters to both these includes follow the same syntax, so we could have used the all keyword instead of the class name on line 7. You can also uses a comma-separated list for both stub and client; this is useful for including a specific set of stub classes (stub=Test,OtherClass) or to include a specific portion of the JavaScript library (`client=main,util`). The header also includes a small amount of CSS (lines 9–14) used to style the element to which we will be outputting messages.

Lines 16–29 include the JavaScript code that provides functionality to this page. First it defines a setup of callback functions (lines 17–26); then it creates an instance of the remote stub class (line 28). In the callback definition, we define one method for each method on the stub class. Lines 18–21 define the callback for the `serverTime` method; this code outputs the results of `serverTime()` to the target DIV prepended with a small message. Lines 22–26 do the same tasks for the `echoString` method, except that they use a different label. Line 28 finishes the process by creating an instance of the remote stub passing in the `callback` variable defined above it. If no callback was passed into the constructor, the remote class would still work, but it would run in synchronous mode, returning results directly and locking the user interface until the request was done.

The rest of the listing creates the user interface for the page, creating links to call the methods on the remote class. Line 33 is for the `serverTime` method, and line 36 is for the `echoString` method. Line 39 creates the output DIV, using the CSS rule defined earlier to give it a border.

9.1.4 Using `HTML_AJAX_Action`

`HTML_AJAX_Action` is a PHP class that allows you to specify the JavaScript callback of a PHP function from within PHP code. On the JavaScript side, you create a remote stub class, but instead of passing in an object containing your custom callback functions, you pass in an empty hash, like so:

```
var remote = new remoteClass({});
```

The PHP class that you are registering for remote access returns an instance of `HTML_AJAX_Action` to specify what the JavaScript should do. `HTML_AJAX_Action` provides the ability to set attributes on arbitrary DOM nodes, create new DOM nodes, and run any JavaScript code. When working with DOM attributes, you can prepend to the property, append to it, or clear it. These operations are most useful with the `innerHTML` property, but they can also be useful with other properties that can take multiple values. One example of such a property is className. Listing 9-5 shows an example of a PHP class that returns `HTML_AJAX_Action` events.

Listing 9-5

Action.class.php

```php
1   <?php
2   require_once 'HTML/AJAX/Action.php';
3
4   class Action {
5     function changeColor() {
6       $haa = new HTML_AJAX_Action();
7
8       // pick a random color
9       $r = rand(0,255);
10      $g = rand(0,255);
11      $b = rand(0,255);
12      $haa->assignAttr('target',
13             array('style' => "color: rgb($r,$g,$b)"));
14      return $haa;
15    }
16
17    function alert() {
18      $haa = new HTML_AJAX_Action();
19
20          $haa->insertAlert('This is a message from PHP');
21          return $haa;
22    }
23  }
```

Because we are going to be creating HTML_AJAX_Action objects, we need to start out by requiring the needed code; this is done on line 2. Then, we define the Action class. The class contains two methods. The first method, changeColor (lines 5–15), uses the assignAttr method to set the style attribute of the target node. To do this, we create a new HTML_AJAX_Action instance (line 6), create three random values to use as our color (lines 8–11) and then run assignAttr (line 12). The first parameter to assignAttr is the ID of the element to update; the second parameter is an associative array of attributes to update. The key of the array is the attribute, with its value being the new value to set. You could include multiple attributes to set, including innerHTML. To finish the method, we return the HTML_AJAX_Action instance on which we've been working (line 14).

The second method alert (lines 17–22) uses HTML_AJAX_Action's ability to inject new JavaScript into the page. On line 18, we create a new HTML_AJAX_Action instance, and then on line 20, we call its insertAlert method. The method takes a single parameter, which is the message to alert. We also could have used the insertJavaScript method and written alert("message"); directly. The function finishes by returning the HTML_AJAX_Action instance (line 21). While not shown here, HTML_AJAX_Action allows you to combine multiple actions in one method; you just keep calling the various methods on the instance before returning it. The order that you call the methods will be the order that the actions are processed in the browser.

9.1.5 JavaScript Behaviors

JavaScript Behaviors are pieces of JavaScript code applied to DOM elements through the use of CSS selectors. They are an effective way to keep HTML code free from hundreds of onclick attributes. HTML_AJAX includes behavior support through its inclusion of a modified version of Ben Nolan's Behavior library. Behavior is extremely easy to use; it has one public method, Behavior.register, which takes a CSS selector as its first parameter and a JavaScript function that is run on each matching element. These registrations can take place in the header of the HTML document. A good strategy is to put them into an include file and create a common set of behaviors to use throughout a site just like you would for CSS. Listing 9-6 gives an example that shows the basics of JavaScript behaviors.

Listing 9-6

HTML_AJAXBehavior.html

```
1   <html>
2   <head>
3   <title>HTML_AJAX: Behavior</title>
4   <script type="text/javascript"
5     src="server.php?client=all"></script>
6
7   <script type="text/javascript">
8   Behavior.register(
9       ".alert",
10      function(element) {
11          element.onclick = function() {
12              alert('I alert on click');
13          }
14      }
15  );
16  Behavior.register(
17      ".green",
18      function(element) {
```

```
19          element.onmouseover = function() {
20              element.style.color = 'green';
21          }
22      }
23 );
24 </script>
25 </head>
26 <body>
27 <p class="alert">
28 I am a paragraph that alerts when you click on me
29 </p>
30 <p class=" alert green">
31 I am a paragraph that alerts on click
32 and turns green on mouse over
33 </p>
34 </body>
35 </html>
```

Behavior is provided by HTML_AJAX, so we get support for it when we include the entire HTML_AJAX JavaScript library; this is done on lines 4 and 5. On lines 7–24, we define two JavaScript behaviors. The first behavior (lines 8–15) applies to the CSS selector .alert, which is any element with a class of alert. On the page load, Behavior passes each matching class to the processing function (lines 10–14); this function adds an onclick event handler, which alerts a message. The second behavior (lines 16–23) has a similar selector; this time, the behavior applies to the green class. The processing function for it (lines 18–22) adds an onmouseover handler, which sets the color of the element to green (line 20).

The rest of the page (lines 26–35) provides some sample HTML elements to which to apply the rules. On lines 27–29, we define a paragraph element with the class alert; when you click this class, it will alert a message because of the behavior applied to elements within the alert class. Lines 30–33 define another paragraph. This paragraph has two classes (in CSS, multiple classes are separated by spaces): alert and green. This value for class means it will get both behaviors, alerting a message when clicked and turning green on a mouse over.

9.1.6 JavaScript Utility Methods

HTML_AJAX contains a number of JavaScript utility methods located in the HTML_AJAX_Util class. Some of these methods, such as quickPrint and varDump, are useful for debugging, whereas others help in cross-browser compatibility. Some of the most widely applicable functions are shown here.

9.1.6.1 `quickPrint`

Method signature:

```
HTML_AJAX_Util.quickPrint(input)
```

The `quickPrint` method takes an input variable and iterates over it, printing out each member on its own line in the format of `name:value`. This is useful for quickly identifying the values of the properties of an object. The input is an object written in object literal notation. Example output of `quickPrint` follows.

```
Input: {property1:'one',innerHash:[4,5,6,7],anotherProp:true}

Output:
property1:one
innerHash:4,5,6,7
anotherProp:true
```

9.1.6.2 `varDump`

Method signature:

```
HTML_AJAX_Util.varDump(input)
```

`varDump` takes an input variable and recurses over it, producing an output similar to PHP's `var_dump` method, including type information. When dealing with DOM objects or other variables that have a large number of children, you will get an extremely large output from `varDump`. Example output of `varDump` follows:

```
Input: {property1:'one',innerHash:[4,5,6,7],anotherProp:true}

Output:
object(Object) (3) {
  ["property1"]=>
  string(3) "one"
  ["innerHash"]=>
  array(5) {
    [0]=>
    number(4)
    [1]=>
    number(5)
    [2]=>
    number(6)
    [3]=>
    number(7)
```

```
    ["_____array"]=>
    string(11) "_____array"
  }
  ["anotherProp"]=>
  boolean(true)
}
```

9.1.6.3 getElementsByClassName

Method signature:

```
HTML_AJAX_Util.getElementsByClassName('CSSClass',parent);
```

The getElementByClassName function allows you to get an array of the DOM elements that have the provided CSS class. The second parameter, parent, is optional; if specified, the search happens against the child elements of the parent node. If it's not specified, the search is done against the entire document. The document we're searching against contains the following HTML:

```
<p class="test">Test Nodes</p>
<div class="test"></div>
<span class="test"></div>
<div class="test2"></div>
```

To find the nodes in the document with a class of test, you would run the following:

```
var nodes = HTML_AJAX_Util.getElementsByClassName('test');
```

This gives you an array with three elements. You could then loop over this array, changing the style of the elements or updating their content using innerHTML.

9.1.7 PHP Utility Methods

HTML_AJAX also includes a class of PHP utility methods that help perform common functions related to JavaScript generation. The methods are located in the HTML_AJAX_Helper class, which is included in a PHP script by use of the following:

```
require_once 'HTML/AJAX/Helper.php';
```

The most commonly used methods are jsonEncode and encloseInScript. The jsonEncode method takes a PHP variable and returns a JSON string, which can be outputted directly to JavaScript, like so:

```
var jsVar = <?php echo $helper->jsonEncode($phpVariable); ?>;
```

The `encloseInScript` method takes a string input, encloses it in JavaScript script tags, and then returns it. It is commonly used when generating JavaScript from PHP, which would be like this:

```
echo $helper->encloseInScript($generateJavaScript);
```

9.1.8 HTML_AJAX Development Tips

HTML_AJAX can be used out of the box, but if it doesn't meet your needs, it can also be used as a building block for your own custom AJAX library. The following are some tips to keep in mind while using HTML_AJAX:

- The HTML_AJAX wiki (http://htmlajax.org) contains more information about HTML_AJAX, including a mailing list by which you can ask questions of its developers.

- If you register lots of classes with `HTML_AJAX_Server`, you can use its `initMethod` functionality to include classes only as they are requested, decreasing the amount of PHP processing done per request.

- HTML_AJAX turns native data types into strings using serialization classes; this process is customizable, so if JSON doesn't meet your needs, you can replace it with whatever does.

9.2 Summary

HTML_AJAX provides easy communication between PHP server-side code and JavaScript code on the browser. This allows you to focus on building backend logic or a frontend user interface instead of worrying about the communication between them. HTML_AJAX also includes helper classes for both PHP and JavaScript that help simplify the AJAX development process. HTML_AJAX's main features include the following:

- Easy movement of PHP data to JavaScript and vice versa

- Export of PHP APs to JavaScript

- A simple JavaScript API for making standard AJAX requests

- The ability to perform basic DOM interactions without writing JavaScript

- JavaScript Behaviors for tying JavaScript code to HTML without populating the HTML with extra markup

- JavaScript helper methods for JavaScript debugging

- PHP helper methods for generating JavaScript

In Chapters 10–12, we will use the libraries shown in Chapters 8 and 9 in real-life cases. As we look at the use cases, will see some of the solutions that AJAX can provide to common Web development problems. We also will see how the choice of library affects the implementation of those solutions.

Chapter 10

Speeding Up
Data Display

In this chapter

Acommon Web development task is showing large data sets. To navigate through the dataset, the user is forced to reload the entire Web page, which makes data browsing a slow process. The example we will build in this chapter is a graph of the time the sun rises and sets for different cities. It will also include a table showing the data from which it's built; this data browsing is especially handicapped by the constant reload process. The actual graph generation is a slow process, and because it shows data for the entire year, it doesn't need to be updated as you look through the data month by month. In this chapter, I will show how you can use the AJAX technique of subpages to greatly speed up data browsing.

10.1 Overview of the Sun Rise and Set Data Viewer

In this chapter, we look at a specific case that illustrates the general problem of slow data display. Our case is a small PHP and HTML site that displays the data for the time that the sun rises and sets in various cities. The page includes a graph of a full year of this data, and it includes a table that shows one month of the data. The overall layout of the site is shown in Figure 10-1.

Many times, when you display large amounts of data in a table, you use a user interface (UI) element called a *pager*. A simple example of this is shown in Figure 10-2. This sun rise and set viewer uses a simpler version of this because the data can easily be divided into months. The pager for the viewer (see Figure 10-3) divides the data set by month and puts all the options in a drop-down widget because the number of possible pages is only 12.

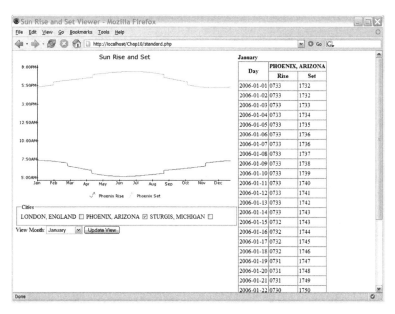

FIGURE 10-1
Basic site interface

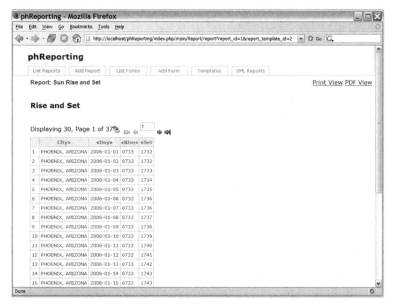

FIGURE 10-2
Example pager

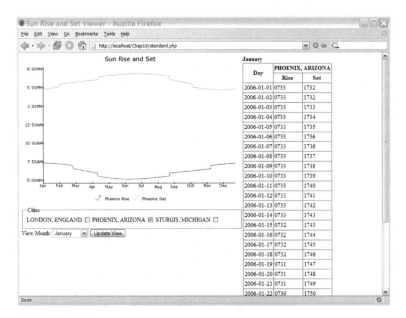

FIGURE 10-3
Month selector

10.2 Building the Non-AJAX Version of the Sun Rise and Set Viewer

This use case starts by building a standard HTML version, which means we're using AJAX as an enhancement at the end of the development process. This is a common AJAX approach, and it follows the basic pattern of building a site, finding its problem areas, and then updating those problem areas with AJAX to improve the user experience. This approach can have some disadvantages, especially on complex multipage sites, because adding in AJAX might cause workflows to be changed, causing large parts of the site to be updated. However, it does work well if you focus on specific tasks that can be upgraded.

This example stores its data in a MySQL database, so we need to start by setting it up. If you're not used to using a database with PHP, don't worry; the AJAX changes are usable with any server-side language. PHP just provides the needed code to have a fully working example. First, you need to create a database named `rise_set`. This can be accomplished in an admin tool such as phpMyAdmin or by running `create database rise_set;`. Once you have the database created, you need to create the table in which to store the data. To do this, load the SQL that is in Listing 10-1.

Listing 10-1

Schema.sql

```
CREATE TABLE `rise_set` (
  `city` varchar(150) NOT NULL default '',
  `day` date NOT NULL default '0000-00-00',
  `rise` varchar(4) NOT NULL default '',
  `set` varchar(4) NOT NULL default '',
  PRIMARY KEY  (`city`,`day`)
) ENGINE=MyISAM DEFAULT CHARSET=utf8;
```

After the table is set up, you're ready to import some sun rise and sun set data. The data has been gathered from the U.S. Naval Observatory Web site (http://aa.usno.navy.mil/data/docs/RS_OneYear.html). Data for two example cities has already been prepared and can be used by running the SQL located in `data/phoenix.sql` and `data/sturgis.sql`. The script that generated these SQL files (`data/dataToSql.php`) is also provided, and you can use it to prepare data for other cities. First, get a dataset for a city by filling out the form at the U.S. Naval Observatory Web site, and then copy the data into a text file. (You want just the data, not HTML tags). Then you can run the `dataToSql.php` script over the file and redirect its output to an SQL file, which can then be loaded into your database server. Here's an example command loading in data for London, England:

```
php DataToSql.php london.txt > london.sql
mysql -u root rise_set < london.sql
```

Now that we've done the prep work, let's look at the overall design of this site. It consists of three parts:

- The `SunRiseSet` class grabs data from the database and performs any needed formatting.

- The `Graph.php` page generates the graph using data from the `SunRiseSet` class.

- The `Standard.php` page builds the interface and displays a month of data at a time in a table.

Each part will get more coverage in the following sections, but the important part is `Standard.php` because it creates the HTML user interface that you will enhance with AJAX.

10.2.1 `SunRiseSet` Class

The `SunRiseSet` class is a simple class that connects to the database and provides methods for the other pages to access the data that's been loaded into the database. Because all database access takes place through this class, you can easily update it to support a different back end. If you want to run the examples on your own server, you may need to update the database connection information; these variables are located on lines 4–7 of `SunRiseSet.class.php`.

The `SunRiseSet` class, shown in Listing 10-2, contains two setter methods that are used to configure the user-selectable components of the data access. The `setMonth` method allows you to set the month of data that will be returned by the `monthsData` method, and it is used by the table that is rendering code. The `setCities` method allows you to set the city to which the data will be limited. Along with these setters, five data access methods are provided: `possibleCities()`, `monthList()`, `monthsData()`, `graphData()`, and `minRise()`. More details about these methods are shown later as we walk through the code of the class. The class also contains a number of methods for querying the database; these internal methods are prefixed with an underscore (_) to show that they shouldn't be used outside of this class.

Listing 10-2

SunRiseSet.class.php

```
1   <?php
2   // manage requesting data from a mysql database
3
4   $dbHost = 'localhost';
5   $dbUser = 'root';
6   $dbPass = '';
7   $dbName = 'rise_set';
8
9   class SunRiseSet {
10     var $_conn;
11     var $month;
12     var $year = '2006';
13     var $cities = array();
14     var $citiesIn = '';
```

```
15
16     function setMonth($month) {
17       $this->month = $month;
18     }
19
20     function setCities($cities) {
21       $this->cities = $cities;
22       foreach($cities as $key => $city) {
23         $cities[$key] =
24                   "'".
25                     mysql_real_escape_string($city)
26                   . "'";
27       }
28       $this->citiesIn = implode(',',$cities);
29     }
30
31     function possibleCities() {
32       $sql = "select
33                     distinct city
34                     from rise_set
35                     order by city
36                   ";
37       return $this->_querySingleArray($sql);
38     }
39
40     function monthList() {
41       $ret = array();
42       for($i = 1; $i < 13; $i++) {
43         $ret[$i] = date('F',mktime(1,1,1,$i));
44       }
45       return $ret;
46 }
47
```

The class starts with some basic setup. Lines 4–7 contain the basic database connection parameters. $dbHost contains the DNS name or IP address of the MySql server, $dbUser contains the username with which to connect, $dbPass contains the password, and $dbName contains the name of the database. After that, we start the class definition (line 9). Inside the class, we define five properties (lines 10–14), which the methods of the class use to hold settings and shared variables. $_conn holds the database connection resource and is set by the _connect method (line 95) and used by the _query method (line 112). $month holds the selected month and is set by the setMonth method on line 16; $year holds the current year and is simply set to 2006. $cities contains an array of all the selected cities; it is set by the setCities method on line 20. Note that $citiesIn also contains a list of selected cities, this time formatted to be used in an SQL in clause.

Lines 16–46 contain the two setter methods and several basic data access methods. The method `setMonth` (lines 16–18) takes a single parameter, the integer value of the selected month, and sets it to `$this->month`. The `setCities` method (lines 20–29) performs a similar action, only this time, it takes an array of cities. It also builds the `citiesIn` method. This method takes an array and turns it into a quoted comma-separated string. If the array had two values, one for Phoenix and one for Sturgis, it would equal `'PHOENIX, ARIZONA', 'STURGIS,MICHIGAN'`.

The `possibleCities` method (lines 31–38) returns an array that contains an entry for each city in the database. This array is used to build the interface for selecting cities. The list is built from the query `"select distinct city from rise_set"`, which returns one row for each city in the `rise_set` table. The helper function `_querySingleArray` is used on line 37 to return the values from this query. The `monthList` function (lines 40–47) creates an associative array containing 12 months; the key of the array contains the values 1–12, with their matching values being generated by the PHP date function. You can see sample output from these functions by running the `SunRiseSetDemo.php` example page. Listing 10-3 continues the `SunRiseSet` class.

Listing 10-3

`SunRiseSet.class.php` ***Continued***

```
48    function monthsData() {
49      $sql = "select *
50        from
51          rise_set
52        where
53          `day` between
54          '{$this->year}-{$this->month}-1' and
55          '{$this->year}-{$this->month}-31'
56          and city in($this->citiesIn)
57        order by
58          `day`, city";
59
60      $data = $this->_queryAll($sql);
61
62      $ret = array();
63      $i = 0;
64      $currentDay = $data[0]['day'];
65      foreach($data as $row) {
66        if ($row['day'] != $currentDay) {
67          $currentDay = $row['day'];
```

```
68              $i++;
69          }
70          $key = array_search($row['city'],
71                      $this->cities);
72          $ret[$i][$key] = $row;
73      }
74      return $ret;
75  }
76
```

Lines 48–76 define the `monthsData` method. This method queries the database and returns an array of data containing one month of rise and set data for the selected cities. The cities are chosen using the values set by `setCities`, and the month is chosen by the value set by `setMonth` along with the `$this->year` property. The SQL query is built on lines 49–58. This query is then executed using the `_queryAll` helper method (line 60). This returns a multidimensional array, with the first level being the row index and the second level being the values of the row in an associative array. We then loop through the results (lines 65–74), which builds an array one row per day, with subentries under that row for each city. Listing 10-4 shows an excerpt of that output.

Listing 10-4

Sample Output of `monthsData()`

```
[0] => Array
    (
        [0] => Array
            (
                [city] => PHOENIX, ARIZONA
                [day] => 2006-01-01
                [rise] => 0733
                [set] => 1732
            )

        [1] => Array
            (
                [city] => STURGIS, MICHIGAN
                [day] => 2006-01-01
                [rise] => 0809
                [set] => 1722
            )

    )
```

Listing 10-5

SunRiseSet.class.php **Continued**

```
77 function graphData($city) {
78       $sql = "select * from rise_set
79       where city = '".mysql_real_escape_string($city)."'
80       order by `day` ";
81
82       return $this->_queryAll($sql);
83    }
84
85    function minRise() {
86       $sql = "select
87                   min(rise) mr
88                   from rise_set
89                   where city in($this->citiesIn)
90               ";
91       $data = $this->_queryAll($sql);
92       return $data[0]['mr'];
93 }
94
```

Lines 77–93 define two functions that are used by Graph.php to load its data. The Image_Graph graphing engine loads its data based on the concept of data sets, so instead of grabbing a combined array, like the month data case, we return the data one city at a time. The graphData method on lines 77–83 accomplishes this process by building a query limited to the passed-in city and then returning all its results using the _queryAll helper function.

The minRise method defined on lines 85–93 is used by the graphing code to set the bottom value on its Y axis. Because this minimum SunRise value needs to take into account all the cities being displayed, the query looks for the minimum rise value where the city is among the currently selected cities in the $this->citiesIn list. A single time value is returned from the function.

Listing 10-6

SunRiseSet.class.php **Continued**

```
95     function _connect() {
96       if ($this->_conn) {
97         return true;
98       }
99       global $dbHost, $dbUser, $dbPass, $dbName;
100
```

```
101      $this->_conn = mysql_connect($dbHost,
102                          $dbUser,$dbPass);
103
104      if (!$this->_conn) {
105        die(mysql_error());
106      }
107
108      mysql_select_db($dbName,$this->_conn);
109    }
110
111
112    function _query($sql) {
113      $this->_connect();
114      $res = mysql_query($sql,$this->_conn);
115      if (!$res) {
116        die(mysql_error($this->_conn));
117      }
118      return $res;
119    }
120
121    function _queryAll($sql) {
122      $res = $this->_query($sql);
123
124      $ret = array();
125      while($row = mysql_fetch_assoc($res)) {
126        $ret[] = $row;
127      }
128      return $ret;
129    }
130
131    function _querySingleArray($sql) {
132      $res = $this->_query($sql);
133
134      $ret = array();
135      while($row = mysql_fetch_row($res)) {
136        $ret[] = $row[0];
137      }
138      return $ret;
139    }
140  }
```

The rest of the class (lines 95–140) defines the database connectivity and utility methods. They provide a basic wrapper around the MySql database functions. The _connect method on lines 95–109 connects to the database. If there is a problem, it stops script execution and shows an error message. The _query method (lines 112–119) executes an SQL query and does basic error handling. Lines 121–129 define the _queryAll method, which uses _query to execute an SQL query and then loops over its results, grabbing an associative array for each row. The `_querySingleArray` method (lines 131–138) is similar to `_queryAll`. The only difference is that instead of returning an associative array for each row; it uses the value of only the first column for each row.

10.2.2 Graph.php

The graph on the viewer is generated using a PEAR library called Image_Graph (http://pear.php.net/Image_Graph). To run the examples locally, you need to install the library, which can be accomplished by running `pear install Image_Graph-alpha`. I won't walk through all the graphing code, because it's not necessary to understand it to understand how the example works. The graph is generated by the `Graph.php` script, which will be used as the URL for an image on the HTML page in which it's displayed. The graph takes the GET parameter of cities and uses it to select which cities will appear on the graph. The graphing period is one year, meaning the graph uses 365 points per city. This large number of points causes much of the slowdown in the graphing processes, but dynamic image generation is usually a slow area in any Web site, no matter how much data it's working with. This slow speed is due to the complexity of the image generation process.

In this example, the slow processing point is this graph, but this slow processing could be replaced by any number of other problems. On another site, you may have some database queries that are slow and impossible to speed up, or you might have some other visualization with lots of processing overhead. In many cases, page loads can be slow simply due to the large amounts of information and the formatting of the HTML that is being used. In other cases, the page performs fine, but the user experience isn't great due to the constant reload process that browsing through data causes.

10.2.3 Standard.php

`Standard.php` generates the HTML that makes up our sun rise and set viewer. This page contains a form that is used to change which cities are displayed and which month of data the table shows. It also links in the graph and generates the data table. This page contains a minimal amount of PHP code, most of it being `foreach` loops to build the options for the form or the data in the table. This separation of the bulk

of the logic from the building of the HTML is important because it will make the
creation of an AJAX version much easier. Listing 10-7 presents the code.

Listing 10-7

Standard.php

```php
1   <?php
2   // non-AJAX version of a sun rise/set viewer
3
4   // include data class
5   require_once 'SunRiseSet.class.php';
6   $data = new SunRiseSet();
7
8   // defaults
9   $month = 1;
10  $cities = array('PHOENIX, ARIZONA');
11
12  // load options
13  if (isset($_GET['month'])) {
14      $month = (int)$_GET['month'];
15  }
16
17  if (isset($_GET['cities'])) {
18      $cities = (array)$_GET['cities'];
19  }
20
21  // Set the selected options on the data class
22  $data->setMonth($month);
23  $data->setCities($cities);
24
25  // build the graph query string
26  $graphOptions = '';
27  foreach($cities as $city) {
28      $graphOptions .= "cities[]=$city&";
29  }
30
31  $action = htmlentities($_SERVER['PHP_SELF']);
32  $months = $data->monthList();
33  ?>
34  <html>
35  <head>
36      <title>Sun Rise and Set Viewer</title>
37  </head>
38  <body>
39  <div style="float:left; width: 610px">
40  <img src="Graph.php?<?php echo $graphOptions; ?>"
41      width="600" height="400" alt="sun rise and set">
```

```
42
43  <form action="<?php echo $action; ?>">
44  <fieldset>
45    <legend>Cities</legend>
46    <?php foreach($data->possibleCities()
47      as $city) { ?>
48    <label><?php echo $city; ?>
49      <input type="checkbox" name="cities[]"
50      value="<?php echo $city; ?>"
51      <?php if(in_array($city,$cities)) {
52        echo "CHECKED"; } ?>
53    </label>
54
55    <?php } ?>
56  </fieldset>
57  <label>View Month:
58  <select name="month">
59  <?php foreach($months as $key => $m) { ?>
60    <option value="<?php echo $key;?>"
61    <?php if($key == $month) {
62      echo 'SELECTED'; } ?>>
63      <?php echo $m; ?></option>
64  <?php } ?>
65  </select>
66  </label>
67  <input type="submit" value="Update View">
68  </form>
69  </div>
```

The first 33 lines of `Standard.php` do the basic PHP setup. On line 5, we require the `SunRiseSet` class that gives us access to the data in the database. On line 6, we create an instance of it, and then we start the process of setting its defaults. First, we set some default values to use throughout the page if nothing is passed in by the form (lines 9–10); then we check for month and cities being passed in by the form and, if so, overwrite our default values with those from the form. On lines 22–23, we use those values and set the month and cities on the `SunRiseSet` instance. To finish up the setup portion, we format the `$cities` variable so that it can be passed in a query string (lines 26–29), set the URL from the form to which to submit (line 31), and put our list of months into the variable `$months` so that it can be used later on.

Lines 34–68 add the graph and the form to the page. These elements float to the left, so as long as you have a wide enough screen, you'll be able to see the data table next to them on the right. The graph is added to the page on lines 40–41. We add

$graphOptions to its query string, which lets us set the cities the graph will display. On lines 43–68, we build the form that provides the viewing options for this page. The page submits using GET to the $action variable, which we set to the current page on line 31.

The first element in the form is a fieldset that contains a checkbox for each possible city (lines 44–56). We get the list of options using the possibleCities method (line 46) and loop over the array; in each iteration, a checkbox element is created (lines 49–53). Line 48 outputs the name of the city to use as a label, and line 50 outputs $city again (this time as the value of the checkbox). Lines 51–52 finish up the output for the checkboxes, checking whether the city is currently selected; if it is, it outputs CHECKED.

The next section of the form builds the selected drop-down element for picking which month to view. The element is started on line 58 and is named month. Lines 59–64 contain a loop that produces the drop-down's option elements. The values from those options are pulled out of the $months variable that was set on line 32. Lines 61–62 check to see if the current element is selected and if it is, outputs SELECTED. The form finishes up with a Submit button on line 67.

Listing 10-8

Standard.php *Continued*

```
70   <div>
71   <b><?php echo $months[$month]; ?></b>
72   <table cellpadding="2" cellspacing="0"
73     border="1">
74   <thead>
75     <tr>
76       <th rowspan="2">Day</th>
77   <?php foreach($cities as $city) { ?>
78       <th colspan="2"><?php echo $city; ?></th>
79   <?php } ?>
80     </tr>
81     <tr>
82   <?php foreach($cities as $city) { ?>
83       <th>Rise</th>
84       <th>Set</th>
85   <?php } ?>
86     </tr>
87   </thead>
88   <tbody>
89   <?php foreach($data->monthsData() as $row) { ?>
```

```
90    <tr>
91      <td><?php echo $row[0]['day']; ?></td>
92    <?php foreach($row as $city) { ?>
93      <td><?php echo $city['rise']; ?></td>
94      <td><?php echo $city['set']; ?></td>
95    <?php } ?>
96    </tr>
97  <?php } ?>
98  </tbody>
99  </table>
100
101 </div>
102 </body>
103 </html>
```

The page finishes by producing the data table. On line 71, a label for the table is created, showing the currently selected month. Then on line 72, the actual table starts; the table is given some basic formatting, some cell padding, and a border of 1 pixel. Then we move on to its dynamic aspects. First, we create the header for the table (lines 74–87). The header has two rows: The first displays the name of each selected city, and the second subdivides each city column into a rise and set column. We create the list of cities in the foreach loop on lines 77–79, looping over the $cities variable, which contains our currently selected cities, and outputting each one with a colspan of 2. We then loop over the same variable again (lines 82–85); this time, two cells are outputted: one for rise and one for set.

The table is finished up by a loop on lines 89–97 that generates the table body. We get the data for this loop from the monthsData method (line 89); if you look back at the explanation of monthsData shown in Listing 10-3, you'll remember that it contains a subarray for each city. Thus, we start off a row by outputting a cell for the date (line 91). We then read the date from the first city's data, knowing that all the dates are the same. Then we loop over the $cities arrays, printing out rise and set times (lines 93–94) for each. This completes the page, giving us a graph, a form, and a data table.

10.3 Problems with the Non-AJAX Viewer

Now that we've implemented the viewer, we can see that it has a number of problems. The first problem is performance. Generating the graph—especially for a large number of cities—can take three to five seconds. This is further aggravated by the fact that obtaining a new set of monthly data takes a page reload. It might be possible to eliminate some of this performance penalty though caching or other graphing speedups, but that's not a reusable solution, and if we would add any more interactive features, such as highlighting a day on the graph, the caching would be unworkable.

The viewer also gives poor user feedback because of how the browser handles loading the slow images. In Internet Explorer, the user will see an empty box where the image will be shown (see Figure 10-4), whereas in Firefox, the old image will be shown until the reload finishes. Firefox's behavior around image loading (see Figure 10-5) is especially problematic because it makes the page look like it's done loading even though the cursor still has a loading icon and is waiting for the graph to finish loading.

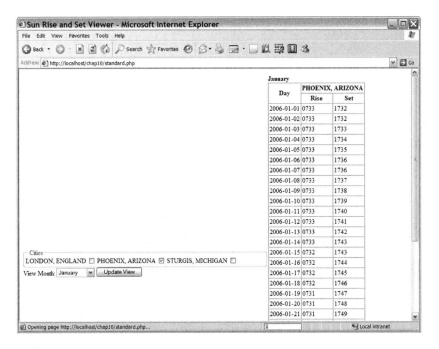

FIGURE 10-4
Internet Explorer's slow image-loading behavior

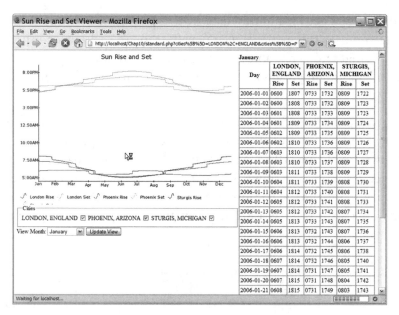

FIGURE 10-5
Firefox's slow image-loading behavior

10.4 Improving Viewing with AJAX

Because the biggest problem with the viewer is that it's reloading content that's not changing, we want to look at AJAX patterns that we can use to avoid this. We have a number of options, but they all end up having the same effect: Instead of treating the viewer as one monolithic page, we get to treat it as a number of sub-pages. This allows us to load data for each section independently, which will keep us from needing to reload the slow graph when we just want to view the next month's data. This independent loading gives us a speed advantage over a mono-lithic approach. We end up with three different sections, one for each of the main elements. (These sections are shown in Figure 10-6.) Each section can be updated independently from the others, and in this case, input from the form section controls what the other sections do. Any change to the form, either in the selection of a different city or in the changing of the month, causes the data section to update. The graph will only be updated when the selected cities are changed.

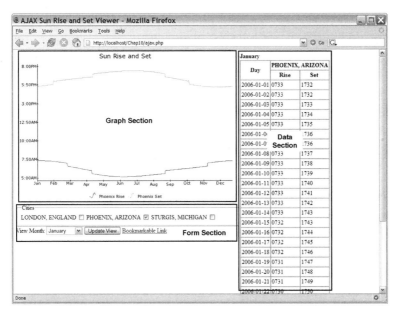

FIGURE 10-6
Viewer with sections labeled

Sectioning a page is an easy AJAX pattern to implement, but it's not without its disadvantages. The biggest disadvantage is that the actions you perform are no longer directly bookmarkable. You can add a bookmark link that always contains the URL to get to your current view, but users might not recognize it and will just bookmark the page like normal, getting its default value instead of the current one. There are some solutions to this problem. They involve using the fragment part of the URL (the value after the #), but they suffer from browser compatibility problems and complex programming models. The fragment solutions also have a hard time fixing both the Back and Forward buttons and booking at the same time. Eventually, there will be an easy solution to the bookmark problem, but it's not ready today.

10.4.1 Viewer HTML Updated for AJAX

To implement our AJAX actions, we start by adding a submit handler to the form:

```
<form action="<?php echo $action; ?>" onsubmit="return updatePage(this)"
id="form">
```

This function returns `false`, canceling the normal form submission process. Now that we have client-side code in control of the submission process, we can figure out what needs to be updated. This means we need some code to always update the data section and to update the graph section only when the selected cities have changed. Using HTML_AJAX, updating the data section is simple, as shown here:

```
var queryString = HTML_AJAX.formEncode(form);
var callback = function(result) {
    document.getElementById('table').innerHTML = result;
}
HTML_AJAX.grab('ajaxTable.php?'+queryString,callback);
```

We start the process by using the `HTML_AJAX.formEncode` method to turn the values of the form into a queryString. This string is the same one that you can see after the "?" in the URL when doing a normal form submission. Then, we build a callback function that will be called when the HTTP request to the server is complete. We then call `HTML_AJAX.grab` against the `AjaxTable.php` page, passing in the queryString we built from the form and the callback we just built. The new PHP script will be explained later in section 10.4.2 (Viewer PHP Script Updated for AJAX), but it follows the same subpage split, generating just the data table section.

Figuring out if the currently selected cities have changed is more difficult. The basis of this process is a function that looks at the form and creates a hash of its current check status. This function will run on page load and then again each time we detect a change so that we have a value to compare against the next time. The code for this function is shown here:

```
function updateCurrentCities() {
  var els = document.getElementById('form').elements;
  for(var i = 0; i < els.length; i++) {
    if (els[i].name == 'cities[]') {
      cities[els[i].value] = els[i].checked;
    }
  }
}
```

The `cities` variable is defined outside of this function as `var cities = {};`, which puts it in the global scope and lets other functions use it. The `updateCurrentCities` function works by first getting all the elements of the form and then looping over them to look for `cities` elements. Because each checkbox has the same name (`cities[]`), we can use those elements that are checkboxes for city selection; if the elements had different names, an easy solution would be to give them all the same CSS class. The value of each checkbox is the name of the city, so we use that as the key in the `cities` hash and then store if the box is checked as the value.

In our form-handling function, we'll loop over the elements again, comparing each value against the value stored in the hash. If any one of the checkboxes doesn't match, we stop the comparison, update the `src` property of the graph, causing it to reload, and then run `updateCurrentCities` again. The code that does this is shown here:

```
// check whether the cities have changed (graph reload)
var els = form.elements;
for(var i = 0; i < els.length; i++) {
  if (els[i].name == 'cities[]' &&
    cities[els[i].value] != els[i].checked) {
    document.getElementById('graph').src =
      'Graph.php?'+queryString;
    updateCurrentCities();
    break;
  }
}
```

Now that we have the basic AJAX functionality added to the page, we are ready to start improving its usability. The first step is adding a link that can be bookmarked and will return you to the current set of data you're viewing. Upon page load, this link will contain the same URL as the form, so we can use the `$action` PHP variable again:

```
<a id="blink" href="<?php echo $action; ?>">Bookmarkable Link</a>
```

Once the link has been added to the page, we need to add code to update it when the form is submitted. This code is pretty simple: It checks the current `href` on the blink tag to see if it has a "?" in it. If it does, all the content after it is removed. Then, we append the new `queryString` to the link. This is the same string we send to the `AjaxTable.php` script. The code that performs this bookmark link updating is shown here:

```
// update bookmarkable link
var blink = document.getElementById('blink');
if (blink.href.indexOf('?') > 0) {
    blink.href = blink.href.substring(
        0,blink.href.indexOf('?'));
}
blink.href = blink.href+'?'+queryString;
```

Adding in the bookmark link helps solve some of the usability problems caused by AJAX, but it doesn't do anything for the page's original usability problem, which is poor feedback. To do this, we need to add a feedback mechanism to the loading of the graph. The basic way this works is that we create a DIV element and position it over the graph. It will contain the message "Loading, please wait" and can be further formatted using CSS to make it look nice. This DIV will be hidden by an onload handler that we will add to the image. To improve the look of this loading notice, we'll use some visual effects from the scriptaculous library. These steps are accomplished by using the startLoad function, which is shown in Listing 10-9. The startLoad function takes as its single parameter the element to which to add the loading effect.

Listing 10-9

The startLoad *JavaScript Function*

```
1   function startLoad(element) {
2       if (!element.loading) {
3           element.loading = document.createElement('div');
4           element.loading.className='loading';
5           element.loading.innerHTML='Loading, please wait';
6           element.loading.style.height =
7                   element.clientHeight+'px';
8       element.parentNode.appendChild(element.loading);
9           element.onload = function() {
10              new Effect.Fade(this.loading);
11          }
12      }
13      else {
14          new Effect.Appear(element.loading);
15      }
16  }
```

In basic operation, the startLoad function takes the loading div and shows it using the Appear effect (line 14); it then sets up a Fade effect to hide the div when the page is loaded (lines 9–11). The rest of the function (lines 2–8) handles the initial case where we dynamically create the loading div. As we create the div, we assign it to a property on the element to which we're adding the message. Doing this makes the code reusable and helps make it clear to what element the loading div belongs. Line 3 creates the div, line 4 sets its CSS class and lets it be styled, and line 5 sets the height of the element. Width can be easily set in CSS because a width of 100% works, but percentage heights don't work in IE, so we need to calculate the absolute height that is needed to cover the area where the element will be loaded.

The setup finishes by appending the loading node to the parent of the element to which it will be applied. This means that the image tag for the graph must be created inside another element, but this works fine because we will want that wrapper `div` for CSS purposes.

The final usability change to make is to replace the default HTML_AJAX loading feedback effect with a custom one. Because updating the data table is normally a fast process, we want to highlight the table when it has been updated. Without this visual queue, users might not notice that something has changed. We'll also change the cursor to the standard page load progress cursor while the table is updating; that way, the user will get feedback if the loading is delayed by a slow network connection. This is implemented by creating an options hash and passing it to `HTML_AJAX.grab`:

```
var options = {
  Open: function() {
        document.body.style.cursor = 'progress';
  },
  Load: function() {
    document.body.style.cursor = 'default';
    new Effect.Highlight('table');
  }
}
```

This `options` hash creates a custom event handler that is called when a connection to the server is opened, and this handler sets the cursor to progress. Then we create a custom function to be called when the page load is finished. This function sets the cursor back to default and then runs a highlight effect on the table. This effect highlights the table in yellow and then fades out the highlight over a short period of time.

10.4.2 Viewer PHP Script Updated for AJAX

Now that we've looked at the AJAX changes we will be adding, let's look at what other changes need to be made to build an AJAX version of the viewer. The first step is to break the `Standard.php` file into three different files. The first 34 lines of the file are pulled out into a file called `AjaxSetup.php`. This allows the basic setup code and form value loading to be easily done in multiple files. Lines 71–101 of Listing 10-8 are also pulled out into their own file, `AjaxTable.php`. At the top of this new file, we require `AjaxSetup.php`, giving it access to the same variables that were used while the code was still in one file. This file now contains the code used to create the data table section. Finishing up the sectioning, `Standard.php` is renamed to `Ajax.php` so that we can compare the two versions, and the removed code is added back into the page using the `require` function so that the initial page generation happens in the same way. Neither the backend class nor the `Graph.php` script needs to change. Listing 10-10 shows the updated AJAX code.

Listing 10-10

AjaxSetup.php

```php
1  <?php
2  // set up the data instance
3
4  // include data class
5  require_once 'SunRiseSet.class.php';
6  $data = new SunRiseSet();
7
8  // defaults
9  $month = 1;
10 $cities = array('PHOENIX, ARIZONA');
11
12 // load options
13 if (isset($_GET['month'])) {
14   $month = (int)$_GET['month'];
15 }
16
17 if (isset($_GET['cities'])) {
18  $cities = (array)$_GET['cities'];
19 }
20
21 // Set the selected options on the data class
22 $data->setMonth($month);
23 $data->setCities($cities);
24
25 // build the graph query string
26 $graphOptions = '';
27 foreach($cities as $city) {
28  $graphOptions .= "cities[]=$city&";
29 }
30
31 $action = htmlentities($_SERVER['PHP_SELF']);
32 $months = $data->monthList();
33 ?>
```

The `AjaxSetup.php` file contains the first 34 lines of `Standard.php`. Because it's in a standalone file, it can be used in both `Ajax.php` and `AjaxTable.php`, performing the setup duties for each of them. The `AjaxTable.php` file will generate the table data and is shown in Listing 10-7, while `Ajax.php`, shown in Listing 10-1, will be the main entry point for the viewer, creating the main UI and the AJAX code for controlling the viewer.

Listing 10-11

AjaxTable.php

```
1   <?php
2   // build just the data table for the viewer
3   require_once 'AjaxSetup.php';
4   ?>
5   <b><?php echo $months[$month]; ?></b>
6   <table cellpadding="2" cellspacing="0" border="1">
7   <thead>
8     <tr>
9       <th rowspan="2">Day</th>
10      <?php foreach($cities as $city) { ?>
11        <th colspan="2"><?php echo $city; ?></th>
12      <?php } ?>
13    </tr>
14    <tr>
15      <?php foreach($cities as $city) { ?>
16        <th>Rise</th>
17        <th>Set</th>
18      <?php } ?>
19    </tr>
20  </thead>
21  <tbody>
22  <?php foreach($data->monthsData() as $row) { ?>
23    <tr>
24      <td><?php echo $row[0]['day']; ?></td>
25      <?php foreach($row as $city) { ?>
26        <td><?php echo $city['rise']; ?></td>
27        <td><?php echo $city['set']; ?></td>
28      <?php } ?>
29    </tr>
30  <?php } ?>
31  </tbody>
32  </table>
```

AjaxTable.php contains lines 71–101 of `Standard.php` (see Listing 10-13). The only change to this code is the addition of the require_once of AjaxSetup.php at the top. This allows AjaxTable.php to be called directly. Because we use require_once to include AjaxSetup.php, it will be included only once during a page load. This lets Ajax.php require AjaxSetup.php and AjaxTable.php without worrying about the setup code running multiple times.

Listing 10-12

`Ajax.php`

```
1  <?php
2    // AJAX version of a sun rise/set viewer
3    require_once 'AjaxSetup.php';
4    ?>
5    <html>
6    <head>
7        <title>AJAX Sun Rise and Set Viewer</title>
8    <script src="scriptaculous/prototype.js"
9        type="text/javascript"></script>
10   <script src="scriptaculous/scriptaculous.js"
11       type="text/javascript"></script>
12   <script src="server.php?client=all"
13       type="text/javascript"></script>
14
```

In comparison to `Standard.php`, the setup for this page has changed quite a bit. All the PHP setup is now handled in `AjaxSetup.php`, and on the HTML side, we're now including a couple of JavaScript libraries. On line 3, we include the `AjaxSetup.php` file, and we use the `require_once` function to make sure the file gets pulled in only one time. On lines 8–11, we include the scriptaculous library; this library will be used for a number of visual effects. The setup completes on lines 12–13, including the HTML_AJAX JavaScript library. The PHP script, `Server.php`, is identical to the one shown in Listing 9-1.

Listing 10-13

`Ajax.php` *Continued*

```
15  <script type="text/javascript">
16  var cities = {};
17
18  function updatePage(form) {
19      var queryString = HTML_AJAX.formEncode(form);
20
21      // check if the cities have changed (graph reload)
22      var els = form.elements;
23      for(var i = 0; i < els.length; i++) {
24          if (els[i].name == 'cities[]'
25          && cities[els[i].value] != els[i].checked) {
26              startLoad(document.getElementById('graph'));
27              document.getElementById('graph').src =
28                  'Graph.php?'+queryString;
29              updateCurrentCities();
30              break;
```

```
31              }
32          }
33
34          // when the AJAX request is done, we replace the
35          // current table with a new one
36          var callback = function(result) {
37              document.getElementById('table').innerHTML
38                = result;
39          }
40
41          // change the cursor to indicate loading
42          var options = {
43              Open: function() {
44                  document.body.style.cursor = 'progress';
45              },
46              Load: function() {
47                  document.body.style.cursor = 'default';
48                  new Effect.Highlight('table');
49              }
50          }
51
52          // make the ajax request
53          HTML_AJAX.grab('AjaxTable.php?'+queryString,
54              callback,options);
55
56          // update bookmarkable link
57          var blink = document.getElementById('blink');
58          if (blink.href.indexOf('?') > 0) {
59              blink.href = blink.href.substring(
60                  0,blink.href.indexOf('?'));
61          }
62          blink.href = blink.href+'?'+queryString;
63
64          return false;
65      }
66
67      // update the cities, marking which ones are checked
68      function updateCurrentCities() {
69          var els = document.getElementById('form').elements;
70          for(var i = 0; i < els.length; i++) {
71              if (els[i].name == 'cities[]') {
72                  cities[els[i].value] = els[i].checked;
73              }
74          }
75      }
76
77      // show the loading effect on the image
78      function startLoad(elem) {
79          if (!elem.loading) {
80              elem.loading = document.createElement('div');
81              elem.loading.className= 'loading';
```

```
82          elem.loading.innerHTML= 'Loading, please wait';
83          elem.loading.style.height =
84              elem.clientHeight+'px';
85          elem.parentNode.appendChild(element.loading);
86          elem.onload = function() {
87              new Effect.Fade(this.loading);
88          }
89      }
90      else {
91          new Effect.Appear(elem.loading);
92      }
93  }
94  </script>
```

Lines 15–94 contain the JavaScript needed for the viewer. Its different components have already been explained; they provide AJAX loading of page sections and various feedback effects. Line 16 defines the `cities` hash; it is used to see if the selected cities to view have changed. Lines 18–65 define the `updatePage` function; this function is called by the `onsubmit` handler on the form and takes that form as its parameter. Line 19 processes the form into a query string. Then, lines 21–32 check whether any of the cities have changed and reload the graph as needed. Lines 34–54 set up the AJAX call and then make the call to update the data table. In this area, lines 36–39 set up the callback, lines 41–50 define the feedback options, and lines 53–54 make the AJAX request using `HTML_AJAX.grab`. The `updatePage` function finishes by updating the bookmark link (lines 57–62). Lines 68–75 define the `updateCurrentCities` function, which populates the `cities` hash. The JavaScript section finishes with the `startLoad` function on lines 78–93, which handles creating and showing the graph-loading message.

Listing 10-14

`Ajax.php` *Continued*

```
95   <style type="text/css">
96   .loadable {
97       position: relative;
98   }
99   .loading {
100      position: absolute;
101      background-color: #eee;
102      text-align: center;
103      top: 0;
104      left: 0;
105      width: 100%;
106  }
```

```
107 #table {
108     float: left;
109 }
110 </style>
```

Lines 95–110 (Listing 10-14) contain some CSS rules that style the elements used in the loading effects. The .loadable rule on lines 96–98 is applied to the container outside the element that will be loaded; making its position relative allows it to be the parent element for the absolutely positioned loading DIV. Lines 99–106 contain the rules for the loading DIV; they position it absolutely to cover the entire graph and give it a gray background. The CSS rules finish up with a rule (lines 109–110) that floats the table to the left. This rule is needed to keep the highlight effect from bleeding out onto the rest of the page, and it is needed only because we're using floats on other parts of the page.

Listing 10-15

Ajax.php *Continued*

```
111 </head>
112 <body onload="updateCurrentCities()">
113 <div style="float:left; width: 610px;">
114
115 <div class="loadable">
116 <img src="Graph.php?<?php echo $graphOptions; ?>"
117     id="graph" width="600" height="400"
118     alt="sun rise and set">
119 </div>
120
121 <script type="text/javascript">
122 startLoad(document.getElementById('graph'));
123 </script>
124
125 <form action="<?php echo $action; ?>" id="form"
126     onsubmit="return updatePage(this)">
127 <fieldset>
128     <legend>Cities</legend>
129     <?php foreach($data->possibleCities()
130         as $city) { ?>
131     <label><?php echo $city; ?>
132         <input type="checkbox" name="cities[]"
133         value="<?php echo $city; ?>"
134         <?php if(in_array($city,$cities)) {
135             echo "CHECKED";
136         } ?>>
137     </label>
138
```

```
139      <?php } ?>
140 </fieldset>
141 <label>View Month:
142 <select name="month">
143 <?php foreach($months as $key => $m) { ?>
144     <option value="<?php echo $key;?>"
145     <?php if($key == $month) { echo 'SELECTED'; } ?>>
146         <?php echo $m; ?></option>
147 <?php } ?>
148 </select>
149 </label>
150 <input type="submit" value="Update View">
151 <a id="blink" href="<?php echo $action; ?>"
152     >Bookmarkable Link</a>
153 </form>
154 </div>
155
156 <div id="table">
157 <?php include 'AjaxTable.php'; ?>
158 </div>
159 </body>
160 </html>
```

Little has changed in the rest of the document when compared to the non-AJAX version. Line 112 contains an onload call to updateCurrentCities; this populates which cities are selected at the time of the page load. The graph output on lines 115–123 also has a number of changes from the standard version. The graph now has an ID so that its src value can be changed later, and its container div has the loadable class applied to it. Finishing up the graph code is a call to startLoad to pass in the graph; this provides a loading message on the initial page load.

Lines 125–153 contain the form code; the form contains several small changes. The form definition now contains an ID and an onsubmit property that calls pageUpdate (lines 125–126). It also has a bookmark link added to it (lines 151–152). On page load, this link is the same value as the form submit and is updated by the pageUpdate JavaScript function as AJAX requests are made. Finishing up the document, we include AjaxTable.php, which renders the data table.

10.5 Summary

In this chapter's use case, we looked at how you can use the subpage AJAX pattern to improve the performance of displaying data. This AJAX pattern breaks up large pages and lets you update one section of the page at a time. It can greatly improve the user experience by increasing the efficiency of the site and reducing the time users spend waiting for content to load. This pattern will be used over and over in your AJAX implementations, because it represents basic AJAX functionality, updating one part of a page without affecting the rest. The major points we can take from experience are as follows:

- Browsers handle slow-loading images poorly.

- JavaScript can be used to add nice image-loading effects.

- Sectioning pages can reduce overall loading times by allowing fast-loading content to be updated without affecting slow-loading content.

- Loading page sections with AJAX is a reusable pattern that is useful in many situations.

In the next use case, we will reuse much of what we learned here; however, instead of focusing on improving performance, we will look at how you use AJAX to add new features without a major application redesign.

Chapter 11

Adding an AJAX Login to a Blog

In this chapter

A common feature of many Web logs is the ability to leave comments. When these systems were first implemented, they allowed anyone to fill in a couple of fields and post a comment directly to the site. Today, however, most blogs have some sort of moderation system with which the blog owner can approve—or disapprove—comments. In an effort to streamline this process, many blogs also use logins. The problem with a login to a site like a blog is that it's not something you need to do until you go to post a comment. This makes a standard login process involving a couple of different redirects annoying, especially if you've already filled out a comment before attempting to log in. AJAX offers you the ability to streamline this process because you need to submit only the login form, not the entire page.

11.1 Why Logins Work Well with AJAX

A login is a type of application that fits into an AJAX paradigm well. Logins are forms that need to be submitted, but they generally take up only a small part of a page. On public sites, you might want to log in multiple times, generally in relation to another action that you've already performed, such as filling out a comment form. A login form also needs the ability to show login failure messages and make it easy for the user to type in his or her password again. To sum up, a Web site login is generally a few square inches on a Web site, and it's handy to have the login on every page of a site. Treating it as its own separate entity works well, and using AJAX so that only the login section submits when logging into the site makes for a much nicer user experience. AJAX-based logins are used by many of the Google sites. An example of Google's AJAX login is shown in Figure 11-1.

11.2 Building an AJAX Login

Building an AJAX login is a simple process if you're using an AJAX library that supports submitting a form using AJAX. If your library of choice doesn't do that, you have a bit of work to do, but it's only two fields, so grabbing their values by hand isn't too hard. Our first login implementation will use HTML_AJAX and its `formSubmit` method; this is the simplest AJAX login case, but it may not work in all cases due to its limited flexibility.

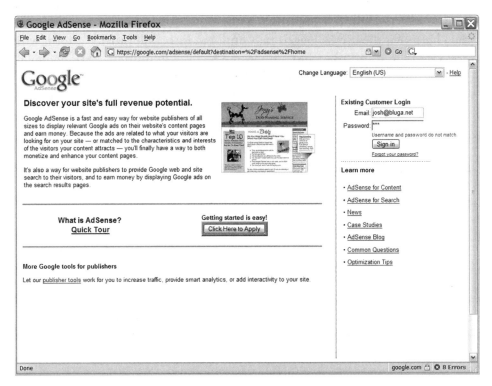

FIGURE 11-1
Google's AJAX login

Although it's possible to use other methods, the easiest way to create an AJAX login system is to use cookie-based logins. PHP has a system called sessions that makes this easy to do. Before outputting any content, run the `session_start()` function; if a session ID cookie exists, PHP uses this ID to load any data associated with this ID from where it is stored on the server. If the session ID cookie doesn't exist, PHP generates a random string that identifies this session and adds a header to send to the browser. Other server-side languages offer similar features, either built-in or through standard libraries. The important part of a session-based approach is that it stores only an ID in the browser cookie; all other data is stored on the server.

The AJAX login form works by updating information in the session to say that the user is logged in. Because the data is stored on the server, other pages don't need to be notified that a login has occurred. If the other pages submit any data, the server can check that the user is logged in. Our login form will provide a form with inputs for a username and password. When the form is submitted, PHP code will update the session storing the username for latter use. The PHP page will then generate a logout button, because redisplaying the form doesn't make sense. In review, the workflow of login form is shown in Figure 11-2.

1. Include a login form in a normal page.

2. Submit the form over AJAX.

3. The PHP script processes the login and updates the session.

4. The contents of the form are regenerated.

5. The JavaScript code uses `innerHTML` to replace the contents of the form with the new version.

To start this process, we need a Web page into which we want to log. This page needs to run `session_start()` before outputting content, and it needs to include the HTML_AJAX JavaScript libraries. Last, it needs to include the login form. A minimal sample page is shown in Listing 11-1.

Listing 11-1

`index.php`

```
1   <?php
2   session_start();
3   ?>
4   <html>
5   <head>
6   <title>Sample Page</title>
7   <script src="server.php?client=all"
8     type="text/javascript"></script>
9   </head>
10   <body>
11
12   <p>
13   This page might contain a blog post, or
14   any other content where a login
15   might be useful.
16   </p>
17
```

```
18   <div id="loginForm" style="
19     border: solid 1px black;
20     width:250px; padding: 2px">
21   <?php
22     include 'SimpleLogin.php';
23   ?>
24   </div>
25   </body>
26   </html>
```

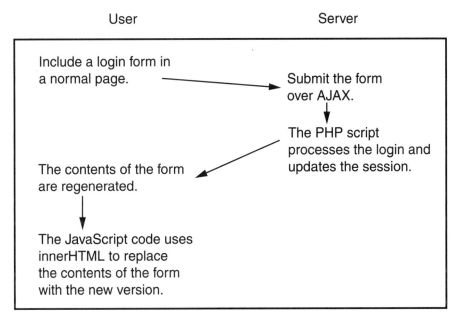

User   Server

Include a login form in
a normal page.   Submit the form
                                    over AJAX.

                                    The PHP script
                                    processes the login and
The contents of the form   updates the session.
are regenerated.

The JavaScript code uses
innerHTML to replace
the contents of the form
with the new version.

FIGURE 11-2
Workflow of the AJAX login process using HTML_AJAX

This sample page could hold any kind of content, but it must meet the require-ments for the embedded login form. Line 2 starts the session. Because this com-mand adds HTTP headers to the response, it needs to be done before any content is generated. Lines 7–8 include the HTML_AJAX JavaScript libraries; you always want to include JavaScript files in the head section of the HTML document because they will slow the display of any HTML that follows the `includes`. Lines 18–20 contain a wrapper DIV for the form. When the form is submitted, the `innerHTML` of this DIV will be replaced with updated content. Line 11 includes an external

PHP file that generates the login form. The basic form could be produced directly in this page, but having the form always generated by the same code helps in its maintenance. The rest of the page could be any HTML content; in this case, it's just a paragraph of text (lines 12–16). Finishing the basic login system is the SimpleLogin.php file (see Listing 11-2).

Listing 11-2

SimpleLogin.php

```
1   <?php
2   if (!session_id()) { session_start(); }
3   $message = "";
4   if (isset($_POST['ajaxLogin'])) {
5     // hard coded login, use the application's
6     // normal login code here
7     if ($_POST['username'] === 'jeichorn' &&
8       $_POST['password'] === 'test') {
9       $_SESSION['login'] = true;
10    }
11    else {
12      $_SESSION['login'] = false;
13      $message = "Login Failed";
14    }
15  }
16  if (isset($_POST['ajaxLogout'])) {
17    $_SESSION['login'] = false;
18    $message = "Logout Complete";
19  }
20  ?>
21  <form method="POST" action="SimpleLogin.php"
22  onsubmit=
23  "return !HTML_AJAX.formSubmit(this,'loginForm');">
24  <?php
25  echo "<p>$message</p>";
26
27  if (!isset($_SESSION['login'])
28    || $_SESSION['login'] == false) {
29  ?>
30
31  <b>Login</b><br>
32  <label>Username:
33    <input name="username">
34  </label><br>
35  <label>Password:
36    <input name="password" type="password">
37  </label><br>
```

```
38 <input type="hidden" name="ajaxLogin" value="1">
39 <input type="submit" value="Login">
40
41 <?php } else { ?>
42
43 Logged in as Test<br>
44 <input type="hidden" name="ajaxLogout" value="1">
45 <input type="submit" value="Logout">
46
47 <?php } ?>
48
49 </form>
```

The first 20 lines of SimpleLogin.php handle processing the form. This code logs the user in or out and creates a $message variable that can be used to tell the user that a login has failed. On line 4, the code checks whether the hidden variable ajaxLogin is set; if it is set, we perform a login. Line 2 starts a session if it hasn't already been; this allows this page to be included in another page or to work stand-alone. The actual login check is hard-coded to a username of jeichorn and a password of test (lines 7–10). If the login succeeds, we set a flag in the session (line 9). If the username or password does not match, we set the session login flag to false (line 12) and set $message to a failure message (line 13). Lines 16–19 contain code for handling logout. If the hidden field ajaxLogout exists, we set the session login flag to false and add a notification message to $message.

The rest of the page generates the login form or the logout form. The form tag is generated on lines 21–23. Its method is set to POST, and its action is set to this same page, SimpleLogin.php. When the form submission button is clicked, the onsubmit handler on the form (line 23) calls HTML_AJAX.formSubmit. The first parameter is the form to process; the value this, which means the current form, is used. The second parameter is the ID of the element to update with the results. Line 25 contains PHP code to output the message that was set up during the login processes. Lines 27–28 check to see which mode the form is in. If the login flag isn't set at all, or if it's set to false, then we produce a login form (lines 30–40). If the login flag is set to true, we produce a logout form (lines 42–46). The login forms are minimal—just a login and password field or a logout button. You can see what this basic form looks like in Figure 11-3.

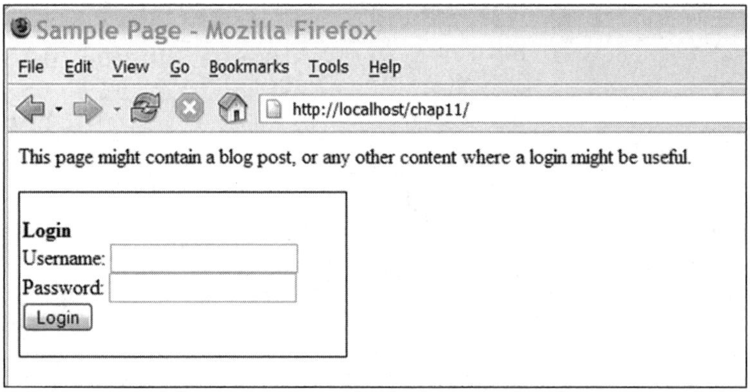

FIGURE 11-3
Basic login form

11.3 Extending the Login Form

With some basic formatting, we now have an AJAX login form that easily meets the needs of pages that need a login. However, in the case of a blog, you usually want to load some profile information into the current page as well. To do this, we need to make some data available to the rest of the site and update the login form. The Comment section of my blog is shown in Figure 11-4; you can see that we also want to load the user's name, email address, and Web site. On some sites, you might hide these fields after a login because the values from the user's profile will be used, but we will just update these fields directly, allowing the user to change the information for this post.

From a user interface standpoint, this form will be easy to extend. There is room to the right of the informational fields to add a login box. The login form will be submitted over AJAX, and instead of returning a logout form, it will return some JavaScript that will populate the fields with information from the user's profile. If the user is already logged in when he or she comes to this page, he or she will just get the prepopulation of his or her profile information. The user will not get a logout button, because logging out from this area of the user interface doesn't make a lot of sense. This approach can be accomplished in this fashion because our AJAX library is doing a lot of work for us.

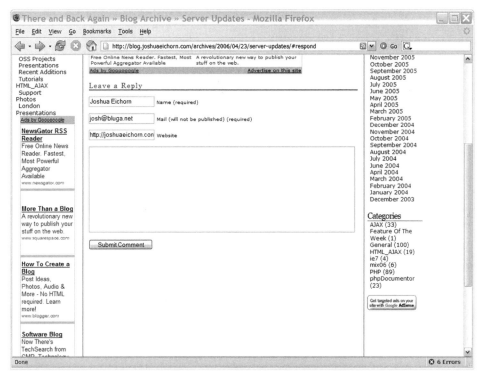

FIGURE 11-4
Comment form from my blog

When you add new content to a document using `innerHTML`, the JavaScript included in it isn't run; HTML_AJAX includes code to pull the JavaScript code out and evaluate it (returning to code). An updated comment form with a login added is shown in Figure 11-5. The code that builds this form is shown in Listing 11-3.

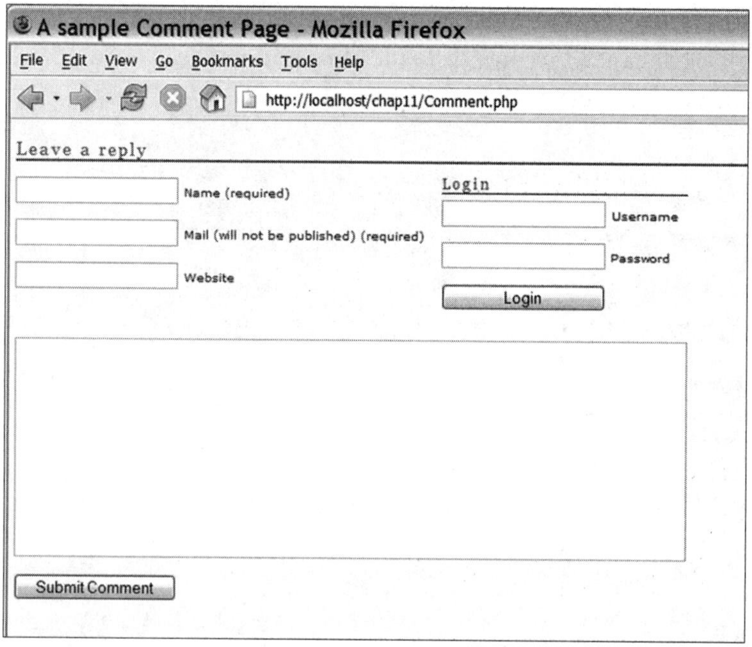

FIGURE 11-5
Sample comment form with a login

Listing 11-3

Comment.php

```php
1   <?php
2   session_start();
3   ?>
4   <html>
5   <head>
6   <title>A sample Comment Page</title>
7   <link rel="stylesheet" type="text/css"
8     href="Comment.css" />
9   <script src="server.php?client=all"
10    type="text/javascript"></script>
11  </head>
12  <body>
13  <h3>Leave a reply</h3>
14  <form action="Comment.php" method="post">
15
16  <div id="inputFields">
17  <p><input name="author" id="author"
```

```
18     size="22" type="text">
19   <label for="author"><small>Name
20     (required)</small></label></p>
21
22   <p><input name="email" id="email"
23     size="22" type="text">
24   <label for="email"><small>Mail (will not be
25     published) (required)</small></label></p>
26
27   <p><input name="url" id="url"
28     size="22" type="text">
29   <label for="url"><small>Web site
30     </small></label></p>
31   </div>
32   <br style="clear:both" />
33
34   <p><textarea name="comment" id="comment"
35     cols="100" rows="10"></textarea></p>
36
37   <p><input name="submit" id="submit"
38     value="Submit Comment" type="submit">
39   </p>
40
41   </form>
42   <div id="loginForm">
43   <?php include 'CommentLogin.php'; ?>
44   </div>
45   </body>
46   </html>
```

Comment.php is mainly a form (lines 14–41) for submitting a comment to a blog. In the example shown in Listing 11-3, submitting the form doesn't do anything, but the goal isn't to show how to submit comments. The goal is to show how a login form that loads profile data could be integrated with a comment system. To make this integration work, the page starts a session on line 2 and then pulls in the needed JavaScript library files on lines 9–10. A CSS file is also included. This file handles the formatting of the page and the positioning of the login form. Forms can't be nested, so if you want that visual effect, you'll need to accomplish it with a positioning effect. The login form is included on line 43; it sits inside a DIV with the ID of loginForm. This wrapper DIV helps in positioning the form and gives it an element to update with its results. The login code from Listing 11-2 was updated to work with this comment form, loading profile data when a login is complete; this code is shown in Listing 11-4.

Listing 11-4

CommentLogin.php

```php
1   <?php
2   if (!session_id()) {
3       session_start();
4   }
5   $message = "";
6
7   if (isset($_POST['ajaxLogin'])) {
8     // hard coded login, use the application's
9     // normal login code here
10     if ($_POST['username'] === 'jeichorn' &&
11        $_POST['password'] === 'test') {
12
13        $_SESSION['clogin'] = true;
14        $_SESSION['profile'] = array(
15        'name' => 'Joshua Eichorn',
16        'email'=> 'josh@bluga.net',
17        'url'  => 'http://blog.joshuaeichorn.com'
18        );
19     }
20     else {
21        $_SESSION['clogin'] = false;
22        $message = "Login Failed";
23     }
24     }
25     if (!isset($_SESSION['clogin'])
26     || $_SESSION['clogin'] == false) {
27  ?>
28  <form method="post" action="CommentLogin.php"
29  onsubmit=
30  "return !HTML_AJAX.formSubmit(this,'ajaxForm')">
31  <?php
32  echo "<p>$message</p>";
33  ?>
34
35  <h4>Login</h4>
36  <p>
37  <input name="username">
38  <label><small>Username</label>
39  </p>
40
41  <p>
42  <input name="password" type="password">
43  <label>Password</label>
44  </p>
45
46  <input type="hidden" name="ajaxLogin" value="1">
```

```
47 <p><input type="submit" value="Login"></p>
48
49 </form>
50 <?php
51 }
52 else {
53     require_once 'HTML/AJAX/Helper.php';
54     $h = new HTML_AJAX_Helper();
55     $var = 'var profile = '.
56         $h->jsonEncode($_SESSION['profile']);
57     $js = "
58     $var;
59     document.getElementById('author').value =
60         profile.name;
61     document.getElementById('email').value =
62         profile.email;
63     document.getElementById('url').value =
64         profile.url;
65     ";
66     echo $h->encloseInScript($js);
67 }
68 ?>
```

Like the login code in Listing 11-2, the first part of CommentLogin.php takes care of processing POSTs from the login form. On lines 2–4, we start a session if one hasn't already been started. Then on lines 7–24, we process the login. The information is again hard-coded to keep the example clear. If the username and password match jeichorn and test (lines 10–11), we set a flag in the session and add some profile information to the session. In some applications, this information could include other demographics and various application details, such as the user's ID or what permissions he or she has. If the login fails, the clogin flag is set to false, and a message is provided.

The form generated by CommentLogin.php has two modes: One is a normal login form (lines 28–49), whereas the other produces some JavaScript that updates the comment form. We check which mode we're in on lines 25–26, which show the login form when we're not logged in. Lines 35–47 produce the actual elements of the form, giving us username and password inputs as well as a submit button and a hidden field to let this page know we are trying to log in.

The logged-in mode of the form uses the HTML_AJAX_Helper class to help it produce some JavaScript. We include this class on line 53 and then create an instance of it on line 54. On lines 55–56, we use the helper's jsonEnode method to turn the session's profile data into a JSON string that can be directly used in the JavaScript we're writing. We then write the rest of the JavaScript, updating each field in the comment form, using the user's ID and the matching value from the profile. After that, we use another helper method to quickly add a script tag around this JavaScript. Because this login code is session driven, the logged-in mode will be used each time the parent Comment.php page is reloaded after a single login has happened. With this design, you need to close your browser to log out, but you normally put a Logout button somewhere else on the page where it would make sense.

11.4 Implementing the AJAX Comment Login System Using XML

The HTML_AJAX-powered implementation of an AJAX login form was easy to implement, but it is tightly tied to the HTML_AJAX library. You could implement it in a similar fashion with another library that has the same features, but you need to take a different approach if you're using a lighter weight library. Because the HTML_AJAX approach generates JavaScript on the fly, it can be especially hard to do if your language of choice doesn't have JSON support. XML is often a good alternative if you lack JSON support, because it's easier to create by hand and more mature; therefore, it has wider language support. Any of the communications patterns that were covered at the beginning of this book are a possibility, but you'll find the ones that use a more standard page-based approach will be easiest to integrate into existing sites. RPC-based approaches can also be useful, but they introduce a different style of interaction into your Web-based applications. Thus, you'll need to think about them from the start, if you're planning on using them.

To give a better idea of what an alternative implementation would look like, I've implemented the same comment updating system using Sarissa and XML. The back end is still written in PHP, but instead of generating HTML and JavaScript, it will now generate XML code that is used by client-side JavaScript. This will increase the amount of JavaScript you need to write, but it may well be worth it, especially if you're already using XML throughout your site.

In this example, we start with the back end script XMLCommentLogin.php, because the JavaScript code doesn't make sense until you see the XML with which it is working. All the XML messages are contained within the root node of login. When a login fails, an XML message like the one shown here can be returned:

```
<login>
      <result>fail</result>
      <message>Login Failed</message>
</login>
```

If a login was attempted, a message should always be provided. An alternate version of this response with no message nodes can be received on the initial page load. This alternate response happens when the login status is read from the session. The other case is, of course, the XML that is shown when a user is logged in. This response contains profile data; using XML for data like this is nice because it makes it easy to extend for future purposes. An example of the XML returned by a successful login is shown here:

```
<login>
      <result>success</result>
      <profile>
                  <value name="name">Joshua Eichorn</value>
                  <value name="email">josh@bluga.net</value>
                  <value name="url">http://blog.joshuaeichorn.com
                  </value>
      </profile>
</login>
```

In a successful case, a result message and profile data are returned. The value tags within the profile tag store the actual profile information. In this example, the name attribute matches the ID of the field we want to update, but in most cases, this mapping wouldn't work and you would have to add code to match the XML nodes and the field IDs. In the initial page load case, the same response as a successful login is used. The code that generates these messages is shown in Listing 11-5.

Listing 11-5

XMLCommentLogin.php

```
1   <?php
2   if (!session_id()) {
3        session_start();
4   }
5
6   function profileXML($profile) {
7        $xml = "<profile>";
8        foreach($profile as $key => $val) {
9             $xml .= "<value name='$key'>$val</value>";
10        }
11        $xml .= "</profile>";
12        return $xml;
13   }
```

```
14
15   if (isset($_GET['ajaxLogin'])) {
16       $xml = "<login>";
17       // hard-coded login, use the application's
18       // normal login code here
19       if ($_GET['username'] === 'jeichorn' &&
20           $_GET['password'] === 'test') {
21
22           $_SESSION['profile'] = array(
23               'name'  => 'Joshua Eichorn',
24               'email' => 'josh@bluga.net',
25               'url'   => 'http://blog.joshuaeichorn.com'
26           );
27           $xml .= "<result>success</result>";
28           $xml .= profileXML($_SESSION['profile']);
29
30           $_SESSION['xlogin'] = true;
31       }
32       else {
33           $xml .= "<result>fail</result>";
34           $xml .= "<message>Login Failed</message>";
35           $_SESSION['xlogin'] = false;
36       }
37       $xml .= "</login>";
38   }
39   else if (isset($_SESSION['xlogin'])
40       && $_SESSION['xlogin'] == true) {
41       $xml = '<login><result>true</result>'.
42           profileXML($_SESSION['profile'])
43           .'</login>';
44   }
45   else {
46       $xml = "<login><result>fail</result></login>";
47   }
48
49   if (!isset($inline)) {
50       header("Content-type: text/xml");
51   }
52   echo $xml;
53   ?>
```

Like the other login pages, Listing 11-5 is included directly in the main content page to produce the loading of default values. Unlike the other pages, it needs a specific flag set to know this is happening. It needs this flag because it sends a content-type header on line 50, and we want to do that only in the stand-alone case. The page starts by initializing the PHP session; like all the login examples, the actual status of the login is stored on the server. Just as in normal Web development, storing the login status on the client is a big security problem. Next (lines 6–13), we set up a helper function, profileXML, which loops over profile data and generates XML for it. It's in a helper function because we need to be able to access it in two places: once for a successful login (line 28), and once for the already logged-in case (line 42).

Lines 15–47 handle the actual login processing. We're using GET requests in this case because they are easier to accomplish with Sarissa, but this could cause some future problems. GET requests can be cached, unlike POST requests, which could make it hard to use this same code as a method to reload profile data. On line 15, we check whether we have a login attempt; if so, we start building our output xml string (line 16) and then do a login check (lines 19–20). If the login succeeds, we set the session flag (line 30) and load the user's profile into the session (lines 22–26). The successful login process is completed by outputting the needed XML. The successful login code first outputs a result tag (line 27) and then the profile data (line 28) by calling the profileXML helper function.

If the login fails, we output a result tag with a value of fail (line 33) and add a message tag whose value will be displayed on the login form (line 34). The failed login process is finished by setting the SESSION flag to false (line 35). Lines 39–47 contain the two default loading cases. If the user is logged in, we generate the profile XML (lines 41–43); if the user isn't logged in, we output the failure XML with no messages (line 46). The file finishes by outputting an XML Content-type header (line 50), which is needed because PHP generates HTML files by default, and then we display the xml (line 52). This example is used by a comment page, shown in Listing 11-6, which has been updated to use the Sarissa library to consume the XML.

Listing 11-6

XMLComment.php

```
1   <?php
2   session_start();
3   $inline = true;
4   ?>
5   <html>
6   <head>
7   <title>A sample Comment Page</title>
8   <link rel="stylesheet" type="text/css"
9     href="Comment.css" />
10  <script type="text/javascript"
11      src="sarissa/sarissa.js"></script>
12  <script type="text/javascript"
```

```
13          src="sarissa/sarissa_ieemu_xpath.js"></script>
14  <script type="text/javascript">
15  var loginData =
16     "<?php include 'XMLCommentLogin.php'; ?>";
17
18  function processForm(form) {
19      var remote = Sarissa.getDomDocument();
20      remote.onreadystatechange = function() {
21          if(remote.readyState == 4) {
22              var result =
23              remote.selectSingleNode('//result');
24
25          if (result.firstChild.nodeValue
26              == 'success') {
27              loadProfile(remote);
28              }
29              else {
30                  var message =
31                  remote.selectSingleNode('//message');
32                  var el =
33                  document.getElementById('message');
34                  el.innerHTML =
35                  message.firstChild.nodeValue;
36              }
37          }
38      }
39
40      var url = "XMLCommentLogin.php?ajaxLogin=1";
41      url += "&username="+
42          escape(form.elements.username.value);
43      url += "&password="+
44          escape(form.elements.password.value);
45
46      remote.load(url);
47
48      return false;
49  }
50
51  function loadInline() {
52      var parser = new DOMParser();
53      var loginXML = parser.parseFromString(
54          loginData, "text/xml");
55      loadProfile(loginXML);
56  }
57
58  function loadProfile(doc) {
59      var nodes = doc.selectNodes('//profile/value');
60      if (nodes.length > 0) {
61          document.getElementById('loginForm').style.display = 'none';
62      }
63      for(var i = 0; i < nodes.length; i++) {
```

```
64              var name = nodes[i].getAttribute('name');
65              document.getElementById(name).value =
66                  nodes[i].firstChild.nodeValue;
67      }
68  }
69
70  </script>
```

XMLComment.php provides the same comment form as the Comment.php example. Because it's using the Sarissa library, the code quickly diverges because it defines
several JavaScript functions to handle the XML. The page starts with some basic
PHP setup, starting the session (line 2) and setting $inline to true so that the
XML-generating page knows not to send Content-type headers. The page then
includes the same CSS (lines 8–9) and the Sarissa library (lines 10–11), including
its XPath support (lines 12–13). Then, we move into the JavaScript. The first item
we define is the loginData variable, which will contain the XML generated by
XMLCommentLogin.php. This variable allows us to load the profile data at page
load if the user is already logged in.

After that, we define a function that will handle submitting the login form (lines
18–49). It starts by getting a Sarissa DOM Document (line 19); it then sets up its
onreadystatechange handler (lines 20–38). When the page is loaded
(readyState == 4), this handler will use an XPath query to grab the result node
(lines 22–23) and then check to see whether its value is successful (lines 25–26). If
the value is success, the profile information will be loaded using the
loadProfile function. If the value isn't success, an XPath query will be used to
load the message node (lines 30–31), and then the content of this message will be
added to the paragraph element with an ID of message (lines 32–35).

Once the handler is set up, the URL to be used in the request is created (lines
40–44). Because we're making a GET request, the data is appended to the query
string. The values are read from the form using the elements.elementName syntax. Each value read from the form is escaped; this escaping makes sure that we
won't get a broken URL. Once we have a URL, we use the DOM document's load
method to make the request (line 46) and then return false (line 48) so that the
form won't do a normal submission. Lines 51–56 define the loadInline function;
this function is called at page load, and it uses a DOMParser to load the XML from
loginData and then calls loadProfile on it.

The JavaScript code finishes up by defining the loadProfile function; this
function takes a login result DOM document and loads the profile data into the

comment form. It does this by making an XPath query that loads all the value nodes into an array (line 59). If that query succeeds, it first hides the login form (line 61) and then loops over the array (lines 63–67), grabbing the name of the value from its name attribute, grabbing the HTML element with an ID that matches that name, and then setting that element's value to the value of the tag. If the names do not match, you can loop over the nodes, creating a hash with the name as the key, and then write out each update by hand.

Listing 11-7

XMLComment.php ***Continued***

```
71   </head>
72   <body onload="loadInline()">
73   <h3>Leave a reply</h3>
74   <form action="Comment.php" method="post">
75
76   <div id="inputFields">
77   <p><input name="author" id="name"
78     size="22" type="text">
79   <label for="author"><small>Name
80     (required)</small></label></p>
81
82   <p><input name="email" id="email"
83     size="22" type="text">
84   <label for="email"><small>Mail (will not be
85     published) (required)</small></label></p>
86
87   <p><input name="url" id="url"
88     size="22" type="text">
89   <label for="url"><small>Web site
90     </small></label></p>
91   </div>
92   <br style="clear:both" />
93
94   <p><textarea name="comment" id="comment"
95     cols="100" rows="10"></textarea></p>
96
97   <p><input name="submit" id="submit"
98     value="Submit Comment" type="submit">
99   </p>
100
101  </form>
102  <div id="loginForm">
103  <form onsubmit="return processForm(this)">
104  <h4>Login</h4>
105  <p id="message"></p>
106  <p>
107  <input name="username">
108  <label><small>Username</label>
```

```
109  </p>
110
111  <p>
112  <input name="password" type="password">
113  <label>Password</label>
114  </p>
115
116  <input type="hidden" name="ajaxLogin" value="1">
117  <p><input type="submit" value="Login"></p>
118  </form>
119  </div>
120  </body>
121  </html>
```

The rest of the page builds the user interface. It has a few changes from Comment.php. The big one is that the login form is defined directly on this page instead of being included. On line 72, we set an onload handler. This handler called loadInline loads any current profile data. After that, we have just the standard comment form until line 102, where we define the login form. The only difference in this form is that it is now calling the processForm function in its onsubmit handler. This event handler will start the AJAX submit process when the user clicks the Submit button. The data flow of the user filling out a comment, logging in, and then submitting his or her comment is shown in Figure 11-6; this data flow is identical in both the HTML_AJAX and Sarissa XML cases.

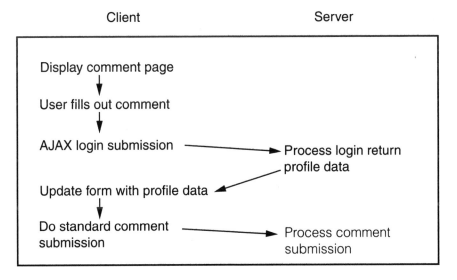

FIGURE 11-6
Workflow of the AJAX login process using Sarissa

11.5 Summary

In this chapter's use case, we focused on submitting forms over AJAX and then updating parts of the document using the returned information. You can implement this pattern in many different ways, but it's common to use a library's AJAX form submission features to do so. This form submission feature is especially powerful if the library supports adding JavaScript to the page along with HTML when doing the update. Be careful when deciding which parts of a page to upgrade with AJAX in this fashion; if you start making one form update many different parts of a page, you can make it hard for a user to see what is happening. Thus, this updating strategy actually works best for self-contained actions or for those that seem related. Even in related cases, you may want to add some visual effects, such as highlighting the changed elements, to make it clear that something has happened.

The page segmenting pattern can be especially useful in cases where you need to look up information while completing another form. This could be anything from selecting a billing address on a shopping cart to selecting a permissions group in a user editor. When designed correctly, you can often package these components in your server-side framework in such a way that they can be reused without your having to write any JavaScript for their subsequent uses. In the next chapter's use case, we look at some other reusable components and how standard ones can be combined to build a small application.

Chapter 12

Building a Trouble-Ticket System

In this chapter

When developing with AJAX, the first decision you need to make is how much you're going to rely on it. It's possible to use it as an optional HTML enhancement, as an integral part to specific features, or as the driver for an entire site. In this chapter's use case, we build a small trouble-ticket system using a design that is 100 percent AJAX powered. Moving to this extreme can be problematic on public sites, but it's a great choice for an internal application like this. Using this case, we can see the differences that having AJAX and JavaScript as the driving force of our development can make. We'll also see a number of techniques and design decisions that can be used in any application—no matter how you're using AJAX.

12.1 Trouble-Ticketing System

Many information technology groups use some kind of Web-based trouble-ticket system to support their users. These applications allow users to report problems; they also allow support personnel to respond and manage the issue's life cycle. In this use case, we'll be building a small-scale trouble ticketing system. This system works, but it doesn't have all the features you might need in a true production system. This sample application will be fully reliant on AJAX communications, setting it on the far right of the reliance scale.

The trouble-ticketing system has two main components:

- The first component is the back end, which handles database updates, queries, and authentication.

- The second is the JavaScript/HTML front end, which uses AJAX to talk to the back-end services infrastructure.

You may hear a design like this called a Service-Oriented Architecture (SOA), but besides helping us communicate with those familiar with the term, it doesn't help us along the learning process, so you can file away the buzzword for future use. This JavaScript front end will replace the control logic you would normally write on the server. If you're used to a model view controller (MVC) programming abstraction, you can think of moving the view and most of the controller code to the client. Not all of the controller code can be moved though, because the client is still an untrusted entity; in addition, authentication, data cleaning, and mapping service requests to a particular piece of code still have to happen on the server.

The overall design of the JavaScript system is one based on components. Each component contains some HTML code and some JavaScript code that powers it. In other scenarios, you might want to also include the CSS style information directly in the component, but in this case, the style rules were left at a global level. The components are designed so that their HTML is present on the page from its initial load, sitting inside a DIV container that has a display attribute of none. When one of the components is needed, its container is shown. This process reveals the HTML and allows the user to interact with it.

A similar component design can be used in an application that uses AJAX as an enhancement tool. If AJAX components are designed to provide generic user-interface components, they can be used in other projects, but you'll generally still want to make customized versions of them. These versions would do specific tasks, such as providing AJAX logins or searching for users. In this project, the components are application specific; this specificity helps lower their complexity and makes it easier to understand them. It also makes their development faster; many times, I find it useful to wait until after I have done two or three specific implementations of a component before I make a generalized one. This lets you learn about the problem space, and it makes it easier to build a truly reusable component instead of one that works only in cases that match its original use.

To understand the code of our trouble ticket system, we must first look at the tasks it must perform:

- Register new users
- Log in users
- Update user accounts
- Create tickets
- Update tickets
- Assign tickets to users
- Give users a way to see all their assigned tickets

A system that has this level of functionality provides a relatively basic trouble-ticket system, and it offers us more then enough functionality to understand the process of building a fully AJAX-powered application.

12.2 AJAX Reliance Scale

You can use AJAX such that it's 100 percent optional, and your application will be just fine with JavaScript turned off. This type of AJAX usage is usually accomplished by developing an application and then adding small amounts of JavaScript to enhance specific functions. JavaScript behaviors are a great technique to use in this approach. At the opposite end of the spectrum, you have a pure AJAX application; in a case like this, the back-end Web server provides only a set of services (such as creating users, listing tickets, and so on). The entire user interface and the logic that drives it are built in JavaScript. A Web application with AJAX enhancement follows the normal Web pattern; forms post like normal to the server and pages reload on a regular basis. An AJAX application breaks out of that mode: The site is loaded once, and from that point on, all interaction with the server is controlled by JavaScript, with requests being made as needed and the DOM being updated as well.

These two styles of AJAX development create two ends of a scale. Although both these approaches have their merits, most applications won't fit neatly into either of the categories. Instead, you'll have a mix somewhere in the middle; an enhanced application will add features such as user selection that work only with AJAX support, but other functions will submit like normal. You might also have a page with few normal reloads. It will not quite fit into the AJAX application structure because the majority of the logic rests on the back-end server.

One important item to remember is that although applications can exist all along the scale, you'll have a hard time moving an application from one end to the other. If your design is structured around server-side logic, you can easily make features that require AJAX optional again by providing non-AJAX versions of them. However, you might have a tough time getting rid of all the page reloads, because you'll find yourself having a large amount of duplicated client and server logic that will be hard to keep in sync. Making a completely AJAX-driven application not rely on AJAX communications will offer these same types of problems, because you'll have to duplicate large amounts of logic on the server to make the switch. If you're making a mixed application, you won't have this problem, because moving small features that cause normal refreshes to an AJAX request will be easy. An AJAX reliance scale with a number of AJAX applications placed on it is shown in Figure 12-1.

The trouble ticket system built in this chapter will rely on AJAX for server communication needs past the original page load. This puts the application at the far right of the scale, with applications like Mp3act, which is described in Chapter 4, "Adding AJAX to Your Web Development Process." Heavy reliance like this can make supporting old browsers extremely difficult, but old browser support isn't usually needed for internal applications, so this isn't an issue for the trouble-ticket system.

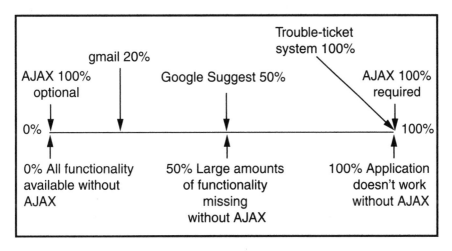

FIGURE 12-1
AJAX reliance scale

12.3 Creating the Back End

The first step to building our application is creating the back-end services that will perform all the database work. Think of the functions as a set of services that will be exposed to the client application. In some cases, these services might already exist and are offered to other applications using SOAP or some other Web services technology, but in most cases, you'll be creating them just for your AJAX application. Because the trouble-ticket application is offering only basic functionality, the back end in this case can be quite simple. In this case, it's grouped into a single class, but as the application grows, you may want to factor it into multiple classes to keep it manageable.

Because the focus of this use case is AJAX, we're not going to look at the back-end code in detail. The back end is implemented in PHP and uses a lightweight class to talk to a MySql database. The code is in `Ticket.class.php`, with the SQL to set up the database in `Ticket.sql`. If you want to run the example on your own server, you'll need to edit the first six lines of the `Ticket.class.php` file, updating its database connection settings. A nice aspect about a back end like this is that it can be easily implemented in any language that has a library to expose the services provided by the class using a JSON RPC mechanism or something similar. We'll be using HTML_AJAX to expose the class from PHP and will cover that in detail once we cover the API provided and the results to expect from each method.

All interactions with the back end are performed by using the API provided by the `Ticket` class. The methods perform actions against the database that has two tables. The basic definition of the Tickets and Users tables is shown in Figure 12-2.

Tickets	
Field	Type
ticket_id	int(11)
creator	int(11)
assigned	int(11)
title	varchar(255)
description	text
status	enum('new', 'open', 'assigned', 'fixed')
created_time	datetime
last_change	datetime

Users	
Field	Type
user_id	int(11)
username	varchar(100)
password	varchar(32)
email	varchar(255)

FIGURE 12-2
Database definition of Tickets and User Tables

The addUser method creates a new user; it takes three parameters: the new user-name to use, the password, and the email address. The method does basic validation requiring that none of the fields is empty; if any are, the method returns false. If a user is successfully added, the method returns true. The method's signature is

```
addUser($username,$password,$email)
```

The updateUser method updates information about the currently logged in user. If no user is logged in, the method returns false. If the update succeeds, an associative array containing the user's profile is returned. The method takes a single parameter, which is an associative array containing the fields to update. updateUser's signature is

```
updateUser($fields)
```

An example input is as follows:

```
$fields = array(
        'email' => 'new email',
        'password' => 'new password'
);
```

Although we store a user_id, username, password, and email address for each user, only emails and passwords can be updated; user_id is auto_created, and username can be set only when an account is created. An example profile array that would be returned by this method is as follows:

```
array
  'user_id' => '1'
  'username' => 'josh'
  'email' => 'josh@bluga.net'
  'loggedIn' => true
```

The listUsers method returns an array containing a list of all the users in the system. The key of the array is the user_id, and the value is the username. The array is ordered by the username. The listUsers method takes no parameters:

```
listUsers()
```

An example output is shown here:

```
array
  1 => 'josh'
```

The `addTicket` method adds a new trouble ticket to the system. It takes two parameters: the title of the ticket and a descriptive text field. The user must be logged in to submit a ticket; if the user isn't logged in, this method returns `false`. On successful creation of a ticket, the method returns the new `ticket_id`. `addTicket` has a signature of

```
addTicket($title,$description)
```

`getTicket` grabs an associative array with all the information about a ticket. This method can be used without logging in. The returned array contains two sub-arrays: the first subarray with a key of `users` contains the output from `listUsers`, whereas the second subarray with a key of `ticket` is the ticket information. The `getTicket` method's signature is

```
getTicket($ticketId)
```

Example output is shown here:

```
array
  'users' =>
    array
      1 => 'josh'
  'ticket' =>
    array
      'ticket_id' => '1'
      'creator' => 'josh'
      'assigned' => '1'
      'title' => 'Test Ticket'
      'description' => 'Test'
      'status' => 'new'
      'created_time' => '2006-02-26 12:38:32'
      'last_change' => '2006-02-26 12:38:32'
      'assigned_to' => 'josh'
```

The `updateTicket` method updates the fields of a ticket. It has a method signature of

```
updateTicket($ticketID,$fields)
```

The first parameter is the ID of the ticket to update, and the second is an associative array of the fields. All the ticket fields except for the `ticket_id` can be updated using this method. The `last_change` field is automatically set to the current time when this method is run. The user must be logged in to use this method; `false` is returned if the user isn't logged in. When the update is completed, an associative array containing the same output as `getFields` is returned. Ticket status can be updated with this method; possible status values are `new`, `assigned`, `open`, and `fixed`. An example input value for the attribute `$fields` is shown here:

```
$fields = array(
            'title' => 'New Title',
            'description' => 'New Description',
            'status' => 'open',
            'assigned' => 1
        );
```

The `assignTicket` method assigns a ticket to a specific user. It takes two parameters: a `$ticket_id` and a `$user_id`. The user must be logged in to use this method; if he or she is not, it returns `false`; after the ticket is successfully updated, output that matches `getTicket` is returned. If `$userId` is set to `false`, the ticket is unassigned. This method will also automatically update the status of the ticket; if the current status of the ticket is `new` and `$userId` isn't `false`, then the status will be changed to `assigned`. If the current status of the ticket is `assigned` and `$userId` equals `false`, then the status of the ticket will be changed to `open`. Note that `updateTicket` uses this method if its assigned field is set. The value of this field is passed in as `$userId`. `assignTicket`'s signature is

```
assignTicket($ticketId,$userId)
```

The `listUnassignedTickets` method lists all the tickets in the system that haven't been assigned to a user. The array is ordered by the `last_change` date of the tickets. The `listUnassignedTickets` signature is

```
listUnassignedTickets()
```

Example output is shown here:

```
array
  0 =>
    array
      'ticket_id' => '1'
      'creator' => 'josh'
      'assigned' => null
      'title' => 'Test Ticket'
      'description' => 'Test'
      'status' => 'new'
      'created_time' => '2006-02-26 12:43:39'
      'last_change' => '2006-02-26 12:43:39'
      'assigned_to' => 'Not Assigned'
```

The `listAssignedTickets` method returns a list of tickets that are assigned to the currently logged in user. If this method is called without the user being logged in, `false` is returned. The array is ordered by the `last_change` date of the tickets. The `listAssignedTickets` method has no parameters and has a signature of

```
listAssignedTickets()
```

Example output is shown here:

```
array
  0 =>
    array
      'ticket_id' => '1'
      'creator' => 'josh'
      'assigned' => '1'
      'title' => 'Test Ticket'
      'description' => 'Test'
      'status' => 'assigned'
      'created_time' => '2006-02-26 12:43:39'
      'last_change' => '2006-02-26 12:43:39'
      'assigned_to' => 'josh'
```

The `listUpdatedTickets` method provides a way to get updated information about tickets that are assigned to the currently logged in user and that have changed since the last time you checked with the back end. This method tries to return a minimal number of ticket records, but in cases where tickets have been unassigned, it sets a flag to note that the table displaying the data needs to be rebuilt and returns the full output of `listAssignedTickets`. When the rebuild flag is set, the ticket data is returned under a `tickets` index.

```
listUpdatedTickets($last_call_time, $current)
```

An example of output returned in normal mode and then in rebuild mode is shown in Listings 12-1 and 12-2. In normal mode, only new and changed tickets are sent to the client where the table displaying them is updated. In rebuild mode, all the tickets are sent to the client, where the entire table is rebuilt.

Listing 12-1

Normal `listUpdatedTickets` *Output*

```
array
  0 =>
    array
      'ticket_id' => '1'
      'creator' => 'josh'
```

```
'assigned' => '1'
'title' => 'Test Ticket'
'description' => 'Blah blah'
'status' => 'assigned'
'created_time' => '2006-02-26 13:21:11'
'last_change' => '2006-02-26 13:21:12'
'assigned_to' => 'josh'
```

Listing 12-2

Rebuild Mode `listUpdatedTickets` ***Output***

```
array
  'rebuild' => true
  'tickets' =>
    array
      0 =>
        array
          'ticket_id' => '2'
          'creator' => 'josh'
          'assigned' => '1'
          'title' => 'test ticket'
          'description' => 'blah blah'
          'status' => 'assigned'
          'created_time' => '2006-02-26 13:39:06'
          'last_change' => '2006-02-26 13:39:06'
          'assigned_to' => 'josh'
```

The `login` method logs a user into the system, storing this status in the user's session. It takes two parameters: the username and the password. If the login is unsuccessful, `false` is returned; if the login is successful, the user's profile information is returned. The method signature is

```
login($username,$password)
```

An example profile output is shown here:

```
array
  'user_id' => '1'
  'username' => 'josh'
  'email' => 'josh@bluga.net'
  'loggedIn' => true
```

The `isLoggedIn` method returns `true` if the user is logged in and `false` if the user isn't. This method isn't usually called by a JavaScript client but is instead used by other methods in the `Ticket` class. `isLoggedIn` has a signature of

```
isLoggedIn()
```

The `profile` method is used to get information about a user's profile. The method takes one optional parameter: `$field`. If `$field` is set, that value from the user's profile will be returned; otherwise, the entire profile will be returned. If the user isn't logged in when this method is called, `false` will be returned. The profile output is identical to the output of a successful login. The `profile` method has a signature of

```
profile($field = false)
```

The `logout` method logs the current user out of the system and destroys the user's current PHP session. This method always returns a value of `true`. `logout` has no parameters; its signature is

```
logout()
```

12.4 Exporting the Back End

Now that we've reviewed the functionality provided by the back-end `Ticket` class, let's look at what we need to do to export it to a JavaScript client. We have a number of options, including generating an XML file from the output of each `Ticket` method, creating chunks of HTML for each method, or having JSON encode the data. XML would work for an application like this, but there is no standard for describing PHP data structures in XML with which JavaScript automatically knows how to deal. An HTML chunk option is less than ideal because it would entail writing more PHP code and would limit flexibility. JSON is a great choice for an application such as this because code is available for PHP to encode its data structures into JSON, and JavaScript can directly evaluate the data it sends. In addition, JSON is a smaller encoding format than the other options, which helps keep our application running quickly. For these reasons, we will use JSON.

Now that we've decided that were going to use JSON, we need to figure out how we're going to make it accessible to the client. One option is to create a PHP page for each method; that page will look at the incoming POST data, transform it to PHP data types, call the method of the `Ticket` class, and then return its output formatted as JSON. An example of what this would look like for the `login` method is shown in Listing 12-3.

Listing 12-3

Login.php

```php
1  <?php
2  require_once 'HTML/AJAX/Serializer/JSON.php';
3  require_once 'Ticket.class.php';
4
5  $rawin = file_get_contents('php://input');
6
7  $serializer = new HTML_AJAX_Serializer_JSON();
8  $in = $serializer->unserialize($rawin);
9
10 $ticket = new Ticket();
11
12 $out = $ticket->login($in->username,$in->password);
13
14 echo $serializer->serialize($out);
15 ?>
```

Lines 2–3 include the classes needed for this page. We're using the JSON serializer code from HTML_AJAX, but any PHP JSON library would work. Line 5 reads the raw POST input, with lines 7 and 8 using the JSON Serializer class to decode it into a PHP object. On line 10, we create a new Ticket instance, calling the login method on line 12. We then send the output to the client on line 14, serializing it into the JSON format. An example HTML page that can be used to test this login page is shown in Listing 12-4.

Listing 12-4

Login.html

```html
1  <html>
2  <head>
3  <title>Login Tester</title>
4  <script type="text/javascript"
5  src="server.php?client=all"></script>
6  <script type="text/javascript">
7  var s = new HTML_AJAX_Serialize_JSON();
8  function callback(result) {
9    var profile = s.unserialize(result);
10   document.getElementById('target').innerHTML =
11     HTML_AJAX_Util.quickPrint(profile);
12 }
13 var options = {
14 args: s.serialize({username:'josh',password:'test2'})
15 };
16
17  function login() {
```

```
18    HTML_AJAX.grab('Login.php',callback,options);
19 }
20 </script>
21 </head>
22 <body>
23 <a href="javascript:login()">Run a test login</a>
24 <pre id="target">
25 </pre>
26 </body>
27 /html>
```

In Listing 12-4, we're again using the HTML_AJAX libraries to handle some of the AJAX grunt work. On lines 4–5, we include the HTML_AJAX JavaScript library. On lines 6–20, we define some functions to test making a JSON request to log in. On line 7, we create an instance of HTML_AJAX_Serialize_JSON; this instance will be used to transform JavaScript data to JSON strings and JSON strings back to JavaScript. Lines 8–12 define a callback function; this function will be called when our AJAX request is complete. It takes the resulting AJAX string and turns it into a profile object (line 9); it then uses a utility method to print its contents to a target element.

Lines 13–15 set up an options object, which contains a JSON string that will be posted to the PHP page. Lines 17–19 define the login function that makes the AJAX request. The request will be made to Login.php, calling the callback function when it's complete, and will pass in the serialized JSON string we set up in the options object. Line 23 provides us with a function to test it. When you run the login function, you will get output from the server that contains the user's profile, because that's what a successful login returns. An example is shown here:

```
user_id:1
username:josh
email:josh@bluga.net
loggedIn:true
```

This system works by sending the JSON-encoded string to the server; in this case, the string would be like so:

```
{"username":"josh","password":"test2"}
```

The server decodes that into a PHP object that looks like this:

```
object(stdClass)
  var 'username' => 'josh'
  var 'password' => 'test2'
```

The `login` method on the `Ticket` class is called; this method returns a profile array. This array is turned into a JSON string, which is sent back to the client. This JSON string looks like this:

```
{"user_id":"1","username":"josh","email":"josh@bluga.net","loggedIn":true}
```

This string is then decoded to a JavaScript object, where it can be used, or in the test case, where it is displayed in the target element.

We could follow this same pattern to create a PHP page for every `Ticket` method, but fortunately, we have a simpler option. HTML_AJAX provides code to automatically expose the `Ticket` class's methods in a similar fashion. On the PHP side, this functionality is provided through the HTML_AJAX_Server class. An example of exporting the `Ticket` class is shown in Listing 12-5.

Listing 12-5

`Server.php`

```
1   <?php
2   require_once 'HTML/AJAX/Server.php';
3   require_once 'Ticket.class.php';
4
5   $server = new HTML_AJAX_Server();
6   $server->registerClass(
7     new Ticket(),
8     'Ticket',
9     array(
10       'addUser',
11       'updateUser',
12       'listUsers',
13       'addTicket',
14       'updateTicket',
15       'getTicket',
16       'assignTicket',
17     'listUnassignedTickets',
18     'listAssignedTickets',
19     'listUpdatedTickets',
20       'login',
21       'isLoggedIn',
22       'currentUserId',
23       'logout'
24   )
25 );
26 $server->handleRequest();
27 ?>
```

This page is fairly simple. It creates a new HTML_AJAX_Server, registers the `Ticket` class with it, and then has the server handle requests to the page. Lines 2–3

include the required classes for the page. Line 5 creates the new
`HTML_AJAX_Server` instance. Lines 6–25 register the class. Line 7 is the instance
of the `Ticket` class, line 8 is the name to export it to JavaScript as, and lines 9–24
are an array of `Ticket` methods to export. These methods don't have to be specified; if they are not specified, PHP introspection is used to detect them, but if you're
running on PHP 4, PHP can't detect the case of the functions; this can be annoying when we look at the JavaScript side of the equation because all the methods will
be exported in lowercase—no matter what they look like in the PHP code.

On the JavaScript side, HTML_AJAX provides a stub class that has all the methods that were exported. When you call one of these methods, an AJAX call is made
against the server. When working with this setup, it's important to remember that
you don't have a PHP object being remotely controlled through JavaScript. Instead,
you have an automatic wrapping of a JavaScript method to an AJAX call. Each
method call takes an HTTP request, which means you have a new instance of the
PHP `Ticket` class for each response; this process is shown in Figure 12-3.

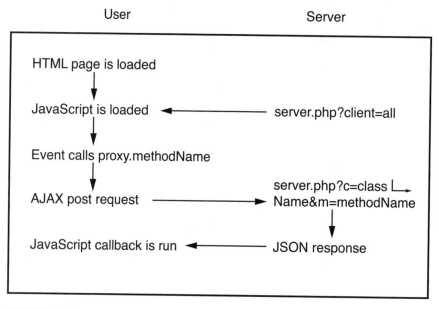

FIGURE 12-3
Data flow of multiple requests to PHP using HTML_AJAX's generated JavaScript proxy

To create this JavaScript class, you simply need to add another `include` to your HTML file. The syntax is `Server.php?stub=Name`. This includes the JavaScript class definition. When you create an instance of this class, you pass it in a single parameter, which is the callback object to use. Matching methods on this callback object will be used to handle the response of the AJAX request. For example, if you call `ticket.login`, the login method on the callback object will be called when the request is complete. An example of calling the `login` method using HTML_AJAX's auto class export is shown in Listing 12-6.

Listing 12-6

LoginStub.html

```
1   <html>
2   <head>
3   <title>Login Tester</title>
4   <script type="text/javascript"
5   src="server.php?client=all"></script>
6   <script type="text/javascript"
7   src="server.php?stub=Ticket"></script>
8   <script type="text/javascript">
9   var callback = {
10    login: function (result) {
11      document.getElementById('target').innerHTML
12      = HTML_AJAX_Util.quickPrint(result);
13    }
14  }
15
16  var ticket = new Ticket(callback);
17
18  function login() {
19    ticket.login('josh','test2');
20  }
21  </script>
22  </head>
23  <body>
24  <a href="javascript:login()">Run a test login</a>
24  <pre id="target">
25  </pre>
26  </body>
27  </html>
```

Using the stub class helps reduce the complexity of our JavaScript code because it makes the AJAX request look much like a normal AJAX call. JSON serializing and unserializing happens automatically, so you only deal with JavaScript data types. The big changes from Login.html are as follows: including the `Ticket` stub (lines 7–8), making the callback a hash (lines 9–14), and using a remote stub object to make the AJAX call (lines 16 and 19). The other item to note is that the code doesn't worry about any of the data serialization, letting us move to another format at any time without changing any application code.

12.5 Building the JavaScript Application

Now that the back end of the application is complete, we need to look at building the front end. This code needs to build the user interface, manage the application flow, and communicate with the back end. To help manage this process, we;ll be breaking the application into a number of different components. Each component is made up of an HTML file and a JavaScript file, and each component performs one action, such as logging a user into the site or adding a ticket. The various components will be tied together by some simple JavaScript code that controls the site.

The JavaScript controller is a simple design; it is based around the idea of showing and hiding DIV elements to enable a current section of the site. All the JavaScript and HTML code will be loading into the browser on the initial page load and then will use a function to pick which code to deal with. Each part of the application with which you can interact is called a *section*, and it could be made up of multiple components, if needed; note, however, that in this case, each section will contain just one.

The basic site setup is a PHP page that loads the application; this page includes `ticket.js`, which contains JavaScript shared throughout the entire site. It also includes all the HTML code for the various components and their associated JavaScript files. The components are used to build the various sections of the application, and only one is visible at a time. There is also a site sidebar that always shows the login component. This setup was used because some features, such as viewing a ticket, can be used without logging in, but other features, such as adding a new ticket, require the user to be logged in. The basic layout of the user interface can be seen in Figure 12-4.

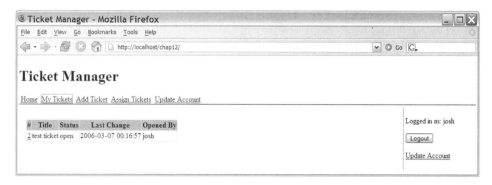

FIGURE 12-4
Basic ticket-manager interface

The look of the ticket application is controlled by the `Ticket.css` CSS file. There is no need to cover the CSS in detail because it doesn't do anything AJAX-specific. The one item to note is that it does specify default display types for a number of CSS classes; this allows us to have all of the various sections of the site hidden by default, so you don't see them until they have been selected. Now that you've seen what we're building, let's look at it in detail, starting with the page that pulls it all together (see Listing 12-7).

Listing 12-7

`index.php`

```
1   <?php
2   require_once 'HTML/AJAX/Helper.php';
3   require_once 'Ticket.class.php';
4
5   $app = new Ticket();
6   $ajax = new HTML_AJAX_Helper();
7   $ajax->stubs = array('Ticket');
8   $ajax->jsLibraries = array('All');
9
10  // Load time values
11  $isLoggedIn = $ajax->jsonEncode($app->isLoggedIn());
12  $profile = $ajax->jsonEncode($app->profile());
13  ?>
14  <html>
15  <head>
16  <title>Ticket Manager</title>
```

```
17   <?php echo $ajax->setupAJAX(); ?>
18   <script type="text/javascript"
19   src="scriptaculous/prototype.js"></script>
20   <script type="text/javascript"
21   src="scriptaculous/scriptaculous.js"></script>
22
23   <script type="text/javascript">
24   var app = {
25     isLoggedIn: <?php echo $isLoggedIn; ?>,
26     profile: <?php echo $profile; ?>,
27     setup: [],
28     logout: [],
29     templates: {},
30     since: false
31   }
32   HTML_AJAX.onError = function(e) {
33     alert(HTML_AJAX_Util.quickPrint(e));
34   }
35   </script>
36
37   <script type="text/javascript"
38   src="Ticket.js"></script>
39   <script type="text/javascript"
40   src="components/Login.js"></script>
41   <script type="text/javascript"
42   src="components/EditAccount.js"></script>
43   <script type="text/javascript"
44   src="components/MyTickets.js"></script>
45   <script type="text/javascript"
46   src="components/AddTicket.js"></script>
47   <script type="text/javascript"
48   src="components/TicketEditor.js"></script>
49   <script type="text/javascript"
50   src="components/Register.js"></script>
51   <script type="text/javascript"
52   src="components/Assign.js"></script>
53
54
55   <link rel="stylesheet" href="Ticket.css"
56     type="text/css">
57   </head>
58   <body onload="setup()">
59
60   <div id="header">
61   <h1>Ticket Manager</h1>
62   <div id="nav">
63   <span><a href="javascript:selectSection('front')"
64     >Home</a></span>
65
66   <span class="loggedIn"><a
67     href="javascript:selectSection('myTickets')"
```

```
68   >My Tickets</a></span>
69
70   <span class="loggedIn"><a
71     href="javascript:selectSection('addTicket')"
72     >Add Ticket</a></span>
73
74   <span class="loggedIn"><a
75     href="javascript:selectSection('assign')"
76     >Assign Tickets</a></span>
77   <span class="loggedIn"><a
78     href="javascript:selectSection('editAccount')"
79     >Update Account</a></span>
80   </div>
81   </div>
82
83   <div style="position: relative">
84
85   <div id="body">
86   <div id="front" class="section">
87   Welcome to the Ticket Manager. Log in to add
88   new tickets and view your own.
89
90   <form onsubmit="return viewTicketForm(this)">
91   <p id="frontMessage"></p>
92   <label>ID</label> <input name="id" size="4">
93   <input type="submit" value="View Ticket">
94   </form>
95   </div>
96   <?php include 'components/Register.php'; ?>
97   <?php include 'components/EditAccount.php'; ?>
98   <?php include 'components/MyTickets.php'; ?>
99   <?php include 'components/AddTicket.php'; ?>
100  <?php include 'components/Ticket.php'; ?>
101  <?php include 'components/Assign.php'; ?>
102  </div>
103
104  <div id="sidebar">
105  <?php include 'components/Login.php'; ?>
106  </div>
107
108  </div>
109
110  </body>
111  </html>
```

The first 57 lines of index.php do the JavaScript setup for the entire application. This includes setting up our interaction with the HTML_AJAX-powered back end and including the JavaScript for the various components. Each component has its own JavaScript file, which is great from a development point of view but could become a scalability problem over time due to the number of HTTP requests required to load them all. You could easily replace all the individual JavaScript `includes` with a request to a PHP script that combined the files automatically, if that ever became a problem.

Lines 2 and 3 require the PHP classes that will be used to build this page. One of these is the `HTML_AJAX_Helper` class (line 2), which we will be using to output some JSON-encoded strings and to quickly build the JavaScript `include` line for the HTML_AJAX libraries. The `Ticket` class (line 3) will be used to get the user's current login status. Outputting this information in `index.php` keeps us from having to do an AJAX call at page-load time to figure out if the user is already logged in. Line 5 creates an instance of the `Ticket` class, which will be used later, and lines 5–8 create an `HTML_AJAX_Helper` instance and then configure it. Setting its stub property to `Ticket` sets it to load the generated JavaScript stub class for the PHP `Ticket` class we registered in `Server.php`. Setting its jsLibraries to `All` gives us the entire set of HTML_AJAX JavaScript libraries; you could limit this to just the components you're using to reduce the amount of JavaScript code that is required, but most sites don't need that level of optimization. Lines 11 and 12 encode login status and the currently logged in user's profile as JSON strings so that we can use them later.

Line 14 starts the HTML output. The first task is to include the JavaScript libraries we're going to use. Line 17 uses the helper class to output the HTML_AJAX JavaScript `includes` and is followed by the `includes` for scriptaculous on lines 18–21. We will be using HTML_AJAX for communications and scriptaculous for visual effects and drag-and-drop support. The next step (lines 23–35) is to define the JavaScript `app` object; this object is used to hold data that will be reused throughout our JavaScript application. We could use a number of separate variables, but combining them into one object helps us keep track of variables that are safe to use throughout the application; included in this variable are the user's login status (line 25) and the user's profile data (line 26). We also set up a development error handler for HTML_AJAX requests (lines 34–36); you could leave this for production as well, but normally, you'll want to show users a less technical error message.

Lines 37–52 require the JavaScript files that are used throughout the site. The first is `Ticket.js` (see Listing 12-8), which contains the site's shared code, followed by the JavaScript for the various components. The order in which the components are required shouldn't matter because they don't have intercomponent dependencies. All the shared code is included in `Ticket.js`, with interactions of items such as login status handled through the application object or through CSS classes. The setup is completed by including the `Ticket.css` file, which gives the application its basic look and feel.

The rest of the file builds a basic user interface; this includes a navigation menu, a simple front page, and a sidebar. On line 58, we add an `onload` handler to the page, which calls a setup method that exists in the shared `Ticket.js` file. Next, the page defines the header DIV (lines 60–81). This DIV contains the application's name (line 61) and its navigation links (lines 62–80). The navigation links call the `setSection` function to change which section is selected, and they use a CSS class to mark which ones should be shown when the user is logged in. Any element on the page with a CSS class of `loggedIn` will be shown only when the user is logged in. The hiding and showing of these elements is handled in the login component.

Lines 85–102 define the main body of the application. Most of this is just including the HTML for the given modules, but the default view is created right on this page because it is so simple. It contains a form (lines 90–94) that calls the `viewTicketForm` function when submitted. This function is defined in the ticket component. The page finishes by defining a sidebar DIV (lines 104–106) that includes the login component. Having the login on the sidebar allows the user to log in or out at any time.

Listing 12-8

`Ticket.js`

```
1   // set up some function aliases
2   var byClass = HTML_AJAX_Util.getElementsByClassName;
3   var byId = function(id) {
4     return document.getElementById(id);
5   }
6   var d = function(item) {
7     alert(HTML_AJAX_Util.quickPrint(item));
8   }
9
10   function setup() {
11     for(var i = 0; i < app.setup.length; i++) {
12       app.setup[i]();
13     }
14     selectSection('front');
15   }
16
```

```
17  function selectSection(name) {
18
19    if (!app.isLoggedIn &&
20      (name != 'front' &&
21      name != 'ticket' &&
22      name != 'register')
23    ) {
24      name = 'front';
25    }
26
27    var s = byClass('section',byId('body'));
28    for(var i = 0; i < s.length; i++) {
29      if (s[i].id == name) {
30        s[i].style.display = 'block';
31        if (s[i].onDisplay) {
32          s[i].onDisplay();
33        }
34      }
35      else {
36        s[i].style.display = 'none';
37      }
38    }
39  }
40
41  function setMessage(element,message) {
42    element.innerHTML = message;
43    element.className = 'message';
44
45    element.style.display = 'block';
46
47    window.setTimeout(function() {
48      new Effect.Fade(element); },3000);
49  }
50
51
52  // Utility functions
53  function positionOver(element) {
54    var target = element.parentNode;
55    target.style.position = 'relative';
56    element.style.position = 'absolute';
57    element.style.top = 0;
58    element.style.left = 0;
59    element.style.width = '100%';
60    element.style.height = target.clientHeight+'px';
61  }
62
63  function buildTable(data,table) {
64    var tbody = byId(table).tBodies[0];
65    for(var i = tbody.rows.length-1; i >= 0; i--) {
66      tbody.deleteRow(i);
67    }
```

```
68
69    for(var i = 0; i < data.length; i++) {
70      var row = app.templates[table].cloneNode(true);
71      updateRow(row,data[i]);
72
73      byId(table).tBodies[0].appendChild(row);
74    }
75  }
76
77  function updateRow(row,rowData) {
78    row.ticket_id = rowData.ticket_id;
79    var tds = row.getElementsByTagName('td');
80    for(var r = 0; r < tds.length; r++) {
81      tds[r].innerHTML = tds[r].innerHTML.replace(
82      /{\$([a-zA-Z0-9_]+)}/g,
83      function(s,k) {
84        return rowData[k];
85      }
86      );
87    }
88  }
```

Ticket.js contains the JavaScript code that is shared throughout the application. At the start of the file, we define several utility functions that cut down on the amount of typing we have to do while writing the application. The first one, which appears on line 2, is byClass, which is an alias to an HTML_AJAX function that returns an array of elements that have the given CSS class. Lines 3–5 define the byId function, which is a wrapper for document.getElementById, and lines 6–8 define a quick debug function, which is useful during the development process.

Lines 10–15 define the setup function. This function is called by the document's load event and gives each module in the application a way to run some code at load time without first having to register an event handler. This is done by looping over the functions in the app.setup array (lines 11–13) and running them. Because the modules are included before the onload event runs, they can add functions to this array as they are included. The setup finishes by selecting the front section of the application.

The next item defined in Ticket.js is the selectSection function. This function acts as the main controller of the application, selecting which section will be shown. It takes a single parameter, which is the ID of the section to be shown. First, the function checks whether the user is logged in (lines 19–25). Only the front, ticket, and register sections can be used without logging in. By doing this check, we prevent errors from taking the user to a section that won't work. Next the function selects all the sections within the body; each section is marked with `section` class, so we use the `byClass` function to do this. Then we loop over the sections; if the ID matches the section we passed in (line 29), we show it (line 30) and run its `onDisplay` method if it exists. Otherwise, we hide the section (line 27). Running the `onDisplay` method gives the section a way to run code as the section is displayed. This gives it the opportunity to update data or clear out old data.

Lines 41–49 define the `setMessage` function. This is a simple function that allows us to give the user a `success` or `failure` message that will be shown for three seconds and then fade off the screen. The first parameter to the function is the DOM element to fade; the second parameter is the message to use. Depending on your design, you can always use a single message target so that the first parameter isn't needed, but in this case, the flexibility is needed, so the same code can be used for login messages. The fading out of the message is performed by the use of a scriptaculous effect (line 48), which is applied inside a `setTimeout` call; the delay on running the timeout function is in milliseconds, so the value of 3000 equals 3 seconds.

When combined with an alert color, such as yellow or red, notification messages that appear and then fade away after a short period can be very successful in AJAX applications. The disappearing message keeps the alerts timely, and it is needed so that the user can tell which action the message applied to, because a page reload won't be clearing it. The biggest downside of this approach is that the user can lose useful information if it disappears before he or she has read the message. One approach to get around this problem is to add a message history to the application. Instead of being removed completely, the message is added to the message history after three seconds. An example message is shown in Figure 12-5.

The `positionOver` function is used to position a passed-in element over its parent element. This is used when you want to cover an element, such as a form, with an opaque message while it is being AJAX processed. This is a useful loading technique because it will prevent the form from being clicked while you are processing the last request it sent. To use the function, follow these steps:

1.   Create a new element (usually a DIV).

2.   Style it.

3.   Add any messaging it should have.

4.   Append it to the element you want to hide.

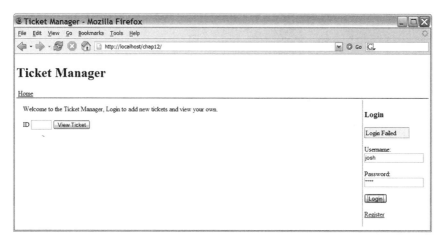

FIGURE 12-5
Message that will fade away after three seconds

Once the element has been added, you run `positionOver(element)`, and the element is positioned to hide all the elements to which it was added. You can show the parent by removing the element from the DOM or setting its display property to `none`. Scriptaculous effects, such as fade, are a good way to remove this element. The positioning elements of this function can be achieved using CSS on some browsers, but if you want it to work everywhere, size the element with CSS.

Another possible approach to preventing a form from being submitted while its results are loading is to disable its form submission button. This is often accompanied with changing the label on the button to a loading message. Both approaches provide good feedback to the users, but positioning a DIV over the form gives the developer the ability to display a larger loading message. Figure 12-6 shows an example of positioning an element over a form as a loading message; Figure 12-7 shows an example of disabling the form submission button.

The last two functions in `Ticket.js` work in concert to allow us to dynamically update tables using a template approach. The first function, `buildTable` (lines 63–75), takes an array of data and the ID of the table to update. It deletes all current rows from the table's body (if you put your headers in the `<thead>` tag, they will not be deleted) on lines 65–67. Then it loops over all the data (lines 69–74), creating a new row by cloning a template node and then runing `updateRow` using that row's data.

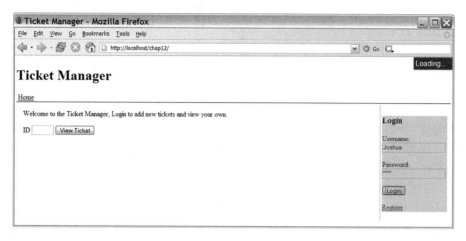

FIGURE 12-6
Providing form-loading status by using the `positionOver` function

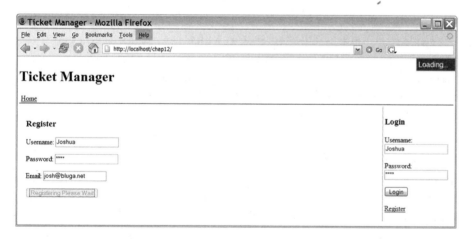

FIGURE 12-7
Providing form-loading status by disabling the form submission button

The `updateRow` function (lines 77–87) takes the data and applies it to the row using a regular expression replacement. The function starts by setting the `ticket_id` on the `tr` element (line 78). This is an application-specific assignment because not all data will contain a `ticket_id` in each row, but similar approaches are often used for other IDs (or even all the row's data) because it makes the data available to later JavaScript code. The actual replacement has to be done by updating the `innerHTML` property of each table cell (`td` tag), because even though the table row (`tr` tag) has an `innerHTML` property, updating it won't work properly. Thus, we get all the `td` tags in the row (line 79) and loop over them, running a replace against their `innerHTML`, with a callback function grabbing the correct data with which to use in the replacement. The regular expression (line 82) is designed to match against strings such as `{$variable_name}`. The name of the variable is passed into our replacement function (lines 82–85) and used to grab the correct index from the row of data. This allows us to create a template like this:

```
<tr><td>#{$ticket_id}</td><td>{$title}</td></tr>
```

This template is used to build each row of output. After replacing its tokens with data that has a matching `ticket_id` and `title` property, you will produce a table row like this:

```
<tr><td>#4</td><td>A Sample Ticket</td></tr>
```

This same replacement approach could be used against many other types of DOM elements; in fact, the most problematic elements for this approach are tables because they don't update properly when working with the `innerHTML` of their individual rows.

12.6 Login Component

The login component provides a login form and a logout form to the ticket manager application. This form is displayed on the sidebar and is always present. Besides providing the user interface in the sidebar, the login component provides hooks for other components to be login aware. This is done by hiding and showing elements that have specific CSS classes. Elements with the `loggedOut` class are shown only when the user is logged out, and elements with the `loggedIn` class are shown only when the user is logged in. The login user interface is shown in logged-out mode in Figure 12-8. It is shown in logged-in mode in Figure 12-9. The HTML that creates the login is shown in Listing 12-9.

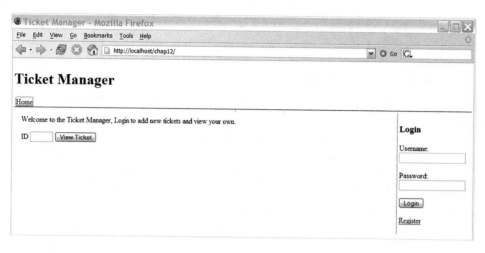

FIGURE 12-8
User is logged out; the login component shows a login form

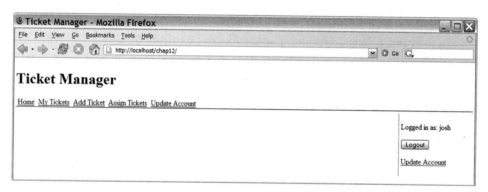

FIGURE 12-9
User is logged in; the login component shows a Logout button

Listing 12-9

`Login.php`

```
1  <div id="login">
2  <form onsubmit="return login(this)" class="loggedOut">
3    <h3>Login</h3>
4    <p id="loginMessage"></p>
5    <p><label>Username:
6    <input name="username">
7    </label></p>
```

```
8    <p><label>Password:
9    <input name="password" type="password">
10   </label></p>
11   <p><input type="submit" value="Login">
12   </p>
13
14   <a href="javascript:selectSection('register')"
15   >Register</a>
16 </form>
17 <form onsubmit="return logout(this)" class="loggedIn">
18   <p>Logged in as:
19   <span id="loginUsername">
20   <?php echo $app->profile('username'); ?>
21   </span>
22   </p>
23   <p>
24   <input type="submit" value="Logout">
25   </p>
26
27   <a href="javascript:selectSection('editAccount')"
28   >Update Account</a>
29 </form>
30 </div>
```

The login component is made up of two parts; the first, Login.php, provides the simple login user interface. The second, Login.js (shown in Listing 12-10), provides the JavaScript logic to power it. The entire interface is created at load time, with parts of it being shown or hidden as needed. There isn't a lot happening here; first the form for logging in is created (lines 2–16), and then the form for logging out (lines 17–29) is created. Both forms are processed through the addition of onsubmit handles; these handles will stop the normal form submission processes and instead perform an AJAX call. The login form contains a message target (line 4) that is used with the setMessage function (from Ticket.js) to display a login failure message. The login form also contains a link to the user registration form, which uses the selectSection function (line 14), whereas the logout form contains a link to the account editing form (line 27), which also uses selectSection.

Listing 12-10

Login.js

```
1  var loginSetup = function() {
2    // Enable logged in sections of components
3    var li = 'none';
4    var lo = 'block';
5    if (app.isLoggedIn) {
```

```
6      li = 'block';
7      lo = 'none';
8    }
9    var els = byClass('loggedIn');
10     for(var i = 0; i < els.length; i++) {
11       if (els[i].tagName == 'SPAN' && li == 'block') {
12         els[i].style.display = 'inline';
13       }
14       else {
15         els[i].style.display = li;
16       }
17     }
18     var els = byClass('loggedOut');
19     for(var i = 0; i < els.length; i++) {
20       if (els[i].tagName == 'SPAN' && li == 'block') {
21         els[i].style.display = 'inline';
22       }
23       else {
24         els[i].style.display = lo;
25       }
26     }
27   }
28   app.setup.push(loginSetup);
29
30   var callback = {
31     login: function(result) {
32       loginComplete(result);
33     },
34     logout: function(result) {
35       logoutComplete(result);
36     }
37   }
38   var rLogin = new Ticket(callback);
39
40  // login component js
41   function login(form) {
42     var username = form.elements.username.value;
43     var password = form.elements.password.value;
44
45     rLogin.login(username,password);
46
47     var div = document.createElement('div');
48     div.className = 'overlay';
49     form.appendChild(div);
50     Element.setOpacity(div,.3);
51     positionOver(div);
52     form.overlay = div;
53
54     return false;
55   }
56   function loginComplete(result) {
```

```
57    var els = byClass('loggedOut',byId('login'));
58    var form = els[0];
59    form.removeChild(form.overlay);
60
61    if (result) {
62      app.profile = result;
63      app.isLoggedIn = true;
64      byId('loginUsername').innerHTML =
65              app.profile.username;
66
67      loginSetup();
68      selectSection('mytickets');
69    }
70    else {
71      setMessage(byId('loginMessage'),'Login Failed');
72    }
73    new Effect.Highlight('login');
74 }
75
76  function logout() {
77    rLogin.logout();
78    return false;
79  }
80
81  function logoutComplete(result) {
82    app.isLoggedIn = false;
83    app.profile = {};
84    loginSetup();
85
86    for(var i = 0; i < app.logout.length; i++) {
87      app.logout[i]();
88    }
89
90    selectSection('front');
91    new Effect.Highlight('login');
92  }
```

The Login.js file provides the functionality behind the login component, processing the forms provided by the user interface and hiding and showing elements as needed. The first part of Login.js is the setup logic; this is composed of the loginSetup function, which will be run at page load, and the creation of a remote AJAX class for accessing the back end. The Setup function (lines 1–27) works by checking whether the user is logged in (line 5) and setting the appropriate style.display value for the logged in case (variable li, line 6) and the logged out case (variable lo, line 7). Once these are set, it's just a matter of using the byClass function to get a list of all the elements with the loggedIn class (line 9), looping over them (lines 10–17), and setting each element's style.display property.

During this process, we also check for span elements because they need to be given the display property of inline, instead of the display property of block. This process is then repeated for elements with the loggedOut class (lines 18–27), with the style properties being set to the opposite values. Once the setup function is defined, it is added to the app.setup array, which will run the loginSetup function on page load.

Next, the AJAX stub class is set up. This class is provided by HTML_AJAX and will call the matching callback function to the method that is called when an asynchronous request is completed. Thus, in the setup process, we define the callback functions (lines 30–37) for the methods that this component needs. To increase readability, these callback functions are kept simple and just call out to other functions that do the real work. An instance of the Ticket stub class is created on line 38; this instance will be used for all AJAX access in the component.

Next, we define the two login functions. First login() is defined; it processes the form and sends an AJAX request. Then, loginComplete() is defined; it takes the results from the AJAX call and updates the user interface. The login function starts by grabbing the username and password from the form (lines 42–43); it then makes an AJAX call (line 45), which performs the login on the server. The rest of the function adds loading notification; this is done by creating a semi-opaque div, which is added to the form and then positioned over it using the positionOver function defined in Ticket.js.

When the AJAX request is complete, loginComplete is run; the result is either false or an array containing the user's profile. The function removes the loading overlay (lines 57–59) and then checks the value of the result. If the result is an object containing the profile, app.profile and app.login are set (lines 62–63), the logout form has the user's username added to it (lines 64–65), and the loginSetup function is called (line 67). The loginSetup function will show all the elements that have a loggedIn class, hiding those with the loggedOut class. The successful login is completed by showing the mytickets section of the application. If the login is unsuccessful, the only action that is taken is the showing of a Login Failed message with the setMessage function. In either case, a scriptaculous highlight effect is used to show that loading has completed and that the login component on the screen has updated its contents.

The last part of Login.js contains the logout() function and its callback function, which is logoutComplete(). The logout process is simpler than the login process because it can't fail. The logout function (lines 76–79) simply calls the `rLogin.logout` method, making the AJAX request. It then returns `false`, canceling the normal form submission. `LogoutComplete` (lines 81–92) is called when the logout is complete on the server; it clears the user's profile, marks the user as logged out, and then calls the `loginSetup` function to show and hide any login-driven visual elements. Next the function calls all the registered logout functions. These work much like setup functions and give the other modules a chance to run code once a logout is complete; usually this code clears data that should be accessible only when the user is logged in. The function finishes by changing the current section to the front page and highlighting the login form to show that it has been changed to a login form.

12.7 User-Registration Component

The user-registration component provides a way for people to register themselves as users of the ticket manager application. It's a simple component, providing a form and the code needed to process that form using AJAX. An example of the form is shown in Figure 12-10, with the HTML that builds the UI shown in Listing 12-11.

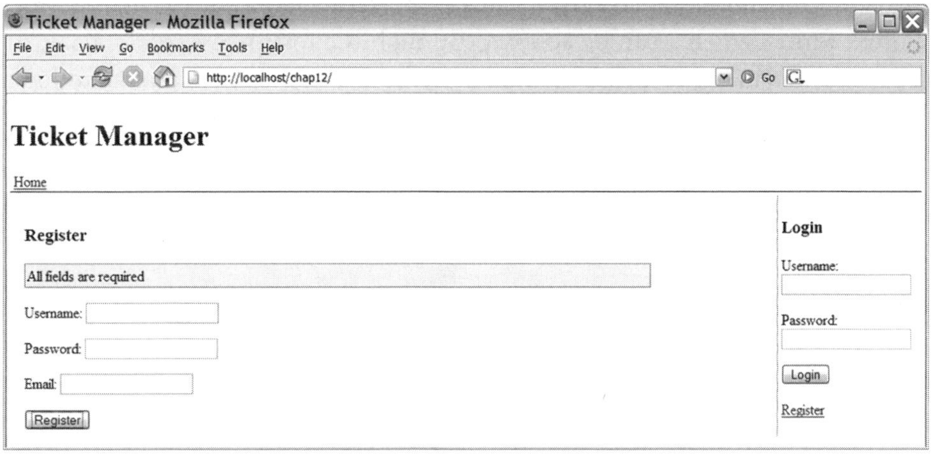

FIGURE 12-10
User registration form

Listing 12-11

Register.php

```
1   <div id="register" class="section">
2   <form onsubmit="return register(this)"
3   id="registerForm">
4     <h3>Register</h3>
5     <p class="message"></p>
6     <p><label>Username:
7     <input name="username">
8     </label></p>
9     <p><label>Password:
10    <input name="password" type="password">
11    </label></p>
12    <p><label>Email:
13    <input name="email">
14    </label></p>
15
16    <p><input name="submit" type="submit"
17      value="Register">
18    </p>
19  </form>
20  </div>
```

Register.php provides the basic form. It calls the register function when submitted (line 2) and has an ID so that it can be easily accessed from JavaScript. All the other form elements can be accessed through the form's elements array, so they need only a name attribute. This access method allows form elements to look just like non-AJAX forms. The form also contains a message target (line 4), which is used to display validation messages. The HTML is powered by the JavaScript added by register.js, which is shown in Listing 12-12.

Listing 12-12

Register.js

```
1   var callback = {
2     addUser: function(result) {
3       registerComplete(result);
4     }
5   }
6   var rReg = new Ticket(callback);
7
8   function register(form) {
9     var u = form.elements.username.value;
10    var p = form.elements.password.value;
11    var e = form.elements.email.value;
12
```

```
13    if (u == '' || p == '' || e == '') {
14      setMessage(byClass('message',form)[0],
15        'All fields are required');
16      new Effect.Highlight(form);
17      return false;
18    }
19
20    rReg.addUser(u,p,e);
21    var els = byClass('loggedOut',byId('login'));
22    els[0].elements.username.value = u;
23    els[0].elements.password.value = p;
24
25    form.elements.submit.value =
26      'Registering Please Wait';
27    form.elements.submit.disabled = true;
28    return false;
29  }
30
31  function registerComplete(result) {
32    selectSection('front');
33    new Effect.Highlight('login');
34    var form = byId('registerForm');
35    form.elements.submit.value = 'Register';
36    form.elements.submit.disabled = false;
37  }
```

The register component doesn't need a `setup` function, so it starts by setting up its AJAX instance (line 6). It defines a single callback, `addUser` (lines 2–4), which calls the `registerComplete` function. Next we define the register function (lines 8–29), which is called when the registration form is submitted. The function grabs the values of the fields it will be submitting (lines 9–11) and then does some basic validation. If the validation fails, we use the `setMessage` function (lines 14–15) to display a warning to the user and stop the form submission by returning `false`. Remember that validation is also enforced on the server, so we're not using this code to protect our back end, just to provide a good user experience. If the validation succeeds, we make an AJAX call to `addUser`, passing in the username, password, and email address (line 20). This call is followed by code that prepopulates the login form with the new username and password (lines 22–23). The next step is to display the loading status, which is done by disabling the submission button of the registration form (lines 25–27).

When the server has returned a response, the `registerComplete` function (lines 31–37) is run by the callback function. This function selects the front page of the application (line 34), highlights the login form (line 33) to show the user that he or she should log in, and then re-enables the registration form (lines 35–36) in case we want to register another user.

12.8 Account-Editing Component

The account-editing component provides a similar form to the registration component, allowing the currently logged in user a way to update his or her password and email address. This page is quite simple and looks just like the registration screen, except that the username input box is disabled because the back end doesn't allow usernames to be changed. An example of the account-editing screen is shown in Figure 12-11; the HTML that generates it is shown in Listing 12-13.

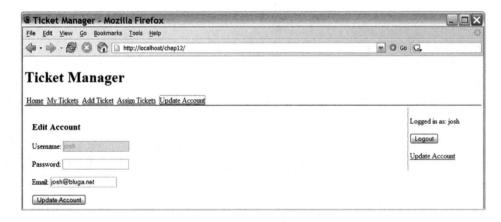

FIGURE 12-11
Account-editing component

Listing 12-13

EditAccount.php

```
1   <div id="editAccount" class="section">
2
3   <form onsubmit="return updateAccount(this)"
4       id="accountForm">
5       <h3>Edit Account</h3>
6       <p class="message"></p>
7       <p><label>Username:
8       <input name="username" disabled="true">
9       </label></p>
10      <p><label>Password:
```

```
11    <input name="password" type="password">
12    </label></p>
13    <p><label>Email:
14    <input name="email">
15    </label></p>
16
17    <p><input name="submit" type="submit"
18    value="Update Account"></p>
19    </form>
20    </div>
```

The HTML for the account-editing component is nice and simple. It creates a form that calls the updateAccount function on submit (line 3). It contains the same fields as the registration form, except that its username field is disabled (line 8). The matching JavaScript for editAccount.js is shown in Listing 12-14.

Listing 12-14

EditAccount.js

```
1  app.setup.push(function() {
2  byId('editAccount').onDisplay = function() {
3    var form = byId('accountForm');
4
5    for(var i = 0; i < form.elements.length; i++) {
6      var n = form.elements[i].name;
7      if (app.profile[n]) {
8        form.elements[i].value =
9          app.profile[n];
10      }
11    }
12  }
13
14  });
15
16 var accountCallback = {
17   updateUser: function(result) {
18     updateAccountComplete(result);
19   }
20 }
21 var rAccount = new Ticket(accountCallback);
22
23 function updateAccount(form) {
24   var update = {
25     password: form.elements.password.value,
26     email: form.elements.email.value
27   }
28   form.elements.submit.value = "Updating please wait..";
29   form.elements.submit.disabled = true;
```

```
30    rAccount.updateUser(update);
31    return false;
32 }
33
34 function updateAccountComplete(result) {
35   app.profile = result;
36   setMessage(byClass('message',
37     byId('editAccount'))[0],'Account Updated');
38   var form = byId('accountForm');
39   form.elements.submit.value = "Update Account";
40   form.elements.submit.disabled = false;
41 }
```

EditAccount.js starts by defining setup and onDisplay functions (lines 1–14). The setup function is used only to register the onDisplay function (lines 2–12). The onDisplay function takes the account form (line 3) and loops over its elements (lines 5–11), setting the value of each field that has a name matching the name of a property in the user's profile. This will populate the account form with the user's account information when the account editor is selected.

On lines 16–21, the AJAX class is set up. This component uses only the updateUser function, so it's the only one with a callback. The response to this method is sent to the updateAccountComplate function. The updateAccount function on lines 23–32 takes the account form and performs an AJAX submission of it. This is done by creating an object containing the form's values (lines 24–27) and then sending it to the server on line 30. The function also contains some basic user feedback; the Submit button's value is changed to a loading message and disabled (lines 28–29). Wrapping up the file is the updateAccountComplete function (lines 34–41), which takes the results from the server, updates the user's profile with them (line 35), and then turns off the loading messages set by the updateAccount function (lines 38–40).

12.9 Ticket-Creation Component

The ticket-creation component provides a form that is used to add a new ticket to the application. The user must be logged in to use this component. The ticket-creation process is kept simple because the form requires only a title and a description; the rest of the information will be pulled in from the user's profile or set later during the editing process. An example of the ticket-creation form is shown in Figure 12-12; the HTML is shown in Listing 12-15.

Listing 12-15

AddTicket.php

```
1   <div id="addTicket" class="section">
2
3   <form id="atForm" onsubmit="return addTicket(this);">
4     <p><label>Title</label><br>
5     <input name="title">
6     </p>
7
8     <p><label>Description</label><br>
9     <textarea name="description" rows=6></textarea>
10    </p>
11
12    <p><input type="submit" value="Add Ticket"></p>
13  </form>
14  </div>
```

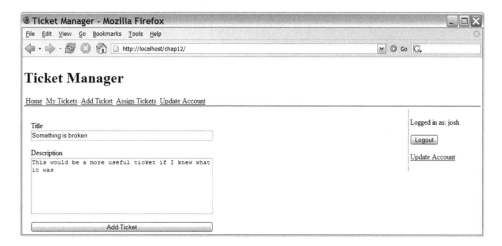

FIGURE 12-12
Ticket-creation form

AddTicket.php contains a simple form. When the form is submitted, the addTicket function is called. This function is shown in Listing 12-16.

Listing 12-16

AddTicket.js

```
1   var atCallback = {
2     addTicket: function(result) {
3       addTicketComplete(result);
4     }
5   };
6   var rAddTicket = new Ticket(atCallback);
7
8   function addTicket(form) {
9     var title = form.elements.title.value;
10    var description = form.elements.description.value;
11    rAddTicket.addTicket(title,description);
12
13    form.submit.value = "Adding ticket please wait ...";
14    form.submit.disabled = true;
15
16    return false;
17  }
18
19  function addTicketComplete(result) {
20    var form = byId('atForm');
21    form.submit.value = "Add Ticket";
22    form.submit.disabled = false;
23    form.title.value = '';
24    form.description.value = '';
25    viewTicket(result);
26  }
```

The HTML that drives the JavaScript for adding a ticket is quite simple. On lines 1–6, we set up the AJAX class; it contains a callback for the `addTicket` method, which calls `addTicketComplete`. The `addTicket` method (lines 8–17) processes the form, the values are pulled from its elements array (lines 9–10), and the values are sent to the server by using the AJAX stub class's `addTicket` method (line 11). The function finishes by adding a loading message to the form's submission button (lines 13–14). The `addTicketComplete` function (lines 19–26) removes the loading indication set by `addTicket`, clears out the form, and then runs the `viewTicket` method, which is defined in the ticket-editor component.

12.10 Ticket-Editor Component

The ticket-editor component provides a form that is used to edit tickets. It allows you to update the ticket's title and description, assign it to a user, and change its status. It also shows some details, including who opened the ticket and when it was last changed. The ticket-editing interface is created by `TicketEditor.php` (see Listing 12-17) and is shown in Figure 12-13.

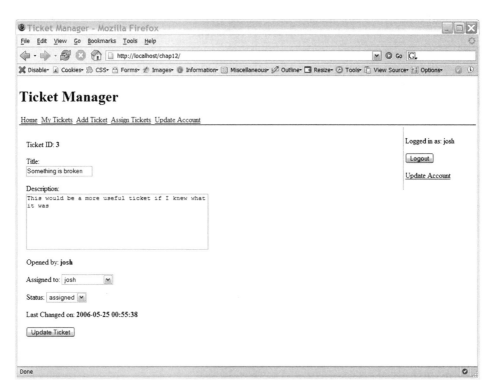

FIGURE 12-13
Ticket editor

Listing 12-17

`TicketEditor.php`

```
1   <div id="ticket" class="section">
2   <form id="tForm" onsubmit="return updateTicket(this)">
3     <p id="ticketMessage" class="message"></p>
4
5     <p><label>Ticket ID:</label>
6     <b><span id="ticketId"></span></b>
7     </p>
8
```

```
9     <p><label>Title:</label><br>
10    <input name="title">
11    </p>
12
13    <p><label>Description:</label><br>
14    <textarea name="description" rows=6></textarea>
15    </p>
16
17    <p><label>Opened by:</label>
18    <b><span id="openedBy"></span></b>
19    </p>
20
21    <p><label>Assigned to:</label>
22    <select name="assigned">
23      <option>Not Assigned</option>
24    </select>
25    </p>
26
27    <p><label>Status:</label>
28    <select name="status">
29      <option>new</option>
30      <option>assigned</option>
31      <option>open</option>
32      <option>fixed</option>
33    </select>
34    </p>
35
36    <p><label>Last Changed on:</label>
37    <b><span id="lastChanged"></span></b>
38    </p>
39
40    <p><input name="submit" type="submit"
41      value="Update Ticket"></p>
42    <input type="hidden" name="ticket_id" value="">
43  </form>
44  </div>
```

The ticket editor contains a larger form than the other components in the application, but from an HTML standpoint, it is not any more complex. When the form is submitted, it will run the updateTicket function (line 2), which performs the AJAX submission. The form contains a message target, which will be used to give the user feedback (line 3). The form also contains a number of spans, which will have their innerHTML updated to show static information (lines 6 and 37). The other new element of the form is the addition of a select element that will be dynamically updated with the users in the system (lines 22–24). The matching JavaScript is shown in Listing 12-18.

Listing 12-18

TicketEditor.js

```
1   var tCallback = {
2     getTicket: function(result) {
3       updateTicketForm(result);
4     },
5     updateTicket: function(result) {
6       updateTicketForm(result);
7       setMessage(byId('ticketMessage'),
8         'Ticket Updated');
9       new Effect.Highlight('tForm');
10    }
11  }
12
13  var rTicket = new Ticket(tCallback);
14
15  function viewTicket(id) {
16    selectSection('ticket');
17    rTicket.getTicket(id);
18  }
19
20  function viewTicketForm(form) {
21    viewTicket(form.elements.id.value);
22    return false;
23  }
24
25  function updateTicket(form) {
26    var fields = {};
27    fields.title = form.elements.title.value;
28    fields.description = form.elements.description.value;
29
30    var a = form.elements.assigned;
31    if (a.selectedIndex > 0) {
32      fields.assigned =
33        a.value;
34    }
35    else {
36      fields.assigned = false;
37    }
38
39    var s = form.elements.status;
40    fields.status = s.options.value;
41
42    rTicket.updateTicket(form.elements.ticket_id.value,
43      fields);
44
45    return false;
46  }
47
```

```
48 function updateTicketForm(values) {
49   if (!values) {
50    setMessage(byId('frontMessage'),
51       "Ticket doesn't exists");
52     selectSection('front');
53     return;
54   }
55
56   var t = values.ticket;
57   var form = byId('tForm');
58   form.elements.title.value = t.title;
59   form.elements.description.value = t.description;
60   form.elements.ticket_id.value = t.ticket_id;
61
62   byId('lastChanged').innerHTML = t.last_change;
63   byId('openedBy').innerHTML = t.creator;
64   byId('ticketId').innerHTML = t.ticket_id;
65
66   var status = form.elements.status;
67   for(var i = 0; i < status.options.length; i++) {
68     if (status.options[i].text == t.status) {
69       status.selectedIndex = i;
70       break;
71     }
72 }
73
74   // remove current user options
75  var a = form.elements.assigned;
76
77   for(var i = 1; i < a.options.length; i++) {
78     a.remove(i);
79 }
80
81   // add users
82   var u = values.users;
83   for(var i in u) {
84     var o = new Option(u[i],i);
85     a.options[a.options.length] = o;
86 }
87
88   // select user
89   if (t.assigned) {
90     for(var i = 0; i < a.options.length; i++) {
91       if (a.options[i].value
92         == t.assigned) {
93         a.selectedIndex = i;
94         break;
95       }
96     }
```

```
97   }
98   else {
99     a.selectedIndex = 0;
100 }
101
102  if (!app.isLoggedIn) {
103    form.submit.value = "Login to Update";
104    form.submit.disabled = true;
105  }
106  else {
107    form.submit.value = "Update Ticket";
108    form.submit.disabled = false;
109  }
110 }
```

This component doesn't require setup methods, but it does have to set up its AJAX class (line 12). We will be using two of the server's methods—getTicket and updateTicket—so callback functions are added for each. The getTicket callback calls the updateTicketForm method when it is called, and the updateTicket method calls that same method. We will also be providing a user feedback message and highlighting the form (lines 7–9).

Lines 20–23 define the viewTicket method; this is used by other parts of the application, such as the add ticket component, to select a ticket to view. This method sets the current section to ticket and does an AJAX call to getTicket. The viewTicketForm method (lines 20–23) calls viewTicket, getting the value of ticket_id from the form that is passed in.

The updateTicket function (lines 25–46) processes a submission of the ticket form. It builds an object that contains the fields to update and then makes an AJAX call to updateTicket (line 42) with that list. The fields object is defined on line 26, and then the easy fields (title and description) are added to it. Next the assigned value is processed (lines 30–37); assigned is set using a select box, and its first option needs a special value. We support this value mapping by checking the select box's selected index (line 31), and if the first option is not selected, using its value. Otherwise, the mapping code uses the value of false. Setting the assigned property to false lets the back end know that the ticket is unassigned and allows it to clean up the database accordingly. Finishing the process, the status property is added to the fields object (line 40), and the AJAX update is performed.

The `updateTicketForm` function updates the form that is used to edit the data. It starts with some basic error checking (lines 49–54). If the server isn't able to find a ticket for a given ID, it returns `false`. Thus, the function checks for a `false` value, sets an error message if it finds one, and then sets the application to the front page. If the ticket exists, we start updating the form. We start with the input boxes, text area, and spans (lines 58–64) and then move on to the select boxes. Status contains a hard-coded set of options, so it can be selected by looping over the list, matching the status value against the options text, and then setting the element's `selectedIndex` property (lines 66–72).

The `users` array is dynamic, so the process has to start by updating the list of users from the data that is returned from the server. This is done by creating a new `Option` instance for each user and adding it to the select element `options` array. With the list updated, we loop over the list as we did in the status case. The only difference is that this time, we compare the option's value because we have a `user_id`. If no user matches, the selected index is set to 0, which is the "not assigned" option.

The function finishes by doing a basic security check. If the user is not logged in, the Submission button is disabled, and a message telling the user to log in to update the ticket is shown. This check allows the same page to be used for authenticated and nonauthenticated users. Like any other security check, this code on the client is there just to provide a good user experience; the back end also enforces security and would prevent any not-logged-in user from updating a ticket, no matter what he or she did to the client's code.

12.11 My-Tickets Component

The my-tickets component is the user's default screen within the application; it provides the user with a list of tickets that have been assigned to him or her. This component does a large amount of dynamic table processing and tries hard to load the minimal amount of data it needs from the server. The data minimization is important because when you're viewing your ticket list, it will poll the server on a 30-second interval, looking for updated tickets. You can see the my-tickets view in Figure 12-14, which is created from `myTickets.php` (see Listing 12-19).

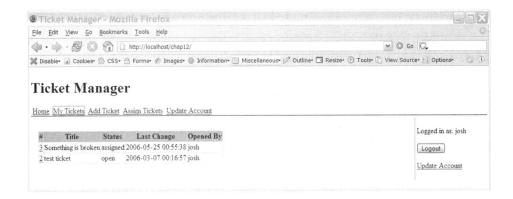

FIGURE 12-14
The my-tickets view

Listing 12-19

MyTickets.php

```
1    <div id="myTickets" class="section">
2    <div style="font-size: 80%; visibility: hidden;"
3      id="mtLoading">Updating ...</div>
4    <table id="mtTable" cellspacing="0">
5    <thead>
6      <tr>
7        <th>#</th>
8        <th>Title</th>
9        <th>Status</th>
10       <th>Last Change</th>
11       <th>Opened By</th>
12     </tr>
13   </thead>
14   <tbody>
15     <tr id="mtTemplate">
16     <td><a href="javascript:viewTicket({$ticket_id});"
17       >{$ticket_id}</a></td>
18     <td>{$title}</td>
19     <td>{$status}</td>
20     <td>{$last_change}</td>
21     <td>{$creator}</td>
22     </tr>
23   </tbody>
24   </table>
25
26   </div>
```

This component has a small template but a large amount of functionality. The template contains two elements: a notice area to display a message when the table is being updated (lines 2–3) and the actual table that shows the user's assigned tickets. The table contains a header, which is contained in the thread tag so that the `buildTable` function won't remove it. It also contains a table in its body, which will be cleared when `buildTable` updates the table. The template is marked with an ID so that it can be pulled out during page load by the component's setup function. The tokens are in the format described in the explanation of the `updateRow` function, so the `{$status}` will be replaced with the corresponding status line from the server. This simple templating system gives a great deal of flexibility, which is shown on lines 16–17, where we add a link around the `ticket_id`. The matching JavaScript that uses this HTML is shown in Listing 12-20.

Listing 12-20

`myTickets.js`

```
1   app.logout.push(function() {
2     var tbody = byId('mtTable').tBodies[0];
3     for(var i = tbody.rows.length-1; i >= 0; i--) {
4       tbody.deleteRow(i);
5     }
6     app.since = false;
7   });
8   app.setup.push(function() {
9
10  function mtOnDisplay() {
11    if (app.since) {
12      startUpdate();
13    }
14    else {
15      app.since = new Date();
16      rMt.listAssignedTickets();
17    }
18  }
19
20  function mtSetup() {
21    app.templates['mtTable'] =
22      byId('mtTemplate').cloneNode(true);
23    byId('mtTable').tBodies[0].removeChild(
24      byId('mtTemplate'));
25
26    byId('myTickets').onDisplay = mtOnDisplay;
27    window.setInterval(
```

```
28   function() {
29     if (byId('myTickets').style.display
30        == 'block') {
31       startUpdate();
32     }
33   },30000);
34
35   }
36   app.setup.push(mtSetup);
37
38   var mtCallback = {
39     listAssignedTickets: function(result) {
40       buildTable(result,'mtTable');
41     },
42     listUpdatedTickets: function(result) {
43       updateTable(result);
44     }
45   };
46   var rMt = new Ticket(mtCallback);
47
48   function startUpdate() {
49     var since = app.since;
50     app.since = new Date();
51
52     var current = [];
53
54     var rows = byId('mtTable').tBodies[0].rows;
55     for(var i = 0; i < rows.length; i++) {
56       current.push(rows[i].ticket_id);
57     }
58
59     byId('mtLoading').style.visibility = 'visible';
60     rMt.listUpdatedTickets(since.getTime(),current);
61   }
62
63   function updateTable(data) {
64     byId('mtLoading').style.visibility = 'hidden';
65     if (data['rebuild']) {
66       buildTable(data['tickets'],'mtTable');
67       return;
68     }
69     var tbody = byId('mtTable').tBodies[0];
70     for(var i = 0; i < data.length; i++) {
71       var row = app.mtTemplate.cloneNode(true);
72       updateRow(row,data[i]);
73
74       var replace = -1;
75       for(var r = 0; r < tbody.rows.length; r++) {
76         if (tbody.rows[r].ticket_id
```

```
77              == data[i].ticket_id) {
78              replace = r;
79              break;
80          }
81      }
82
83      if (replace == -1) {
84          tbody.insertBefore(row,tbody.rows[0]);
85      }
86      else {
87          tbody.removeChild(tbody.rows[replace]);
88          tbody.insertBefore(row,tbody.rows[0]);
89      }
90  }
91 }
```

MyTicket.js starts by creating three setup functions:

- The first is a function to be called when the user logs out (lines 1–7). This function is needed to clear out the user's current tickets so that the tickets currently shown won't be reused if another user logs in from the same browser.

- The second is the onDisplay function (10–18), which runs when the page is displayed and sends an AJAX request to the server to update the list of tickets that are being shown.

- The third is the Setup function (lines 20–36), which runs on page load. This function clones the row template for the table, storing it in the app object (lines 21–24). It registers the onDisplay function (line 26), and it sets up a function to run on a 30-second interval (lines 23–33). This function will run every 30 seconds while this page is loaded. The function does a simple check to see if the user is on the My Tickets section (line 29); if it is, the function starts the update process (line 31).

Lines 38–46 set up the AJAX class for this component. Callbacks are set up for the listAssignedTickets method, which is used on initial page load, and for listUpdatedTickets, which is used to get updates afterward. The Ticket instance is created on line 46.

The startUpdate function (lines 48–61) gets the data needed to call the server's listUpdateTicket method. This method needs the last time an update was asked for, which is stored in app.since (lines 49–50). It also needs a list of the current tickets being displayed, which is created by looping over the ticket table and reading the ticket_id property on each row (lines 54–57). Once this data is ready, a loading indicator is shown (line 59) and the AJAX call is made (line 60).

Finishing up the component is the updateTable function (lines 63–91). This function takes the data returned from the server and updates the ticket table with it. The function starts by disabling the loading indicator set by the startUpdate function (line 64); it then checks to see what type of data was returned. If it is a complete set of data (lines 65–68), then the buildTable function is used, and the function stops. If there is an updated set of data, we loop over the new data, inserting new rows at the top of the table or replacing current ones. Lines 70–71 prepare the new row, using updateRow and its template system. Lines 74–81 determine if we are doing an update or a replace; this check is done by looping over the current tickets and looking for matching ticket_ids. If the ID exists, then we are updating a current row by removing the old row and inserting the new one (lines 87–88). If the ID doesn't exist in the table, we insert a new row at the top of the table.

12.12 Assign-Tickets Component

The ticket-assignment component provides the users of the ticket manager with a quick way to assign unassigned tickets to users in the system. This is done by dragging tickets from a table and dropping them on a box that represents each user. This interface is a good example of the power that fully interactive interfaces give users. A drag-and-drop approach is especially useful for tasks such as sorting or assigning, because they are made up of elements that are mappable and that are often time-consuming with pre-AJAX approaches. The scriptaculous library is used to provide the drag-and-drop logic in this example. The interface of the assign-tickets component is created by Ticket.php (see Listing 12-21) and is shown in Figure 12-15.

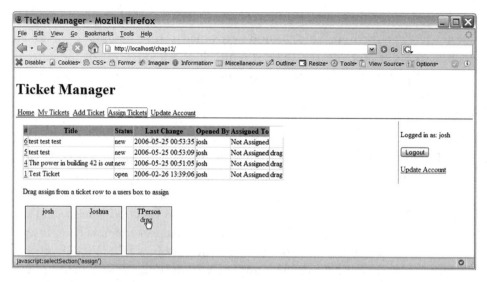

FIGURE 12-15
Assign-tickets component

Listing 12-21

Ticket.php

```
1    <div id="assign" class="section">
2    <table id="aTable" cellspacing="0">
3    <thead>
4      <tr>
5        <th>#</th>
6        <th>Title</th>
7        <th>Status</th>
8        <th>Last Change</th>
9        <th>Opened By</th>
10       <th>Assigned To</th>
11     </tr>
12   </thead>
13   <tbody>
14     <tr id="aTemplate">
15     <td><a href="javascript:viewTicket({$ticket_id});"
16       >{$ticket_id}</a></td>
17     <td>{$title}</td>
18     <td>{$status}</td>
19     <td>{$last_change}</td>
20     <td>{$username}</td>
21     <td>{$assigned_to}</td>
22     </tr>
```

```
23  </tbody>
24  </table>
25
26  <p>Drag assign from a ticket row to a
27    users box to assign</p>
28  <p id="dragMessage"></p>
29  <div id="assignUsers">
30  </div>
31  </div>
```

The `Ticket.php` file provides the interface for assigning tickets to users. This interface is made of two parts: The first is a table that lists unassigned tickets, and the second is a box containing boxes for each user. The table is defined on lines 2–24 and follows the standard, dynamic-table model we've used throughout the application. It contains a `thead` tag (lines 3–12), which contains the headings for the table, and a `tbody` tag, which contains a single row (lines 14–22). This row acts as the template for the `buildTable` and `updateRow` functions in `Ticket.js`. The file also contains a DIV (lines 29–30) to hold the drop targets for the ticket rows. This target is empty now because the targets will be built dynamically from the list of users. The JavaScript that builds the user drop targets and powers the rest of the interface is shown in Listing 12-22.

Listing 12-22

Assign.js

```
1   function aOnDisplay() {
2     rAssign.listUsers();
3     rAssign.listUnassignedTickets();
4   }
5
6   function aSetup() {
7     app.templates['aTable'] =
8       byId('aTemplate').cloneNode(true);
9     byId('assign').onDisplay = aOnDisplay;
10  }
11  app.setup.push(aSetup);
12
13  var aCallback = {
14    listUnassignedTickets: function(result) {
15      buildTable(result,'aTable');
16      makeDraggable();
17    },
18    listUsers: function(result) {
19      buildUserDrops(result);
20    }
21  }
```

```
22  var rAssign = new Ticket(aCallback);
23
24    function makeDraggable() {
25    var tbody = byId('aTable').tBodies[0];
26    for(var i = 0; i < tbody.rows.length; i++) {
27      var td = document.createElement('td');
28      var div = document.createElement('div');
29      div.innerHTML = 'drag';
30      div.className = 'handle'
31      td.appendChild(div);
32      tbody.rows[i].appendChild(td);
33
34      new Draggable(div,
35         {revert:true, ghosting: false});
36    }
37  }
38
39  function buildUserDrops(users) {
40    byId('assignUsers').innerHTML = '';
41    for(var i in users) {
42      var div = document.createElement('div');
43      div.className = 'user';
44      div.innerHTML = users[i];
45      div.userId = i;
46
47      byId('assignUsers').appendChild(div);
48      Droppables.add(div,{
49      accept: 'handle',
50      hoverclass: 'highlight',
51      onDrop: function(element, u) {
52        assignTicket(element,u);
53      }
54      });
55    }
56  }
57
58  function assignTicket(handle,user) {
59    var row = handle.parentNode.parentNode;
60    var title = row.cells[1].innerHTML;
61    var id = row.cells[0].firstChild.innerHTML;
62    rAssign.assignTicket(id,user.userId);
63
64    byId('dragMessage').innerHTML = "Assigned ticket #"+
65      id+" '"+title+"' to "+user.innerHTML;
66
67    row.cells[5].innerHTML = user.innerHTML;
68    new Effect.Highlight(row);
69  }
```

The ticket-assignment component uses both a setup function and an `onDisplay` function, so it starts by setting those up. The `onDisplay` function (lines 1–4) is run each time the user loads the section. In this function, AJAX calls are made to the server to load the users and unassigned tickets in the browser. The ticket information is updated when the section is displayed because you don't want to be in a situation in which you are reassigning tickets that someone else already assigned. This problem can happen if you are working with stale data; updating the data on section display least guarantees you fresh data at the start of the assignment process. The `Setup` function (lines 6–9) loads the template row into the `app` object using `cloneNode` so that it can be used later—even after the source is overwritten. The `Setup` function also registers the `onDisplay` function because that can't be done until the assign DIV is loaded.

The next ten lines take care of setting up the AJAX class. Callbacks for `listUnassignedTickets` and `listUsers` are registered. As in the rest of the application, these callbacks do minimal work, leaving the implementation to functions that are registered later in the file.

The rest of `Assign.js` contains the functions that provide the functionality of the component. `MakeDraggable` (lines 24–37) makes the rows in the ticket table draggable. It does this by looping over the rows in the body of the table and adding a new `td` on the right side. This `td` will contain a `div`, which is the drag handle for the row. The use of the handle DIV makes it clear how you should interact with the table; it works better than directly dragging-and-dropping the table rows because the rows have a variety of bugs in different browsers and they don't always offer a great user experience. The DIV is made draggable on lines 34–35 by creating a new scriptaculous `Draggable` instance; the `revert` option is set to `true` so that the DIV stays in place after it is dragged to a user's drop target.

The `buildUserDrops` function takes a list of users that is returned from the server and dynamically creates a DIV for each user that is used as a drop target for the ticket rows. This process starts by clearing the target DIV (line 40) because drops may already be in place from an earlier view of this section. Then the list of users is iterated over. On lines 42–45, a DIV is created, and it's populated with some of the user's information. Included in this is the user's `user_id` set as a property on the DIV so that it can be accessed by other code when the tickets are dropped. The function finishes by adding the new DIV to the target area (line 47) and making it a drop target (lines 48–54). When we make it a drop target, we set an `onDrop` handler.

This handler calls the `assignTicket` function and gives us a way to tie the drop event from the user interface to the back end.

The `assignTicket` function runs when a drop is completed. The first parameter, `handle`, is the DIV from the ticket row; the second parameter, user, is the user's drop target DIV. The function starts by using the handle's `parentNode` property to get the actual table row (line 59), and then it uses the row to get the title of the ticket (line 60) and the ticket's ID (line 61). With that information, an AJAX call to the server can be made. This call assigns the ticket to the specified users (line 62). The rest of the function provides status feedback to the user; lines 64–65 provide a textual message, and lines 67–68 update the assigned column in the ticket table and highlight the row to show that it's been updated.

12.13 Security Considerations with AJAX Applications

The ticket manager application has a relatively simple security model. There are no different user levels; the only issue to worry about is whether the user logged in. If the user is logged in, he or she has the ability to edit and create tickets; otherwise, he or she can only view them. The user's login status is stored on both the JavaScript side and the server. On the JavaScript side, this status is used to hide the links to actions that the user can't perform. On the server side, the login status is used to enforce what actions the user can perform. This setup highlights an important rule in any Web application: The client can't be trusted.

Often, when we build an AJAX application, we forget that our back-end code is still being exposed through normal HTTP requests. Just because the JavaScript-driven user interface doesn't allow a ticket to be created doesn't mean that an HTTP request directly to the back-end addTicket method can't be made. The methods exposed in the `Ticket` class are a public interface to the application; they need to check login status if a login is required to use the method, and they need to do any required data escaping.

Even though libraries such as HTML_AJAX make it easy to expose a PHP class for AJAX, access doesn't mean that you can remove the controller from your application and expose your data models directly to JavaScript. The code that handles an AJAX request is now the front-line code of your application and needs to take appropriate precautions.

12.14 Comparing Our AJAX-Driven Application against a Standard MVC Model

You have many different design choices that you can make when building a Web application, but one that is often used is the MVC model. In an MVC application, your model code handles interacting with the database, the view manages how the content is displayed, and the controller ties things together. When you move to an AJAX-driven application, this model will still exist, only now you have the possibility of having it twice: once on the server and once on the client. In many cases, the controller and view classes will mainly disappear from the server side because that functionality is transparently provided by the AJAX communications library.

In the ticket manger, the controller functionality was provided by the HTML_AJAX_Server class. The server class takes incoming requests and maps them to the appropriate method on the ticket class; it then takes the output and uses a JSON serialization class as the view. In the ticket manager, the model is less clear, but the model component is still the ticket class. In some ways, the ticket class is still a controller because it handles user input, decides what to do with it, and then returns data or errors. As the ticket manager application grows, a common refactoring approach would be to pull the code that creates the queries into its own classes, leaving only the code for cleaning the input and for picking the entity to work with in the ticket class. You can also build an AJAX-driven application without the use of JSON; instead of returning data to the client, you would return chunks of HTML. In an HTML, chunk-style AJAX application, you would keep the standard view component in the MVC model. (The view component is a template in most Web applications.)

On the JavaScript side of the application, you can also choose an MVC model to drive your application. However, you're less likely to see a pure implementation because most JavaScript code is event driven. (That is, it responds only to user interaction, such as the clicking of a link.) In addition, it is harder to work in a controller model than the standard, URL-driven approach used on the server. A strict view also isn't needed on the JavaScript side because you can interact directly with the DOM, but you may find template-based approaches to be quite useful because the templates make the development processes much simpler. Models follow much of the same pattern; in a simple AJAX application, they can be simple data structures mapped directly from the server using JSON. However, as features are added, you'll find it useful to wrap this data inside JavaScript classes. These classes can take care of caching data in the client, handle validation, and even combine multiple requests to allow you to lower the number of requests you send to the server.

Overall, building an AJAX-driven application has the tendency to lower the amount of code you have on the server and increase what you have on the client. However, even with large amounts of functionality being provided by an AJAX library, the server-side code will still need to provide more than simple data access. All of the application's security will have to be enforced on the server. You'll also need to manage the first-time page generation on the server, which may include pre-loading large amounts of data to save you from doing a bunch of AJAX requests as soon as the page is loaded. The server will also tend to have methods that combine multiple-step processes; due to the high latency of AJAX requests, you will want to minimize the number of round trips to the server that are required to process a single action.

Building a fully AJAX-driven application gives you a lot of power, but be careful when using this approach. You'll have a lot more important logic running on the client, so you'll need to update your testing approaches to account for this. You also want to be careful about ending up with a design that leaves you with a complex back end and then a complex front end that performs many of the same functions. If you have a fully driven AJAX application, you should strive to keep one side of the application as simple as possible. If you're pushing data out using JSON, that side should be the back end; if you're pushing out chunks of HTML, that side is the front end. If you let both sides become complicated, you'll find yourself with two interdependent pieces that are hard to maintain and debug.

12.15 Summary

The ticket manager use case showed us a different development pattern. A lightweight back end exposed services that a heavier front-end JavaScript application used to build the actual ticket manager. This made JavaScript the primary development language and shifted the development processes much further from the standard Web development model than the other use cases. The approaches we covered would also be useful in cases in which JavaScript was taking more of a secondary role. These approaches include the following:

- Exposing back-end functionality as a service gives the most flexibility to your AJAX code.

- JSON's lightweight encoding makes it the perfect fit for heavy AJAX use.

- Building small JavaScript components that are self-contained and have simple rules for interacting with the rest of the application helps manage complexity.

- Usability must be thought about at the initial design stage, not bolted on later.

- Visual sorting is easy to implement and easier for users to understand.

- Creating utility functions for common JavaScript operations can speed development and make code more readable.

The ticket manager is a rich Internet application, offering quick response times, features such as drag-and-drop ticket assignments that are seldom seen in Web 1.0 applications, and high levels of usability throughout. However, it just scratches the surface of what's possible.

AJAX offers the ability to create highly interactive applications. AJAX-powered applications have the ability to help us create a new Web—a Web 2.0. As you walk down the path to AJAX development, you need to be careful to avoid the bumps in the road. Keep your focus on the user's experience, not on technology, and strive to keep your code simple. As you rely more and more on AJAX, you'll want to move complexity to the client code, not create a situation in which both sides of the equation are extremely complex. AJAX development gives you lots of options, from moving data with JSON to updating the page with server-side generated HTML. However, what determines your success won't be what programming strategy you use, but how well you keep your focus on what the user needs.

Appendix A

JavaScript AJAX Libraries

In this chapter

AJAX Toolbox

Web site: http://ajaxtoolbox.com/request/

License: Free to use

AJAX Toolbox is a comprehensive XMLHttpRequest wrapper. It features progress monitoring, request grouping, and AJAX form submission. The project is well documented and includes source code and examples. The main drawback is the nonstandard license.

Bajax

Web site: https://developer.berlios.de/projects/bajax/

License: BSD

Bajax is a small AJAX library with support for asynchronous requests. Automatic URL encoding of parameters is supported, but building the argument list from a form is not. The API is set up to be used as a simple entry point to a URL-encoded RPC system and to easily include new HTML content.

Dojo Toolkit

Web site: www.dojotoolkit.org/

License: New BSD or Academic Free License 2.1

Dojo is a complete framework for building JavaScript applications. It includes support for managing events and AJAX communications and for building widgets using templates. Dojo ships with a wide variety of widgets—from application style menus to Google Map's integration. Dojo is focused on building rich applications and provides a rich set of features for doing so. It's not the sort of library you want to drop in just for AJAX support, but if you want to build applications with JavaScript as a primary development language, it's a good choice. AJAX includes RPC-style calls through JSON support. It also supports AJAX form submission and a document-oriented JavaScript API.

libXmlRequest

Web site: www.whitefrost.com/reference/2005/09/09/libXmlRequest.html

License: Similar to BSD, but with an advertising clause

libXmlRequest is an AJAX communications library with an XML focus. It supports asynchronous and synchronous operation, including support for cached GET requests. The XML support includes an XPath and an XSL wrapper that works in Firefox and IE. Other browsers are supported for basic communication, but the XML features won't work.

MochiKit

Web site: http://mochikit.com/

License: MIT or Academic Free License, v. 2.1

MochiKit is a complete JavaScript library that is designed to be a base for building rich Web applications. Features include visual effects, drag-and-drop support, JSON serialization and safe evaluation, string and date formatting, event management, and a number of other development tools. AJAX communication support is focused on JSON and supports only asynchronous operation. The library is well documented at the API level, but there is little high-level documentation explaining how it all fits together. Although MochiKit is a large library, it takes strides to be well name-spaced so that it can be used with other libraries.

Rico

Web site: http://openrico.org/

License: Apache 2.0

Rico is an AJAX and general DHTML library that provides many effects and tools that are useful in AJAX applications. Rico includes cinematic effects, drag-and-drop support, and widgets called behaviors. Like scriptaculous (described in Chapter 8, "Libraries Used in Part II: Sarissa, Scriptaculous"), Rico builds on the prototype library and is comparable in scope to scriptaculous. Rico is known for its high-quality widgets, such as its accordion and datagrid widgets. Basic AJAX communication support is provided by a singleton communication manager.

Simple AJAX Code-Kit (SACK)

Web site: http://twilightuniverse.com/projects/sack/

License: MIT

SACK is a simple JavaScript library that provides AJAX communication support. Its focus is on ease of use and simplicity. Requests are made by creating a single object, which contains support for URL encoding data. There is no direct support for RPC or JSON, but the library is simple enough that it would be easy to extend. Support for managing errors is minimal, but loading notification is provided by adding event-handling functions.

ThyAPI

Web site: http://sourceforge.net/projects/thyapi/

License: LGPL

ThyAPI is a framework for creating rich applications. It needs a server component but will work with any server-side language that supports XML-RPC. (Currently only a PHP back end exists.) The API is similar to client GUI frameworks, such as Java's Swing, and includes a number of widgets, including a rich text editor, a calendar, dialog boxes, and windows. ThyAPI also supports drag-and-drop support, animations, and sound playback. (Sound playback uses the Flash plug-in.)

Qooxdoo

Web site: http://qooxdoo.org/

License: LGPL

Qooxdoo is a rich-application framework with a focus on AJAX-powered widgets. It has a large set of core features, including browser detection, event management, drag-and-drop support, a cookie API, and AJAX communications. The focus of the project is on API layout and widgets; the API layout provides an experience similar to using standard graphical APIs, such as Swing in Java. Widgets include menus, toolbars, combo boxes, and windows. Qooxdoo is extremely large, so it won't be a good choice for mixing and matching with other solutions.

XHConn

Web site: http://xkr.us/code/javascript/XHConn/

License: Creative Commons Attribution-ShareAlike

XHConn is an extremely lightweight wrapper that provides cross-browser XMLHttpRequest support. It's a good choice if you don't want to bother with cross-browser support but want to take care of the rest of the details yourself. The implementation is simple enough that you could easily make your version using the examples in Chapter 1, "What Is AJAX?"

Yahoo! User Interface Library

Web site: http://developer.yahoo.com/yui/

License: BSD

The Yahoo! User Interface Library is a large JavaScript API that provides support for all aspects of rich-application development. It includes event management, drag-and-drop support, visual effects, animation, and AJAX communications. It also includes a number of widgets (which are called controls); these include an AutoComplete search widget and a calendar widget. The AJAX API is document-based on a single asyncRequest method. AJAX form submission is supported, and an object-oriented API for managing connections and errors is provided. The library includes excellent documentation; it also includes a design patterns library that shows how to combine the various widgets and effects.

Appendix B

AJAX Libraries
with Server Ties

In this chapter

PHP

AjaxAC

Web site: http://ajax.zervaas.com.au/

License: Apache

AjaxAC is a widget-based AJAX library in which minimal JavaScript is written. New widgets are written as PHP classes, and they use an event API for attaching AJAX actions to normal JavaScript events. Small amounts of glue JavaScript are included inside the PHP class, which can make for a complex development process. On the client, a mix of custom, handwritten JavaScript and framework-generated JavaScript is used to implement applications.

HTML_AJAX

Web site: http://pear.php.net/package/HTML_AJAX/

License: LGPL

HTML_AJAX provides a stand-alone JavaScript-and-PHP API for AJAX requests. It's part of the PHP PEAR library project. PHP integration includes exposing PHP classes though proxy JavaScript objects and helper functions for JavaScript generation. RPC communications takes place using JSON, although other formats are supported through a pluggable architecture. Easy AJAX form submission and the generation of JavaScript from AJAX requests are also supported. The library is covered in detail in Chapter 9, "Libraries Used in Part II, HTML_AJAX."

PAJAJ

Web site: http://pajaj.sourceforge.net/

License: LGPL

PAJAJ is an object-oriented, event-driven AJAX library for PHP5. You can develop applications by using the PAJAJ HTML-generation tools to build your HTML and to attach events on the server side; you can also use a JavaScript API to bind events to already-existing HTML pages. PHP classes are exposed to JavaScript by creating a PHP page for each class and having the class extend the `BaseAjaxServer` class. This requirement of extending a base class can be troublesome for some frameworks that already contain base classes. JSON is used for all communication between JavaScript and PHP.

TinyAjax

Web site: www.metz.se/tinyajax/

License: LGPL

TinyAjax is a PHP5 solution that provides a simple API that is similar to SAJAX. It works by exporting individual PHP functions to JavaScript and generating JavaScript from a set of PHP helper methods. These helper methods include functions for grabbing the values from an HTML form and setting the innerHTML of DOM elements. Basic TinyAJAX applications can be written without writing any JavaScript code.

Xajax

Web site: www.xajaxproject.org/

License: LGPL

Xajax works by exporting PHP classes that return AJAX action objects from each call. These return actions can update the attributes of any DOM element and new custom JavaScript to the application. This functionality is similar to HTML_AJAX_Action (Chapter 9) and is designed to allow you to implement AJAX almost completely from the server side. Data serialization is handled using a custom XML format.

XOAD

Web site: http://wiki.xoad.org/index.php?title=Wiki_Home

License: PHP

XOAD provides RPC-style AJAX by exporting PHP classes to JavaScript. It includes a number of helper classes for generating the needed JavaScript during this process. JSON is used for communications between the client and the server.

XOAD also includes a number of additional features, including action-based returns (similar to HTML_AJAX_Action in Chapter 9) and a custom event model. The event model is designed to allow you to fire an event on one client and catch it on another. This makes it easy to write chat applications.

Java

AjaxTags

Web site: http://ajaxtags.sourceforge.net/

License: Apache 2.0

AjaxTags is a set of JSP tags designed to make it easy to add AJAX to Java JSP sites. Each tag implements a specific widget. These tags include support for an auto-complete text box, pop-up balloons, multistep select boxes, tabbed panels, and area displays. Tags are also offered for making HTML content replacement. Prototype, scriptaculous, and OverLIB are used on the client side. XML is used for communication between the client and the server.

Direct Web Remoting (DWR)

Web site: http://getahead.ltd.uk/dwr/overview/dwr

License: Apache

DWR offers an easy way to export Java classes and make them accessible from JavaScript applications. DWR does this by generating JavaScript proxy classes that match the Java ones. This operation works much like HTML_AJAX's RPC mechanism (described in Chapter 9). The Java classes can be configured using XML or annotations. A number of utility JavaScript functions are also included to make standard DOM-manipulation tasks easier.

Google Web Toolkit

Web site: http://code.google.com/webtoolkit/

License: Mix of Apache 2.0 and free-to-use components

Google Web Toolkit allows Java developers to make AJAX applications without writing JavaScript. The heart of the toolkit is a special compiler that translates the Java application into JavaScript and HTML. The toolkit includes a user-interface library with a large number of widgets, including standard HTML form elements, menu bars, trees, tables, dialog boxes, and various panels for managing the layout of the application. A custom event model based on a listener pattern is provided, as is an API for managing style sheets. RPC support is provided using code generation to hide the hard work, and data serialization is provided for most basic Java types. The toolkit also includes back-button management and debugging tools.

ZK

Web site: http://zk1.sourceforge.net/

License: GPL and commercial

ZK is a component- and widget-based AJAX library. It allows you to build AJAX applications without writing JavaScript. Its widgets are geared toward building complete applications; thus, it would be hard from a style-and-usability perspective to integrate it into existing Web sites. (This isn't unique to ZK; many widget-based toolkits have a similar problem.) ZK has a large set of widgets, from standard HTML form elements to trees and modal dialog boxes. ZK applications are developed using a custom ZUML markup language (which is similar to Mozilla's XUL) with embedded Java.

C#/.NET

Ajax.NET

Web site: www.ajaxpro.info/default.aspx

License: Public domain

Ajax.NET provides AJAX support for ASP.NET 2.0 applications. It includes control for AJAX versions of standard HTML elements and allows you to create your own custom controls. It includes the ability to expose .NET classes to JavaScript, handling type mapping automatically. This mapping is implemented using JSON.

Anthem.NET

Web site: http://anthem-dot-net.sourceforge.net/

License: Public domain

Anthem.NET provides AJAX support to ASP.NET 1.1 and 2.0. Like most .NET libraries, it provides indirect AJAX, where portions of your templates are rewritten by the library to make AJAX calls. It works by mapping the standard ASP.NET control model into an AJAX environment. This includes full support for view state and server-side events.

Atlas

Web site: http://atlas.asp.net/

License: Free to use

Atlas is Microsoft's AJAX toolkit that provides tight integration with ASP.NET 2.0 and Visual Studio. The toolkit is designed so that .NET developers can add AJAX to their applications by using widgets and indirect AJAX and without editing code. In indirect AJAX, the Atlas code takes current ASP.NET templates and rewrites their links and form actions, making them post to the server using AJAX calls. The toolkit also includes visual effects, drag-and-drop support, automatic user profiles, data-binding widgets, and support for Windows Live widgets.

MagicAJAX.NET

Web site: http://www.magicajax.net/

License: LGPL

MagicAJAX.NET focuses on providing AJAX support without your needing to write JavaScript code. You can do this by adding an AJAX control to your pages and then rewriting current controls. MagicAJAX.NET also has some support for writing JavaScript from .NET (including helper methods). Communication with the server is done with URL-encoded POSTs to the server. In such situations, the server returns JavaScript code.

Multiple Languages

CPAINT

Web site: http://cpaint.booleansystems.com/

License: GPL and LGPL

Languages: PHP, ASP, and PERL

CPAINT is an AJAX library that is focused on communications and supports XML and text-return types. The JavaScript API supports RPC calls and can be used in asynchronous or synchronous mode. Results are encapsulated in a CPAINT result object and can be generated on the server using a similar API. As an alternative, the results on the server can be generated automatically using a proxy API.

Rialto

Web site: http://rialto.application-servers.com/wiki/

License: Apache

Languages: JSP, JSF, .NET, Python, and PHP

Rialto is a JavaScript widget library with support for a number of different server languages through pluggable back ends. The widgets include drag-and-drop, tree-view, popup, calendar, and forms. The pages are created using an object-oriented API in JavaScript, and page development can be done using pure JavaScript or a server API. Server-specific code includes an object-oriented API for creating widgets as well as an API for dealing with AJAX requests. Java JSP support is the most mature, but others are in early development.

SAJAX

Web site: www.modernmethod.com/sajax/

License: BSD

Languages: PHP, ASP, ColdFusion, Perl, Python, Ruby, LUA, and IO

Sajax is a simple RPC-style AJAX library. Its original focus was PHP, but support for other languages has been added over time. Some of the additional language support is under a different license than the main code. Sajax provides a procedural API and works by registering server methods and having JavaScript stubs generated for them. When you call the stub method, Sajax makes an AJAX request and then calls a callback method with the results.

Appendix C

JavaScript DHTML Libraries

In this chapter

Accesskey Underlining Library (AUL)

Web site: www.gerv.net/software/aul/

License: New BSD

AUL is a JavaScript library that, when included, adds additional behaviors to your HTML page based on existing `accesskey` attributes. It works by taking HTML elements that have `accesskey` attributes and adding underlines under the matching characters within the label. For example, a button defined as `<button accesskey="b">button</button>` would be displayed with an underline under the b. This allows you to easily match `accesskey` display standards without filling your HTML with extra markup.

Behaviour

Web site: http://bennolan.com/behaviour/

License: BSD

Behaviour is a small library that is used to attach JavaScript events to an HTML page without adding additional markup. This is accomplished by using CSS selectors, which apply JavaScript to matching HTML elements. Such a matching system is useful for keeping markup clean, and it helps make your JavaScript more reusable. The library is bundled with HTML_AJAX, and its usage is explained in Chapter 9, "Libraries Used in Part II: HTML_AJAX."

cssQuery()

Web site: http://dean.edwards.name/my/cssQuery/

License: LGPL

cssQuery() is a cross-browser JavaScript function that allows you to query the DOM using CSS selectors. It includes support for CSS1 and CSS2 selectors and for parts of CSS3. It's useful for creating your own behaviors, such as functionality, and for trying out new CSS3 selectors that are not yet supported in all browsers.

Dean Edwards IE7

Web site: http://dean.edwards.name/IE7/

License: LGPL

Dean Edwards IE7 is a browser-compatibility library that uses JavaScript to extend Internet Explorer 5 and 6, giving these browsers support for newer CSS standards. It also fixes various layout bugs and contains a fix for transparent PNGS. It works quite well and can be an easy addition for a site that is targeted toward a standards-compliant browser that later needs to be made to work in IE. On large and complex sites, IE7 can add some additional load times and can cause page reflows after the initial layout is done. However, if you use IE7 enough to understand its drawbacks, it can be a useful tool for supporting IE6.

DOM-Drag

Web site: www.youngpup.net/2001/domdrag/

License: Free to use

DOM-Drag is an extremely lightweight (4Kb) library that makes DOM elements draggable. It includes support for making part of the element the dragging handle and for limiting the area to which the draggable element can be dragged. It doesn't support drop targets or ghosting, as is the case with scriptaculous (see Chapter 8, "Libraries Used in Part II: Sarissa, Scriptaculous"), but it is much smaller.

JavaScript Shell

Web site: www.squarefree.com/shell/

License: GPL/LGPL/MPL

JavaScript shell is a command-line interface for JavaScript and DOM that allows you to interactively write JavaScript code. Accessible as a stand-alone tool or from a bookmarklet, it is useful as a debugging and development tool and includes tab completion of function names. It also includes extra functions for interacting with the DOM.

Lightbox JS

Web site: www.huddletogether.com/projects/lightbox/

License: Creative Commons Attribution 2.5

This is an unobtrusive JavaScript library that makes it easy to overlay images on the current page. It is used on many sites to show the larger images of thumbnails within articles. To use it, you simply need to include the library and add `rel="lightlight"` attributes to an `a href` that links to the image you want to overlay.

Moo.fx

Web site: http://moofx.mad4milk.net/

License: MIT

Moo.fx is a lightweight library for providing JavaScript visual effects. Rather than bundle effects in the manner that scriptaculous does, Moo.fx provides tools to animate the width, height, and opacity of elements. This focus allows for 6Kb of file size for basic operations. An extension package provides a number of additional features including an accordion widget, support for combination effects, memory of last effect position through cookie storage, and text resizing. This doubles the size of the library but adds its features in only a fraction of the size of other libraries.

Nifty Corners Cube

Web site: www.html.it/articoli/niftycube/index.html

License: GPL

With Nifty Corners Cube, you can add rounded corners to HTML elements in a cross-browser manner, without adding additional images or HTML markup to your pages. The library rounds the elements by calling a single JavaScript function and providing CSS selectors for the elements you want rounded. Nifty Corners Cube also provides parameters for controlling transparent display, rounding size, and element size. This allows Nifty Corners Cube to be used for everything from creating buttons to making fake columns.

overLIB

Web site: www.bosrup.com/web/overlib/

License: Artistic

overLIB is a large, feature-filled library for producing ToolTips. It can be used for anything from standard Tool Tips to pop-up message boxes. A plug-in API is provided, and plug-ins are available for tasks such as moving the pop-up message box while scrolling the page or adding drop shadows to the pop-up message box itself. overLIB contains a huge number of features, making it suitable for many tasks, but it can be overkill if you are adding just a few ToolTips to a site.

Sorttable

Web site: http://kryogenix.org/code/browser/sorttable/

License: MIT

Sorttable is an unobtrusive JavaScript library that makes a table's columns sortable without server interaction. Sorting is enabled by giving the table a class of `sortable`. Sorting is allowed on one column per table and works in ascending or descending mode.

Tooltip.js

Web site: http://tooltip.crtx.org/

License: MIT-style

Tooltip.js is an unobtrusive behavior-style library built on top of scriptaculous that adds simple ToolTips to Web sites. ToolTips can be added by using specially named CSS classes or by using a simple JavaScript API. Tooltip.js has fewer features than overLiB, but is much smaller if you are already using scriptaculous. However, if you're pulling in scriptaculous just for ToolTips, then it's the same size.

WZ_jsgraphics

Web site: www.walterzorn.com/jsgraphics/jsgraphics_e.ht`m

License: LGPL

WZ_jsgraphics adds a vector-graphics drawing implementation in pure JavaScript. It supports multiple browsers and allows for drawing anywhere on the Web site's content area. The API provides for basic drawing, including lines, boxes, polygons, and ellipses. Arbitrary positioning of images and text is also supported. The library includes a mode to make the drawings printable and works by building the lines out of DIV elements. Thus, it will have some performance limitations, but it works fast enough for many tasks.

WZ_dragdrop

Web site: www.walterzorn.com/dragdrop/dragdrop_e.htm

License: LGPL

WZ_dragdrop is a DHTML drag-and-drop library; it offers highly functional drag-and-drop support and an additional DHTML API. With this API, you can make elements resizable, clone nodes, and perform basic animation. The only missing functionality is built-in support for drop targets, which is useful for tasks such as sorting or ordering

Index